Becky has nailed it!
I'M BAKING AGAIN!
Thank you so much.

Janet

Becky Excell is an
ANGEL IN AN APRON
sent from the great kitchen in the sky to rescue anyone with a troublesome tummy.

Sue

What I love about Becky and her recipes are that you don't have to buy fancy ingredients. You can just pick up her book and bake, and feel like **YOU'RE NOT MISSING OUT**.

Michelle

MOVE OVER MARY BERRY, there's a new kid on the block.

Nigel

EVERY RECIPE WORKS!
Every. Single. One. I've never experienced that before from a recipe book. My muggle family are constantly requesting I bake more of your recipes and, as a result, I've found a love for baking.

tie

Becky you have
RE-OPENED A WORLD
that I thought had closed to me.

Andrea

Becky's recipes have allowed my daughter to eat food she has never tried before. She really loves the bread rolls, cake recipes and chocolate chip cookies, now her **CLASSMATES LOOK IN ENVY** at her lunch box rather than her missing out.

Ann

Because of you, Becky, I have found my **LOVE FOR BAKING AND FOOD** again!

Becks

I thought becoming gluten- and dairy-free would mean I would never enjoy food again. Becky's recipes have **PROVED ME WRONG!**

Debbie

Becky's books are a must-have on any gluten-free person's shelf! They will **TRANSFORM YOUR GLUTEN-FREE LIFE**, like they did with mine.

Ruth

This book is dedicated
to all the gluten-
free people who have
walked into a bakery and
realised they couldn't
eat a single thing.

How to BAKE *anything* GLUTEN FREE

How to BAKE anything GLUTEN FREE

Over 100 Recipes for Everything from Cakes to Cookies, Bread to Festive Bakes, Doughnuts to Desserts

BECKY EXCELL

Photography by Hannah Hughes

quadrille

WELCOME TO THE BOOK THAT'LL SHOW YOU HOW TO TURN YOUR KITCHEN AT HOME INTO YOUR OWN PERSONAL GLUTEN-FREE BAKERY, FILLED WITH ALL THE BAKES THAT YOU PROBABLY THOUGHT YOU'D NEVER BE ABLE TO EAT AGAIN.

Best of all, nobody would **ever** know that any of your bakes were gluten-free.

Hands up if you've ever:

Walked into a bakery and realized you could only eat the napkins.

Experienced the awkward moment of being unable to eat your own birthday cake.

Remortgaged your home to buy a loaf of gluten-free bread, only to find an enormous hole in the middle.

Watched *The Great British Bake Off* and experienced the mixed emotions of feeling 'hangry'.

Ordered dessert and ended up with a fruit salad.

According to a recent study I just completely made up, **100% of you** have experienced one or more of those situations at some point. If that's the case, then I can wholeheartedly say that this **book was written for you!**

*yes, they do exist!

I'd love to sit here and pretend that my passion for gluten-free baking always came from a place of pure joy and happiness. But in reality, it was the sheer frustration with all of those scenarios that became my infinite well of inspiration. However, that all changed for me when I first stumbled upon an entirely gluten-free bakery* on my travels many, many years ago.

The walls were adorned with fresh bread, proudly on show like trophies – everything from freshly baked French baguettes to a bounty of beautiful boules, alongside a mountainous display of crusty bread rolls.

The counters were crammed with constellations of pastries, cookies, tarts and a seemingly endless amount of fresh desserts that you would happily sell your left arm, leg and any remaining limbs for. And though it was painfully clear that there wasn't a single crumb of gluten on the premises, it still didn't stop me asking, 'is this gluten-free?' a billion times – I just couldn't quite believe my eyes or tastebuds! Nothing looked or tasted gluten-free at all and, up until that point, I thought that was impossible.

My boyfriend Mark and I shared a slice of cake for the first time in years and, not surprisingly, I went back every day without ever eating the same thing twice.

IF I HAD TO SUM UP HOW I FELT AT THAT EXACT MOMENT, IT WOULD BE A STRANGE MIX OF DISBELIEF, EXCITEMENT AND THE SHEER JOY OF JUST FEELING LIKE A 'NORMAL' PERSON AGAIN.

*people who <u>can</u> eat gluten

I immediately wanted to bottle that exact feeling and share it with you, so you could experience it whenever you liked – just like 'muggles'* do, every single day.

And it was that simple sentiment that inspired me to start writing my second book, *How to Bake Anything Gluten Free*. After all, what better way to share that feeling than by showing you exactly how to transform your kitchen into your own **<u>personal gluten-free bakery at home</u>**?

BUT THERE WAS ONE SMALL PROBLEM: HOW ON EARTH WAS I GOING TO CAPTURE THAT INCREDIBLY SPECIFIC FEELING WITHIN THE PAGES OF A BOOK?!

Before I even wrote a single word, first I had to break down that game-changing gluten-free experience.

I instantly realized that the beginning of that magical experience started with the overwhelming feeling of choice. Unfortunately, choice usually goes out of the window* when you embark upon a gluten-free diet. Our choices in bakeries often boil down to one of two options: either the one, token gluten-free option or, even worse – **nothing at all**. So I absolutely had to recreate the excitement that comes with tremendous variety and choice.

*along with gluten

But while choice is always great, it would all be for nothing if everything tasted blatantly 'gluten-free', right? That's when I realized that at the heart of my joyous experience was the fact that nothing in that bakery tasted or looked gluten-free. But wait, isn't that impossible?! Well, that's exactly what I thought before I graced the doors of that gluten-free bakery for the first time. **Eating is believing, trust me!** So naturally, every single bake in this book had to be utterly indistinguishable from its gluten-containing counterpart, with none of the dry, crumbly or dense textures that so often give gluten-free baking a bad name. Fortunately, that's what I've always strived for anyway!

And if I could nail all the above in this book, it would automatically make one important thing possible again: **the ability to share a slice of cake with the people you care about most.** After all, if nothing tastes or looks gluten-free, muggles have no reason to turn their noses up at it, right? It's definitely something I took for granted until I wasn't able to do it anymore and I never realized how much I truly missed it. So naturally, all the recipes in this book had to reach the point where, if you didn't tell someone that your bake was gluten-free, they'd never even notice.

AFTER ALL, HOW ELSE WOULD I BE ABLE TO SHARE MY BAKES WITH MARK LIKE I DID IN THAT GLUTEN-FREE BAKERY?

*what else was there to do all day when COVID-19 was on the rampage and we all had to stay indoors?

*should they be so lucky to get a slice!

Now that I understood what that experience loosely translated to in recipe book form, all that was left to do was make it a reality.

And after months and months of baking across multiple lockdowns* with **a LOT of taste-testing**, thanks to my muggle friends and family, I'm pleased to say that I finally did it. I can honestly put my feet up and say that I've successfully captured the experience that I felt walking into that gluten-free bakery, right here, 'bottled' within the pages of this book.

I proudly present to you an eclectic **choice** of over 100 recipes, including game-changing fresh bread, an entire chapter dedicated to doughnuts, tons of celebration cakes, cookies and show-stopping desserts. And of course, because you'd never know anything was gluten-free, you can share everything with your muggle friends and family as you wish.* This book is packed cover to cover with all the things that gluten-free people could only *dream* of buying from your average bakery.

BUT PERHAPS BEST OF ALL...

I managed to do it without using tons of strange, unobtainable ingredients or a top-secret flour blend – I actually used a simple, commercial gluten-free flour blend from the supermarket for almost every single recipe.

So, needless to say, as you flick through this book, I hope you're filled with the same disbelief and excitement that I felt whenever I walked into that gluten-free bakery, while also feeling confident in the knowledge that you can recreate **the simple joy of feeling 'normal'** whenever you like.

Oh and as my boyfriend Mark is lactose-intolerant, I'll let you know whenever a recipe is (or can be made) lactose-free or dairy-free. Plus, I've done the same for veggie, vegan and low FODMAP options throughout this book, too, so that hopefully nobody misses out on a bite of that magical feeling I experienced.

So if you've become a spectator whenever cake appears, please join me in saying:

'let them eat
(gluten-free) cake'

About me

Here I am, awkwardly introducing myself again – you'd think I'd be used to this by now, right? I'm Becky Excell, I've been gluten-free for over a decade and I share recipes on my blog and social media that you'd never know were gluten-free. Is it frivolous and self-explanatory to say that I'm a cookbook author when you're reading this in my actual cookbook? Oh well, I've done it now. I should probably mention that there are over 350,000 of you lovely people following me online. Something that I'm eternally grateful for and constantly flabbergasted by!

My debut recipe book, *How to Make Anything Gluten Free*, was dedicated to reuniting everyone with all the foods on their gluten-free bucket lists. Thankfully, it wasn't just my mum who bought it, so I'm lucky enough to be here writing the sequel! My second recipe book is dedicated to showing you how to turn your kitchen at home into your very own personal gluten-free bakery. But I guess I should probably talk about myself more first, right?!

When my doctor first diagnosed me with IBS and told me that my relationship with gluten was over, I didn't realize that sentence also roughly translated to 'you're no longer welcome at bakeries anymore'. Bakeries instantly went from a place of joy and wonder to the equivalent of the elephant graveyard in *The Lion King*.

As soon as any cakes, cookies or desserts were involved, I instantly became a spectator. No, seriously – I literally just watched people eat food while I awkwardly waited for them to finish. If I was lucky, I'd get a dry, crumbly gluten-free brownie in a plastic wrapper as a consolation prize, though it was better than nothing. The saddest thing of all is that, over many years, I'd come to accept that this was just how things had to be from now on. And though I often struggled to adjust, I never questioned it.

But after travelling to many of Europe's best gluten-free bakeries, I realized that wasn't how life had to be *at all*. It was the first time I'd ever tried gluten-free bread that both looked and tasted like 'normal' bread. All of their cakes and pastries were edible works of art and it was impossible to even tell that anything was gluten-free.

Until I visited those bakeries, I genuinely believed that achieving muggle-like results in gluten-free baking was utterly impossible. But after tasting the impossible, my entire outlook on gluten-free baking changed that day and, as a budding gluten-free baker, it was a total game-changer. I was suddenly filled with all the fuel I needed to strive for a zero-compromise approach in my own recipes. Now all that was left to do was to convince everyone else!

And that's exactly what I aimed to do in every recipe I've created ever since, especially those tucked away in my first (and now second) book.

But perhaps best of all, sharing my recipes over the last decade has made me realize that *anybody* can become an accomplished gluten-free baker. No, really – I have tons of photos of your successful bakes as proof! With the right recipe, gluten-free baking doesn't have to be any harder than muggle baking. Nor does it have to involve tons of exotic ingredients that you'd have to hunt for outside of the supermarket.

After all, I'm most definitely not a professional chef, baker or scientist. I'm just a fairly ordinary girl from a quiet town who began baking out of sheer frustration with the lack of gluten-free options out there in the world. What I'm badly trying to say is, if I can create these recipes, then you most definitely can too!

Don't forget that my recipes don't end with the last page of this book, either. Please go and check out my blog (glutenfreecuppatea.co.uk), Instagram or YouTube channel for loads more recipes and inspiration too. I'll be posting step-by-step video tutorials to accompany the recipes in this book over on my YouTube channel too. So definitely come over and say hi.

Most importantly, if you do try one of my recipes, please make sure you take a photo, post it on social media and tag me (@beckyexcell) in it. If there's one thing that has got me through the multiple lockdowns of the pandemic, it's been seeing all your wonderful bakes every day. They make my day, every day, and I always look forward to seeing them!

Becky x

A crash-course in PREPARING GLUTEN-FREE FOOD

In some of the gluten-free bakeries I've visited on my travels, they actively stopped anyone from entering if they were clearly holding any food items that could potentially contain gluten. They had a strict zero-tolerance policy on gluten in place and worked diligently to prevent any gluten from ever entering the premises. While that level of safety may not be possible (especially if you live with muggles) we can and always should take the same approach whenever it comes to preparing gluten-free food.

So, with that in mind, it's important to ask yourself these three questions before you even put your apron on:

1.

Do any of the ingredients or products used have any gluten-containing ingredients or relevant allergen warnings?

First of all, triple-check the ingredients list on any products used to ensure that they don't have any gluten-containing ingredients or relevant allergy warnings. Here's a list of common sources of gluten that you'll need to avoid:

- wheat
- barley
- rye
- oats
- spelt

Of course, even if a product doesn't have any gluten-containing ingredients, it can still be cross-contaminated through manufacturing methods.

Even naturally gluten-free products like beansprouts or hazelnuts can sometimes have 'may contain' warnings that makes them unsuitable for most people who are gluten-free. I've even seen 'may contain gluten' warnings on salt and pepper, so it's best to check everything.

I've indicated each ingredient in this book as 'gluten-free' where commonly necessary. But it's still best to triple-check the ingredients and allergy info on the packaging of every product you're using.

2.

How can I store my ingredients or products separately from gluten-containing foods?

If a gluten-free product or ingredient comes into contact with gluten at any point, it's no longer truly gluten-free. So how can you minimize that risk? Here are a few common best practices:

- Firstly, once gluten-free items are removed from their packaging, they must immediately be stored separately from gluten-containing products. This can easily be achieved by using sealed, airtight containers. It's also wise to label the containers so it's clear to everyone what's inside.
- Also, remember: if you butter gluten bread, then put the knife back into the butter, the butter is no longer gluten-free. It's always a good idea to have separate butter/jam/peanut butter and condiments that are clearly labelled as being 'gluten-free only'.

3.

How can I avoid cross-contamination when preparing and cooking gluten-free food?

Carefully considering your cooking methods and any equipment used is vital in preparing gluten-free food. That's especially important if your kitchen or utensils have previously been used to prepare gluten-containing food. So how can you minimize that risk? Here are a few more common best practices:

- Of course, gluten-free food must be cooked *entirely* separately from gluten-containing food.
- When deep-frying gluten-free food, do not reuse oil that has been previously used to cook gluten-containing food.
- Do not place gluten-free bread in a toaster that has been used for gluten-containing bread.
- Do not cut gluten-free bread on a board that has been used for gluten-containing bread, unless thoroughly cleaned.
- But crucially, all utensils, pans and surfaces must be totally cleaned down if they have previously come into contact with gluten. You can happily use regular washing-up liquid and dishwashers to do this.
- Ideally, you'd own utensils, pans, sieves and bread boards that are solely dedicated to cooking gluten-free food.

The moral of the story is that you can never be too careful! Of course, this isn't an exhaustive list, so definitely visit the website of your country's coeliac society for up-to-date info.

Gluten-free

ESSENTIAL BAKING INGREDIENTS

I learned the hard way that attempting muggle recipes and simply swapping wheat flour for gluten-free flour is a bad idea when it comes to baking.

If recipes were stories, with the ingredients being the characters, 99% of the time gluten is the protagonist. And what happens if you remove the protagonist from a story? The story doesn't make sense anymore and it just doesn't work.

So that's why a gluten-free recipe must absolutely be its own story with its own cast of unique characters. And in this chapter, this is where you'll meet them!

I've endeavoured to ensure that over 95% of these ingredients are easily sourced in supermarkets. But you may have to hop online for one or two particular ingredients that are absolutely integral to making gluten-free bread that tastes like the 'real deal'.

This isn't an exhaustive list of every common gluten-free baking ingredient in existence (there are tons more!) just those which I used in this book.

FLOUR

Gluten-free plain (all-purpose) flour

It's always been incredibly important to me that my recipes are all based around simple, commercial flour blends that you can easily source in supermarkets. Otherwise gluten-free baking can seem like a real mission! So not surprisingly, the gluten-free plain flour I use in this book can be easily found in supermarkets (I used Doves Farm's FREEE flour throughout this book) and contains a blend of rice, potato, tapioca, maize and buckwheat flour.

But as gluten-free flour is made from a blend of different flours and starches, they vary in their ratios and ingredients depending on where you live. In certain parts of the world, you might even struggle to find a gluten-free flour blend at all! That's why I've included a gluten-free plain flour blend (page 204) in the essentials chapter for anyone struggling to find one.

The reason I mention this is because results can vary depending on what gluten-free flour blend you use, so definitely bear that in mind. Some flour blends are more absorbent, meaning your pastry dough, for example, may be a little dry and more brittle to work with. That simply means you might need a little more of whatever your 'wet' mixture is for that recipe (just add a little more water for pastry) to compensate. And vice versa for flour blends that aren't so absorbent, which can make dough a little too sticky.

Gluten-free self-raising (self-rising) flour

Generally, gluten-free self-raising flour tends to be almost identical to a plain (all-purpose) gluten-free flour blend, but with added raising agents and a little xanthan gum too. The raising agents are great for cakes where you need a little extra rise, though it's not uncommon to still add baking powder regardless. The xanthan gum helps with binding in the absence of gluten – read on to find a little more about it.

Again, if you can't find gluten-free self-raising flour where you live, use the simple recipe on page 205 to make your own from a plain blend.

Gluten-free white bread flour

Muggle bread flour is extremely high in gluten, making it an essential item in almost all bread recipes. Which is bad news for us! Unlike gluten-containing bread flour, gluten-free white bread flour is unfortunately not something you can use as a like-for-like substitution when following a muggle bread recipe.

It also has very similar ingredients to gluten-free plain (all-purpose) flour, so if you can't find gluten-free bread flour where you live, feel free to use that instead. But since the ingredients are so similar, that also means there's no 'magical' effect like you'd get with strong bread flour.

That's because you'll still need psyllium husk (read more about it opposite) to compensate for the lack of gluten in gluten-free bread flour. The blend of gluten-free bread flour I use is from the supermarket and contains rice flour, potato starch, tapioca starch and xanthan gum.

Cornflour (cornstarch)

Cornflour isn't to be confused with maize flour or cornmeal – it's actually a white starch that is traditionally used to thicken sauce and gravy. But best of all, it's gluten-free and very easy to source in your local supermarket. As it's so incredibly light, it's perfect for adding to cookies and doughnuts for a lighter, fluffier texture, which is always welcome in gluten-free baking!

Tapioca starch

Say hello to yet another white starch, but with slightly different properties to cornflour or potato starch. It's extracted from the roots of the cassava plant and crucially adds a little stretch to your finished baking products. That's why I tend to use it a lot in bread as it's not only incredibly light, but also adds more of a 'tearable' texture. This is one that you'll likely have to hop online to buy, but trust me – it's worth it! As with the next two flours coming up, please ensure there's no 'may contain gluten' warning on the packaging before using.

Gluten-free buckwheat flour

Don't panic! Despite literally containing the word 'wheat' in its name, buckwheat flour is actually derived from fruit seeds. That makes it naturally gluten-free, though you'll still need to watch out for 'may contain' warnings on the packaging as it can often be cross-contaminated during manufacturing. This flour has tons of wholegrain flavour that can be a real asset in baking, as most gluten-free flours and starches often have a neutral flavour.

White rice flour

Made from finely milled rice, this is one of the most common flours you'll find in any gluten-free flour blend – mainly because it has a more neutral flavour. However, as rice is a much harder grain than wheat, that does also mean it doesn't absorb liquid nearly as well. This is why gluten-free flour blends which contain rice often have starches to balance out that effect. The use of rice flour means that you'll notice that some gluten-free recipes (especially anything involving dough) require considerably more hydration than a traditional wheat-flour recipe.

SIMPLE SWAPS

Gluten-free oats

While oats are naturally gluten-free, unless they're labelled as 'gluten-free oats', regular oats will likely be cross-contaminated through manufacturing methods, making them unsuitable for a gluten-free diet. So they must always be clearly labelled as gluten-free!

But even still, a small number of people still struggle to tolerate oats, despite being totally gluten-free, so please be aware of that. In some countries (such as Australia), even *gluten-free* oats aren't considered to be suitable for a gluten-free diet. Due to both of those reasons, I've tried to minimize my use of gluten-free oats in this book – purely to ensure that everyone can enjoy as many of my recipes as possible.

There's no easy like-for-like substitute for gluten-free oats, so you might just have to skip those recipes entirely if you either can't tolerate them, or can't source them.

Gluten-free baking powder

Believe it or not, baking powder is one of those sneaky ingredients that isn't always gluten-free. Some brands of baking powder often add wheat flour to help bulk it out and absorb moisture. Not only does that mean it's no longer gluten-free, but it also makes it worse as a raising agent anyway! So definitely make sure you check the ingredients list on your baking powder to ensure that it's actually gluten-free.

Gluten-free stock cubes

While this isn't an essential 'baking' ingredient per se, you will most definitely need some gluten-free stock cubes to take on the savoury baking chapter. Fortunately, a ton of the stock cubes in supermarkets here in the UK are clearly labelled as being gluten-free, so you shouldn't have too much trouble sourcing them. You can also find gluten-free *and* low FODMAP stock cubes online now too, if you need them.

BINDING

Xanthan gum

Acting as a gluten replacer, this ingredient is key to so many of my recipes working as I intended. While it comes in a powder form, once hydrated it has a 'gummy' property that instantly thickens, stabilizes and binds any mixture. Though definitely nowhere near as effective as gluten, it provides all the binding we need 95% of the time.

Despite the unusual name, it's often very easy to source in supermarkets as it's such a prevalent ingredient in gluten-free baking. Despite being so vital, a little goes a long way, so we'll generally only need this in small amounts throughout this book.

Psyllium husk powder

Psyllium husk powder is as integral to gluten-free bread as gluten is to muggle bread. Playing a similar role to xanthan gum, this magical powder provides not only a binding effect, but the crucial ability to retain moisture and add much needed elasticity.

Psyllium husk is a form of dietary fibre made from the seeds of a *Plantago* plant. When buying it online, firstly make sure it's psyllium husk *powder* as you can also buy a non-powdered version. But most importantly of all, please ensure it's clearly labelled as gluten-free as some can have a 'may contain' warning on them. It's a store-cupboard essential for every aspiring gluten-free bread baker!

You can only currently buy this online, but trust me, it's well worth sourcing if you want to make gluten-free bread that tastes like 'real' bread.

Ensure your psyllium husk powder is blonde, otherwise it can affect the colour of your bread. Just ask me in my Facebook group if you're not sure!

Other handy INGREDIENTS

Eggs

Believe it or not, eggs are an especially vital ingredient in gluten-free baking. Eggs not only provide much needed binding power, but also leavening and structure, all of which help massively in the absence of gluten. I generally use large eggs throughout this book, but, did you know that a large egg in the UK is actually bigger than in the USA, Canada and Australia? Because of this, I've included a handy egg 'conversion' guide at the back of this book on page 216.

Butter

Of course, butter is always a given when it comes to baking, but not just for its lovely, buttery taste. Butter plays an even more important role in gluten-free baking - especially when it comes to making pastry. Think about butter straight out of the fridge - it's hard as a brick! So naturally, when you put your pastry dough into the fridge, as the butter chills once again, it adds much needed strength and malleability to the pastry. Again, this effect is often integral in the absence of gluten.

Greek yoghurt

The easiest and quickest way to make any kind of gluten-free flatbread is by combining Greek yoghurt with a gluten-free flour blend, like you'll find in my pitta bread over on page 151. It has lots of protein, adding both strength and structure and, because it's thick, it creates a dough that isn't sticky and unmanageable. You can also now commonly find lactose-free Greek yoghurt in supermarkets, which is a great lactose-free replacement for sour cream in baking.

Mascarpone

Whenever it comes to using cream cheese in a recipe, I always opt for mascarpone. Why? Well, it has a higher fat content that means your finished bakes will tend to be more stable, with a creamier texture. For example, a no-bake cheesecake using cream cheese will tend to be less firm and stable, meaning it'll start to melt out of the fridge sooner. You're welcome to use cream cheese instead, but my personal preference is always mascarpone (and please always use full-fat).

Black treacle

In case you didn't know, black treacle is the British version of molasses. So whenever you see it mentioned in a recipe, feel free to substitute it like-for-like if it's not available where you live.

Golden syrup

This ingredient is another staple baking essential here in the UK, sometimes known as light or golden treacle. It's essentially a form of inverted sugar syrup with a distinctive, 'buttery' taste. However, it seems to be available all across the world these days, so check the international aisle of your supermarket for it. Trust me, it's worth hunting for as there's nothing else quite like it!

Food colouring paste

I'm very strict with my use of food colouring *paste* throughout this book, not the liquid food colouring you'll commonly find in supermarkets. That's because food colouring paste is highly concentrated, meaning you only need a small amount to achieve an instant, vibrant colour.

Not only does this mean you use less and it lasts longer, but crucially, it means you don't dilute your mixture by adding too much liquid - which is never a good idea in baking! Plus, liquid food colouring in supermarkets never provides a vibrant colour in cakes or buttercream, no matter how much you squeeze in. So, hop online and buy a set of food colouring pastes and thank me later!

Dried active yeast and instant yeast

First of all, ensure that your yeast is gluten-free before even starting your baking session! Most recipes in this book use dried active yeast, which absolutely must be activated first, as you'll see in the first steps of the method when necessary.

Instant yeast on the other hand (sometimes known as easy-bake yeast) can just be chucked in with your dry ingredients as it doesn't require activating. I use both in the bread chapter, so make sure you're using the correct one!

And, of course, always make sure that your yeast is still in date or your dough will never prove.

DAIRY-FREE ALTERNATIVES MENTIONED IN THIS BOOK

Hard margarine (hard dairy-free alternative to butter)

This is also sometimes known as a 'baking block' and is my go-to dairy-free alternative to butter in baking. Despite being a hard block, it's still a little soft no matter how long you leave it in the fridge. Popping it in the freezer until it firms up a bit is always advisable, especially when making buttercream or pastry.

Dairy-free milk

Of course, if you're dairy-free, then use dairy-free milk instead wherever you see it! It very rarely makes a difference, though depending on the milk you use, you may not get that golden finish that dairy milk provides.

Dairy-free double (heavy) cream

Yes, dairy-free cream that whips to soft/stiff peaks like *real* double cream does exist (though it may not always be labelled as 'double cream' or 'heavy cream'). It can be hard to find in supermarkets, depending on where you live and in that case, it's best to turn your searches online. While you can easily find a dairy-free alternative to cream in the supermarket, they rarely have the desired fat content to be 'whippable'.

The key to knowing whether it'll whip or not is its fat content – if it is less than 30% then, in my experience, it won't whip up at all. You can check the fat content by looking at the nutritional info on the packaging.

Dairy-free cream cheese

The same applies to dairy-free cream cheese. For use in some of my no-bake recipes or in whipped cream fillings, the fat content must be 23% as a minimum. You can check the fat content simply by looking at the nutritional info on the back of the packaging.

If it doesn't have a high enough fat content, it won't set in your creation, and instead it'll likely become a sloppy mess that never stabilizes. Unfortunately, with most dairy-free cream cheese I've tried, they have a very low melting point, which means they liquify far sooner than dairy-based cream cheese. This makes dairy-free cream cheese unsuitable as an alternative in baked cheesecakes, or any recipe where the cream cheese is heated.

LACTOSE-FREE ALTERNATIVES MENTIONED IN THIS BOOK

Lactose-free milk

Unlike dairy-free milk, lactose-free milk is *real cow's milk*, but with an enzyme called 'lactase' added to help cancel out the lactose. If you're lactose intolerant or following the low FODMAP diet, feel free to use this instead of milk whenever a recipe calls for it. Lactose-free milk literally has no impact on a recipe because it is real milk, after all!

Bear in mind that dairy-free milk (made from almonds, soy etc.) is also lactose-free. But using lactose-free milk made from cow's milk is always preferable, especially if you're on the low FODMAP diet.

Lactose-free whipping cream

Throughout this book, you'll see that I recommend lactose-free whipping cream as an alternative to double (heavy) cream. That's because, in the UK, you can easily buy it in the supermarkets and it has a similar fat content to double cream, being 30% fat. This is what allows it to whip and stabilize, just like double cream.

Again, lactose-free whipping cream is made from real cow's milk with 'lactase' added to cancel out the lactose. This is ideal if you're following the low FODMAP diet too, as truly dairy-free cream often contains high FODMAP ingredients.

Lactose-free cream cheese

Whenever I use mascarpone or cream cheese throughout this book, I always recommend lactose-free cream cheese as a substitute. It doesn't have quite as high fat content as mascarpone, but generally it works as a like-for-like replacement, though your mixtures may be a little softer as a result. Use the highest fat content lactose-free cream cheese available to ensure your bakes turn out as intended.

Again, this is made from real cow's milk, which is vital if you're following the low FODMAP diet as truly dairy-free cream cheese is often made from high FODMAP ingredients.

Useful EQUIPMENT

Not surprisingly, I have enough tins, pans, mixers and ovenproof dishes to start my own kitchenware shop. But you'll be pleased to discover that I've only listed the things you'll need for this book! Not everything on this list is mandatory, but if you do have all of these, then you're ready to take on every single recipe.

Fan oven

All the oven temperatures stated in this book are based on a fan-assisted oven. Not got a fan oven? No problem! Just remember to use the standard oven temperature given in each recipe instead.

While I'm here, I just also wanted to stress how important it is to get to know your oven when it comes baking. And no, I'm not talking about finding out its hobbies or where it likes to go on holiday! For example:

Does it need longer to preheat than the indicator light lets on? I used an oven thermometer to check this - mine actually needed about 10 minutes longer before it reached the temperature I set it to.

Does it run hotter or colder than your average oven? If your bakes are always underdone or overdone, this could be the case.

Is the back of the oven hotter than the front? Mine definitely is - my muffins at the back always brown more than those at the front.

Is the top shelf hotter than the middle shelf? My cakes on the top shelf always rise more.

And the best way to find all this out is to simply use it a lot. With these questions in mind, you'll soon get to know your oven, which always produces more reliable results.

If using a gas mark oven, see page 216 for a handy temperature conversion guide.

Digital weighing scales

When it comes to baking, using digital cooking scales is highly, highly advised. The difference of 10 grams or millilitres can make a huge difference between a workable dough and a wet, sticky dough. Since we don't have gluten to assist us, this makes the consistency of pastry dough especially, very important - if it's too dry, it'll break too easily. If it's too wet, it'll be too sticky to work with. I've spent many hours getting these measurements to the perfect ratios, so do yourself a favour and take advantage of that with digital weighing scales!

12-hole muffin or cupcake tin (pan)

This is most definitely at the top of my 'essentials' list when it comes to baking. Fortunately, even the cheapest of options seem to last several years as you'll often use cupcake cases to line the tin, meaning it doesn't usually see much rough treatment.

20cm (8 inch) round baking tins (pans)

I always recommend having at least three of these ready for baking. For starters, a sandwich cake wouldn't be much of a sandwich with only one sponge! But most importantly, having a third round baking tin is essential if you want to make one of my three-tier cakes, like my chocolate orange drip cake on page 30. Once mixed, cake batter should be baked in the oven ASAP, otherwise, the longer it's left to rest, the more its ability to rise starts to degrade. You'll also need a *deep* round baking tin for Mark's Japanese-style cotton cheesecake on page 113.

20cm (8 inch) round, loose-bottomed baking tins (pans)

A loose-bottomed (or a springform) baking tin is essential when it comes making the cheesecakes in this book. If you try and make one in a tin without a loose bottom or springform mechanism, you won't have a hope of ever getting it out in one piece! Also, unlike regular round baking tins of the same size, these tend to have much higher sides to accommodate taller creations.

23cm (9 inch) square baking tin (pan)

The number of things you can make in a humble square baking tin never ceases to blow my mind. Think smores brownies (page 62), baked raspberry cheesecake bars (page 56) and millionaire's shortbread (page 61), to name a few. Plus, when you slice your creation up, you'll get perfectly square, equal slices, which you wouldn't get if you used a round baking tin.

25cm (10 inch) round, loose-bottomed chiffon tin (pan)

Unlike a bundt tin, which looks very similar with a hole in the middle, a chiffon tin has a loose bottom. The loose bottom is especially vital if you intend to make Mark's mum's pandan chiffon cake (page 33) - without it, you absolutely wouldn't be able to get it out in one piece. Trust me, it's worth owning one of these as soon as you take a bite of that cloud-like sponge!

23cm (9 inch) fluted tart tin (pan)

If you intend to venture into the wonderful world of gluten-free pastry, a fluted tart tin (preferably with a loose bottom) is always a worthwhile investment. You can use it to make everything from quiche to tarts, and its fluted edges always ensure a perfect finish.

900g (2lb) loaf tin (pan)

Loaf cakes are the perfect place to start if you're new to baking or fancy a nice, simple baking session. Simply whip up your cake batter, pour it in, bake and that's it! They can vary in shape and size - some are wider, which results in a flatter, wider loaf cake that bakes slightly faster. Some are taller, which sometimes means they need a little longer in the oven, so bear that in mind.

25cm (10 inch) bread tin (pan)

Unless fun-size bread is your thing (it definitely isn't mine!), investing in a decent sized bread tin is always a good idea. Mine is 26.2 x 12 x 7.8cm (10 x 4¾ x 3in) and you'll need one for the super seeded sandwich loaf in the bread chapter (page 154). A Pullman loaf tin works here too - mine is 21.5 x 12.3 x 11.4cm (8½ x 5 x 4½in).

Baguette tray

If you miss lovely, long sticks of fresh bread, then this is an absolute essential - mainly because you won't get anywhere without one! Mine is 39 x 16.5 x 2.5cm (15¼ x 6½ x 1in). They're fairly light, compact and inexpensive, so definitely treat yourself to one of these if you can. You can buy trays that fit 2 or 4 baguettes and I'd always recommend getting one that fits 4, if possible.

Proving basket (banneton)

For my boule-shaped loaves, you'll definitely need one of these to prove it in. But it's not just for proving - it actually gives the loaf its lovely shape as it proves, too. Mine is 22cm (8½in) in diameter and I picked it up in the supermarket.

20cm (8 inch) and 28cm (11 inch) skillet or ovenproof frying pan

Though I'm still very bad at maintaining my skillets, you just can't beat them as an ovenproof baking dish when it comes to baking my boule-shaped loaves of bread. A skillet is the perfect tool for the job, with edges that help the bread to maintain its shape as it rises in the oven. A round, ovenproof frying pan of the same size will definitely do the job too if you don't have one. But you can actually pick one up for a very affordable price, if that helps.

Rolling pin

Speaking as someone who once tried to roll out pastry with a can of soup in the absence of a rolling pin, I can confirm that a rolling pin is an essential item! That's especially true if you intend to venture into baking gluten-free pastry or any kind of flatbread. I now have one that comes with a series of ring guides which assist you in rolling your dough out to a specific thickness.

Sieve

Of course, a sieve is perfect for ensuring that some ingredients, especially cocoa powder, are evenly dispersed throughout your mixtures. But there's another very important reason that I mention it here: please ensure that your sieve hasn't previously been used to sieve wheat flour without being thoroughly cleaned! It's definitely worth labelling it so anyone else in your house knows it's for gluten-free flour only.

Non-stick baking parchment

You'll need a healthy supply of this throughout this book to line all of your baking tins. Remember that non-stick baking parchment most definitely comes in different grades, so it's often wise to invest in a more expensive one, if possible. Trust me, it's especially worth it just for avoiding the stress of parchment that's stuck to your otherwise perfect bake!

Stand mixer

Of course, this isn't mandatory for this recipe book, nor is it mandatory for baking in general. However, it can make the difference between baking feeling like hard work or being an absolute breeze. For starters, when making mixtures that require extended periods of mixing (such as buttercream or meringue, for example), you can be completely hands-off. Plus, you can also add ingredients while the mixer is still in motion, which always makes baking an infinitely quicker and easier process. You don't need to break the bank for one as the power of your stand mixer only really comes into play when mixing dough - which isn't commonplace when baking gluten-free bread, believe it or not.

Food processor

While I don't often use this as a 'mixer' as such, my food processor always comes out whenever I need to blitz something, like biscuits for the base of a cheesecake. Again, while you can easily do this by hand, having a food processor will save you time and effort. However, if I had to choose between a stand mixer or a food processor, I'd always choose my stand mixer because it gets used so much more often.

Electric hand whisk

Before I could afford to buy a stand mixer, I used a very basic electric hand whisk for all my baking. It mixes just as well as a stand mixer, but of course, you're the one who has to put the effort in! But for me, an electric whisk still remains the most affordable option for those who are new to baking or don't bake that often, yet still yields extremely similar results.

Digital cooking thermometer

I didn't realize how much I actually needed one of these until I got one. Now I can't live without it! So why is it so important? Crucially, for this book, it's outrageously handy for measuring the temperature of oil when deep-frying - which is essentially the entire doughnut chapter! Plus, it also comes into play when making Italian meringue, caramel and for checking the internal temperature of bread. A digital cooking thermometer just instantly removes all the guesswork and, to me, that's priceless. Of course, there's also the added advantage that you can use it to check the internal temperature of meat, ensuring that not only is it done, but also that it's not getting overdone.

Silicone spatula

This is as essential as it gets when it comes to baking! Nothing can scrape a bowl cleaner than one of these, meaning you waste as little of your mixtures as possible. It's also essential when gently folding in mixtures to ensure you don't lose lots of air that you've probably worked hard to whisk in. If you don't have access to electric mixers, you can achieve the same result with one of these and a simple balloon whisk. At the heart of all baking, they're all you need - as long as you're prepared to put in a little more elbow grease!

Angled palette knife

To me, this is yet another essential tool for baking and I've lost count of all the many ways I use one on a daily basis. A large one comes in handy for applying dollops of buttercream to a cake and a small one is perfect for any task that either requires precision, or where a larger palette knife is simply too big. Use them whenever you want to create a smooth, even finish, whether it's smoothing out cake batter that's about to be baked, or for creating neat, sharp edges when icing a cake.

Wooden spoon

You might be surprised to learn that I very rarely use a wooden spoon when I'm baking (I use a silicone spatula for that). Instead, I use my humble wooden spoon to check the temperature of my oil for deep-frying. Simply pop the handle into the oil for 3-4 seconds - if you see bubbles gently forming around it then it's ready to fry. The wooden spoon handle test has never let me down yet!

Baking beans

As you might expect, there are a lot of delicious, buttery pastry recipes in this book! On occasions where you'll need to blind bake the pastry case first, these are super handy. At a pinch, you can always use rice instead, but it feels like a waste of rice!

Plastic icing scraper

If you want to achieve a professional finish on your rainbow cake, piñata cake or drip cake when it comes to icing, this simple tool is essential. Use it to scrape a crisp, clean edge on the outside of your cakes - couple this with an icing turntable and the job suddenly becomes incredibly easy!

6-hole doughnut tray

For my baked doughnuts, a 6-hole doughnut tray is essential. Simply spoon into the recesses, pop in the oven and you've got doughnuts with no frying required. I'd always recommend getting two, if possible, as otherwise the rest of your doughnut mixture has to wait a while before being baked, which isn't great!

Just as a handy reminder for those still in disbelief: yes, everything in this entire book is gluten-free!

But it's also incredibly important to me that as many people can enjoy my recipes as possible. That's why I've labelled all of them to clearly indicate whether they're dairy-free, lactose-free, low lactose, vegetarian, vegan or low FODMAP.

But even if a recipe isn't naturally suitable for all dietary requirements, watch out for the helpful notes by the key. These will indicate any simple swaps you can do in order to adapt that recipe to your dietary needs, if possible.

If the recipe needs more than a couple of simple tweaks, make sure you check the 'Making it...?' section underneath each recipe for full advice on how to adapt it if possible.

Dairy-free
This indicates that a recipe contains zero dairy products. Ensure that no ingredients used have a 'may contain' warning for traces of dairy and double-check that everything used is 100% dairy-free. Of course, if a recipe calls for a quantity of one of my pastry/buttercream/filling recipes from the Essentials chapter, ensure you make those dairy-free too.

Lactose-free
Lactose-free? Isn't that the same dairy-free? No, it definitely isn't! For example, lactose-free milk is *real* cow's milk with the lactase enzyme added, so while it's definitely not dairy-free, it is suitable for those with a lactose intolerance. The 'lactose-free' label indicates that a recipe is naturally lactose-free or uses lactose-free products. If a recipe calls for a quantity of one of my pastry/buttercream/filling recipes from the Essentials chapter, ensure you make those lactose-free too.

Low lactose
Butter is an integral ingredient in baking and, fortunately, it's also incredibly low in lactose. That means that people with a lactose intolerance will have no problems tolerating it. The same goes for a lot of hard cheeses like Cheddar. So for those ingredients, you won't necessarily need a special 'lactose-free' equivalent. Of course, recipes that use these ingredients aren't technically lactose-free, so they'll be labelled as low lactose for clarity. If a recipe calls for a quantity of one of my pastry/buttercream/filling recipes from the Essentials chapter, ensure you make those lactose-free or low lactose too.

Vegetarian
This indicates that a recipe is both meat-free and fish-free. Fortunately, baking in most cases lends itself well to being vegetarian! However, when it comes to savoury baking, I'll provide simple veggie swaps where necessary and possible. Please make sure all products and ingredients used are vegetarian-friendly.

Vegan
This indicates that a recipe contains no ingredients that are derived from animals. Even if a recipe isn't vegan to start with, look out for those little helpful notes for simple swaps, or check the 'Making it...?' section at the bottom of each recipe. While gluten-free *and* vegan baking is a different matter entirely, if it is easy to make the recipe using vegan alternatives, I'll tell you how in that section. Make sure all products and ingredients used are vegan-friendly.

Low FODMAP
This indicates that one serving of the finished recipe is low FODMAP. The low FODMAP diet was specifically created by Monash University in order to help relieve the symptoms of IBS in sufferers. Brief disclaimer: you should always start the low FODMAP diet in consultation with your dietician.

Also, you might be surprised to find that there's no actual onion or garlic in *any* of the savoury recipes in this book. Why? Well, they're two ingredients that quite a lot of people with IBS can't tolerate – myself included! If you are in the same boat, please ensure that any products you bake with are low FODMAP, and if a recipe calls for a quantity of one of my pastry/buttercream/filling recipes from the Essentials chapter, ensure you make those low FODMAP too.

CAKES AND BAKES

When asked 'what's your favourite gluten-free cake?' my usual answer is 'yes'. That's because if it's gluten-free, yet doesn't taste or look like it is, then it's automatically my favourite by default! I think that's just what going several years of eating dry, crumbly cakes will do to you.

So say hello to a chapter crammed with my 'favourites of all the favourites', all of which you'd find on sale in my imaginary gluten-free bakery. It's a real mix of classic bakes, from fruit scones to angel cake slices, chocolate cake and Battenberg, with a sprinkling of modern crowd pleasers and celebration cakes – rainbow cake, piñata cake, salted caramel cake, whoopie pies, and tons more.

For more classic bakes, check out my blog or Instagram (@beckyexcell) for loads more ideas.

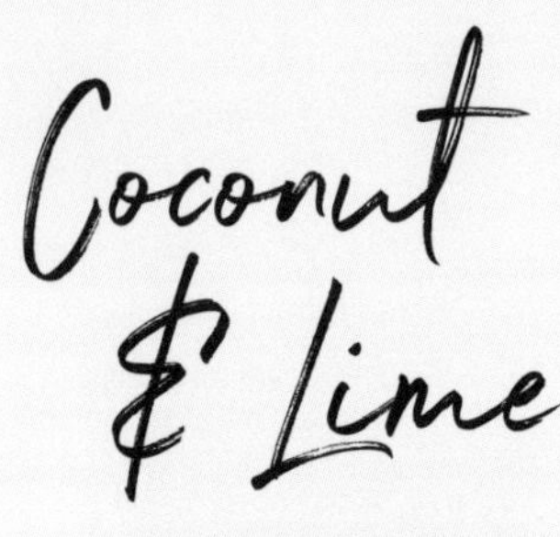

DRIZZLE LOAF CAKE

use a dairy-free butter alternative and dairy-free milk

use lactose-free milk

MAKES · 10 SLICES

TAKES · 1 HOUR 20 MINUTES + COOLING

- 175g (¾ cup plus 1 tbsp) butter, softened, plus extra for greasing
- 175g (¾ cup minus 2 tbsp) caster (superfine) sugar
- Grated zest of 3 limes
- 3 large eggs
- 1 tbsp milk
- 150g (1 cup plus 2 tbsp) gluten-free self-raising (self-rising) flour
- ¼ tsp xanthan gum
- 50g (1¾oz) desiccated (dried shredded) coconut

For the drizzle

- Juice of 2 limes
- 50g (¼ cup) caster (superfine) sugar

For the icing

- 120g (generous ¾ cup) icing (confectioners') sugar, sifted
- Juice of 1–2 limes

To finish

- Grated lime zest
- Desiccated (dried shredded) coconut

This tropical-tinged loaf cake is dangerously easy to make, with a delightful finish that simply involves drizzling over a little icing and topping with lime zest and coconut. The drizzle ensures it's super-moist *and* infused with tons of lime, while the coconut in the sponge adds an instant explosion of tropical flavour. Save me a slice, please!

Preheat your oven to 160°C fan / 180°C / 350°F. Lightly grease a 900g (2lb) loaf tin (pan) and line with non-stick baking parchment.

In a large mixing bowl, cream together your butter and sugar until light and fluffy (I prefer to use an electric hand whisk or a stand mixer for this). Add the lime zest and mix in, then crack in the eggs, one at a time, mixing in between each addition, until well combined. Mix in your milk, then sift in your flour and xanthan gum and fold in. Lastly, fold in your coconut.

Spoon the mixture into your prepared tin and bake in the oven for 45–50 minutes until golden. If it's browning too much on top, cover with foil (shiny-side up) for the final 5–10 minutes. Check that it's cooked by sticking a skewer into the middle – if it comes out clean, then it's done.

While the cake is baking, make the drizzle. Grab a small mixing bowl, add the lime juice and caster sugar, then mix until well combined.

Use a skewer to poke lots of holes all over the top of the cake, while it's still hot, then gradually pour over all of the drizzle. Allow to cool briefly in the tin before transferring to a wire rack to cool completely.

For the icing, gradually add your lime juice to your icing sugar in a medium bowl. It should reach a smooth, slightly thick, spreadable consistency – bear in mind that you might not need all the lime juice, depending on how big your limes are! Once the cake has fully cooled, drizzle the icing all over the top of the cake. Finish with lime zest and plenty of extra desiccated coconut sprinkled on top.

use dairy-free milk

use lactose-free milk

MAKES · 10

TAKES · 30 MINUTES + COOLING

- 120ml (½ cup) milk
- 1 tbsp lemon juice
- 1 large egg
- 170g (¾ cup) butter, softened, plus extra for greasing
- 200g (1 cup) caster (superfine) sugar
- 200g (1½ cups) gluten-free plain (all-purpose) flour
- ¼ tsp xanthan gum
- 60g (⅔ cup) unsweetened cocoa powder
- 1 tsp gluten-free baking powder
- ¼ tsp bicarbonate of soda (baking soda)
- 60ml (¼ cup) hot water

For the filling

- ½ quantity Swiss meringue buttercream (page 210)

OR

- ½ quantity vanilla buttercream (page 209)

OR

- Jar of store-bought marshmallow fluff

If you've never had a whoopie pie before, then now's the time to correct that! Pick either light and fluffy Swiss meringue buttercream, creamy, sweet buttercream, or sticky marshmallow fluff as your filling, then sandwich it between two of the softest mini chocolate sponges on Earth. Then all that's left to do is take one big bite!

Preheat your oven to 170°C fan / 190°C / 375°F. Grease 2 large baking sheets and line with non-stick baking parchment. (Or grease a whoopie pie pan if you have one.)

Put your milk and lemon juice into a jug (pitcher) and briefly mix. Allow to stand for 10–15 minutes until it becomes thicker and a little lumpy. Once it does, crack in your egg and mix together.

In a large mixing bowl, cream together the butter and sugar until light and fluffy (I prefer to use an electric hand whisk or a stand mixer for this).

In a separate, medium mixing bowl, mix together your flour, xanthan gum, cocoa powder, baking powder and bicarb.

Add the dry mixture to the creamed butter mixture a quarter at a time, followed by a quarter of the egg and milk mixture, alternating them and mixing between each addition until everything is incorporated and smooth. Pour in your hot water and briefly mix until combined.

Use an ice-cream scoop to scoop out portions of the mixture, then dollop them onto your prepared baking sheets (at a pinch, a tablespoon will do the job too). Allow space between each dollop as they will spread out as they bake.

Bake in the oven for 9–10 minutes until they spring back when touched. Remove from the oven, allow to cool briefly on the sheets for 5 minutes, then transfer to a wire rack to cool completely.

Once cooled, spread your chosen filling on the flat side of one of your sponges, then sandwich another one top to create your whoopie pies.

TIP:
Flavour the whoopie pie sponges however you like by adding 1 tsp orange or mint extract to the cake batter.

CHOCOLATE Swiss Roll

use dairy-free chocolate, dairy-free cream cheese (minimum 23% fat) instead of mascarpone, and dairy-free cream (minimum 30% fat)

use lactose-free chocolate, lactose-free cream cheese instead of mascarpone, and lactose-free whipping cream (minimum 30% fat)

MAKES · 10 SLICES

TAKES · 50 MINUTES + COOLING

- 2 tbsp oil, plus extra for greasing
- 4 medium eggs
- 100g (½ cup) caster (superfine) sugar
- ½ tsp vanilla extract
- 2 tbsp milk
- 45g (⅓ cup) gluten-free plain (all-purpose) flour
- 15g (1½ tbsp) unsweetened cocoa powder
- ¼ tsp xanthan gum

For the cream filling

- 250ml (1 cup) double (heavy) cream
- 50g (5¾ tbsp) icing (confectioners') sugar, sifted, plus extra for dusting
- 50g (1¾oz) mascarpone

To serve

- 120g (4oz) milk or dark chocolate, finely chopped
- 175ml (¾ cup) double (heavy) cream

This isn't something I ever thought would be possible to make using gluten-free ingredients. But in reality... it was incredibly simple! The chocolate sponge is so light and moist, with a swirl of thick, sweet creamy filling, topped with a game-changing chocolate ganache.

Preheat your oven to 180°C fan / 200°C / 400°F. Grease a 35 x 25cm (14 x 10 in) Swiss roll tin (pan), and line with non-stick baking parchment.

Separate your eggs, placing the egg whites into a small bowl and the yolks into a large mixing bowl.

Add half the caster sugar to the yolks in the large mixing bowl and whisk together until combined. Next, add the vanilla extract, milk and 2 tablespoons of oil and whisk once more.

Sift in the flour, cocoa powder and xanthan gum, and mix well using a balloon whisk until thick, combined and glossy.

In a separate bowl, whisk your egg whites (I prefer using an electric hand whisk or stand mixer for this, but it's entirely doable by hand) until they start to turn white and frothy. Gradually add the remaining caster sugar, whisking continuously until you have medium peaks.

In three stages, fold your egg white mixture into your egg yolk mixture using a silicone spatula. Once fully combined, pour into your prepared tin and gently spread it out to make sure it's even. Bake for 10–12 minutes. While it is baking, place a sheet of baking parchment on your work surface and dust lightly with icing sugar.

When cooked, the sponge should have come away a little from the sides of the tin and be slightly risen. Remove it from the oven and carefully invert it onto the dusted baking parchment. Peel off the lining parchment. Now, while the sponge is still warm, roll it up from a long side, with the parchment inside it as you roll. Place to one side and leave to cool completely while rolled up.

While the sponge is cooling, make your cream filling (again, I prefer to use an electric hand whisk for this). In a large mixing bowl, whisk the cream and icing sugar together until soft peaks form, then fold in the mascarpone until well combined to create a fluffy, stiff cream.

To assemble, carefully unroll the cooled sponge and remove the baking parchment. Spread a layer of cream filling around 1cm (½in) thick over the sponge, leaving a 5mm (¼in) clear border around the edges. Carefully roll the sponge back up and transfer to a serving plate, seam-side down. Chill in the fridge while you make the chocolate ganache topping.

Put your chopped chocolate into a heatproof bowl. Heat your cream in a small pan until just before boiling. Pour the cream over the chocolate and allow it to sit for about 5 minutes without stirring. Then stir together so it's all melted, thoroughly combined and pourable.

Drizzle the ganache over your chilled Swiss roll and allow to fully set before serving.

CHOCOLATE ORANGE

use dairy-free chocolate, milk and cream (minimum 30% fat), and a (hard) dairy-free butter alternative

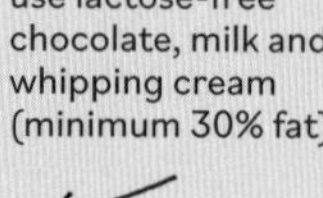

use lactose-free chocolate, milk and whipping cream (minimum 30% fat)

MAKES · 15 SLICES

TAKES · 1½ HOURS + AT LEAST 30 MINUTES CHILLING

- 340g (1½ cups) butter, softened, plus extra for greasing
- 340g (scant 1¾ cups) caster (superfine) sugar
- 6 large eggs
- 4 tsp orange extract
- 285g (2 cups plus 2 tbsp) gluten-free self-raising (self-rising) flour
- ¼ tsp gluten-free baking powder
- ½ tsp xanthan gum
- 50g (½ cup) unsweetened cocoa powder, sifted

For the buttercream

- 300g (10½oz) dark chocolate, broken into pieces
- 500g (scant 2¼ cups) butter, softened
- 1kg (7 cups) icing (confectioners') sugar, sifted
- 3 tsp orange extract
- 1–3 tsp milk, if needed

For the chocolate orange drip

- 80g (3oz) dark or milk chocolate, broken into pieces
- 80ml (⅓ cup) double (heavy) cream
- ½ tsp orange extract (optional)

To finish

- Finely pared zest of 1 orange
- Any chocolate orange-flavoured chocolate bars (optional)

For special occasions, I always whip out my chocolate orange drip cake and each time I do, I'm still in slight disbelief that I was able to make and decorate it all by myself. And trust me, if I can do it, then you definitely can too! Chocolate orange flavour runs through every aspect of this cake, and the finish will have muggles eyeing it up without a doubt.

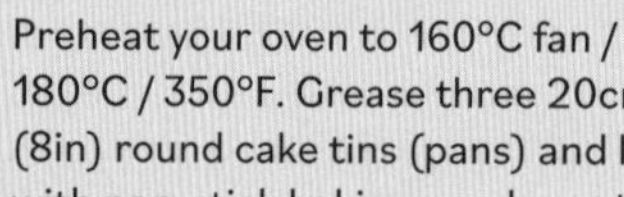

Preheat your oven to 160°C fan / 180°C / 350°F. Grease three 20cm (8in) round cake tins (pans) and line with non-stick baking parchment.

In a large mixing bowl, cream together the butter and sugar until light and fluffy (I prefer to use an electric hand whisk or a stand mixer for this). Add your eggs one at a time, mixing between each addition, then mix in your orange extract. Add your flour, baking powder, xanthan gum and cocoa powder. Mix for a final time until well combined.

Divide the mixture evenly between the three tins and bake in the oven for 25–30 minutes until risen and cooked through – check by poking a skewer into the middle; if it comes out clean, then they're done. Leave the sponges in their tins for about 5 minutes before turning them out onto a wire rack to cool completely.

Once cooled, use a cake leveller (or sharp knife) to trim the risen top of each sponge to create a perfectly level top. Ensure that you don't tear through the cake as you do this.

Next, make your buttercream. I use a stand mixer for this, but an electric hand whisk will do the job just fine too. I wouldn't recommend doing this by hand as it's a large amount of buttercream... however, it is possible!

Firstly, melt your dark chocolate (I do this in the microwave, mixing in between short bursts until melted), then put to one side and allow to cool slightly. Place your butter in the bowl of a stand mixer and mix on a medium speed for about 5 minutes until the butter is fluffy and paler in colour.

Add your icing sugar in two or three stages, beating for about 3 minutes between each addition. Start your mixer slowly (to avoid creating a mini icing sugar explosion) but then increase the speed to medium-high for each of your 3-minute mixing intervals. Add in your slightly cooled, melted chocolate and the orange extract. Mix until fully combined. If the icing seems too thick, just add a little milk (dairy-free or lactose-free if necessary) to loosen it up.

To assemble your cake, place the first sponge on a flat serving plate and spread an even layer of buttercream on top, then add your second sponge on top of that. Spread some buttercream on top of that sponge and finish by placing your final sponge on top (flat-side up).

Continued overleaf...

To smooth over the sides, simply touch the icing with your cake scraper and rotate the cake stand/serving plate until you achieve a smooth finish – an icing turntable comes in handy here but isn't essential. For the top of the cake, smooth the buttercream inwards towards the middle of your cake with your cake scraper to create nice, sharp edges and a smooth top.

To make the chocolate orange drip, place your chocolate and cream into a microwavable bowl and heat for about 20 seconds, then mix. Return to the microwave and continue to blast for 10-second intervals, mixing in between, until the mixture is smooth and completely melted. If using, stir in your orange extract.

Put your chocolate drip mixture into a piping bag and snip the end off, leaving a 3mm (⅛in) hole. Pipe the drip around the very edge of the cake slowly and carefully, encouraging it over the edge every 1cm (½in) or so. Squeeze out differing amounts as you go so that the drips vary in length.

Once the drips are all done, fit a piping bag with a large open star nozzle and fill with the remaining buttercream, then pipe a ring around the top of the cake. Finish with a little orange zest and, optionally, any gluten-free chocolate orange bars you can get your hands on.

Next, apply a crumb coat to the entire cake: this will help to achieve a super-smooth finish to the icing, which is vital for a drip cake. It basically involves applying an extremely thin coating of buttercream, so use a small, cranked palette knife to do exactly that. You should be able to see all of the sponges through the crumb coat.

You should now have a 'naked' finish to your cake. Place the cake in the fridge for 30–60 minutes for the crumb coat to set. Cover the remaining buttercream to stop it from drying out.

Now it's time to ice your cake for real. Use a large palette knife to apply a 5mm (¼in) coating of buttercream to the entire cake, so that it's completely covered and pretty 'rustic' looking.

TIP:

If you remove all the orange extract, you've got a chocolate drip cake. If you replace it with mint extract, you've got a mint chocolate drip cake. Then simply top with gluten-free chocolate that complements your flavours. Use this wisdom as you will!

Mark's Mum's PANDAN CHIFFON CAKE

MAKES · 12 SLICES

TAKES · 1 HOUR + COOLING

- 120ml (½ cup) full-fat coconut milk
- 6 large egg yolks
- 25g (2 tbsp) caster (superfine) sugar
- 2 tsp pandan extract
- 120g (1 cup minus 1½ tbsp) gluten-free plain (all-purpose) flour
- 1½ tsp gluten-free baking powder
- 4 tbsp vegetable oil
- Green food colouring paste

For the egg white mixture

- 6 large egg whites
- ½ tsp cream of tartar
- 75g (6 tbsp) caster (superfine) sugar

This cake is a Malaysian classic that Mark has been enjoying throughout his entire life. I'd never had a slice until he adapted his mum's recipe to be gluten-free for me (that's true love, right?). The cake is fluffy like a cloud, with a subtle coconut flavour and the fragrant, sweet, rice-like flavour of pandan leaves. Trust me – you need to try it! You can find pandan extract in Chinese supermarkets or online.

Preheat your oven to 170°C fan / 190°C / 375°F. Have ready a 25cm (10in) round, loose-bottomed chiffon tin (pan), which will be ungreased and unlined (believe it or not, we *want* the cake to stick to the tin!).

Pour your coconut milk into a jug (pitcher) and give it a good mix as it often separates in the tin.

In a large mixing bowl, whisk the egg yolks and sugar until well combined, then whisk in the coconut milk and pandan extract. Add the flour and baking powder and whisk until smooth. Lastly, whisk in the oil, and enough green food colouring paste to achieve a vibrant green colour.

I use a stand mixer for this next part, but you can easily do this using an electric hand whisk. Doing this process by hand is also doable, but in that case, it's vital that you whisk long enough to achieve stiff peaks.

Whisk the egg whites and mix on a medium speed until bubbly and frothy, then stop the mixer. Add the cream of tartar and return to mixing on a medium speed. Add the sugar in two batches, mixing between each addition. Once all the sugar has been added, turn the speed up to high until stiff peaks form, if they haven't already.

Whisk your green cake mixture briefly to ensure the flour hasn't all sunk to the bottom. Then gently fold the egg white mixture into it, a third at a time, until completely incorporated. Ensure the mixture looks completely consistent and doesn't look marbled – this is a sign that the egg whites aren't fully incorporated yet. Watch out for lumps of egg white too, and fold these in as you see them.

Pour into your chiffon tin and bake for 15 minutes, then reduce the oven temperature to 150°C fan / 170°C / 340°F and bake for a further 20 minutes until risen and golden brown.

Remove from the oven and immediately invert the tin and allow to fully cool, upside-down inside the tin. This cake *must* fully cool upside-down while stuck in the tin; gravity will ensure the cake doesn't sink under its own weight as it cools.

Once fully cooled, smoothly run a palette knife around the edge of the tin, being careful not to 'saw' into the cake. Now the cake has been loosened, you should be able to invert it out onto a serving dish. Carefully run a palette knife between the bottom of the cake and the loose-bottom part of the tin and remove it.

Serve with whipped cream if you fancy, and enjoy. Once cooled, store in an airtight container in the fridge, or freeze for up to 3 months.

TIP:
If you have access to pandan leaves, instead of using pandan extract and food colouring, you can use those instead. Simply place 12 chopped pandan leaves and 2 tbsp water into a food processor and pulse until smooth. Sieve the mixture and add 3 tbsp of the pandan mixture along with the coconut milk.

·JAMAICAN· Ginger Cake

use a dairy-free butter alternative

use a dairy-free butter alternative and 1 tbsp ground flaxseed mixed with 3 tbsp water (allowed to rest) instead of the egg

MAKES · 12 SLICES

TAKES · 1 HOUR 20 MINUTES

- 70g (3½ tbsp) black treacle (molasses)
- 70g (3½ tbsp) golden syrup
- 70g (5 tbsp) dark brown sugar
- 70g (⅓ cup minus 1 tsp) butter, plus extra for greasing
- 70ml (4½ tbsp) water
- 170g (1¼ cups) gluten-free self-raising (self-rising) flour
- ½ tsp xanthan gum
- 3 tsp ground ginger
- 1 tbsp ground cinnamon
- ½ tsp ground nutmeg
- ¾ tsp bicarbonate of soda (baking soda)
- 1 medium egg, beaten

This cake was inspired by the Jamaican ginger cake that my mum always brought home from the supermarket. Sadly, it's been over a decade since I was able to eat it, so I made my own version instead and I'm tremendously glad I did! It's warming, sticky, with a sweet, deep molasses flavour and a pudding-like texture – serve warm with custard and let me know what you think!

Preheat your oven to 160°C fan / 180°C / 350°F. Lightly grease a 900g (2lb) loaf tin (pan) and line with non-stick baking parchment.

In a small saucepan, gently heat your treacle, syrup, sugar, butter and water, stirring until completely melted; don't allow to boil.

In a large mixing bowl, mix your flour, xanthan gum and spices, then pour your warm syrup mixture into it. Mix together until lovely and smooth.

Add half your beaten egg, stir in, then add the other half and stir in until combined.

In a small dish, add 2 tablespoons water to the bicarb, mix until well combined and then add to your cake mixture and stir in to combine. The mixture should now look nice and smooth. Pour into the loaf tin and bake for 60 minutes until a golden dark brown and cooked through (stick a skewer into the middle; if it comes out clean, it's done).

Remove from the oven and allow to cool briefly in the tin before transferring to a wire rack. Serve warm with custard, or on its own at room temperature – the choice is yours!

LEMON & RASPBERRY Battenberg

MAKES · 10 SLICES

TAKES · 1 HOUR + COOLING

- 175g (generous ¾ cup) butter, softened
- 175g (¾ cup minus 2 tbsp) caster (superfine) sugar
- 140g (1 cup plus 1 tbsp) gluten-free self-raising (self-rising) flour
- 50g (½ cup) ground almonds (almond flour)
- ½ tsp gluten-free baking powder
- 3 medium eggs
- Grated zest of 1 lemon (or ½ tsp lemon extract)
- Yellow food colouring paste
- ½ tsp raspberry extract (sometimes also called raspberry flavouring)
- Pink or red food colouring paste

To assemble and finish

- 6 tbsp raspberry jam (ideally seedless)
- 400g (14oz) white marzipan, plus a little icing (confectioners') sugar, sifted, for rolling
- Handful of fresh raspberries
- A little finely pared lemon zest

Lemon and raspberry is one of my favourite flavour combos, never failing to make me feel like I'm sipping an ice-cold pink lemonade on a warm, breezy day. Coupled with the traditional marzipan finish of a Battenberg, there's a wonderful zesty lemon and raspberry Bakewell flavour that I just can't get enough of.

Preheat your oven to 160°C fan / 180°C / 350°F. Line a 23cm (9in) square cake tin (pan) with non-stick baking parchment, so that there is a middle pleat that divides the tin in half. (Or line the tin as normal, then use foil to create a makeshift dam to divide the tin.)

In a large mixing bowl, cream your butter and sugar until light and fluffy (I prefer to use an electric hand whisk or a stand mixer for this). Add the flour, ground almonds, baking powder and eggs, and mix until smooth and combined.

Divide your mixture evenly between two bowls. To one bowl, add the lemon zest (or lemon extract) and enough yellow food colouring paste to achieve a vibrant yellow colour. To the other bowl, add the raspberry extract and enough pink or red food colouring paste to achieve a pastel pink colour.

Pour your cake mixtures into either side of your prepared tin and bake in the oven for 25–30 minutes, or until cooked through. Check by poking a skewer into the middle – if it comes out clean, then they're done. Leave the sponges in their tins for about 5 minutes before turning them out onto a wire rack to cool completely.

Heat the raspberry jam (in the microwave is easiest) so that it is lovely and smooth for sticking together your cakes. Allow to cool.

Trim the edges of both cooled sponges using a sharp knife, and carefully use a cake leveller or knife to remove the tops, revealing all that beautiful colour hiding beneath. Cut two strips out of each sponge that are equal in height and width – I measure the height of the sponge and then use that as a guide for how wide each strip should be. If needed, trim the end of the strips to ensure they're all identical in length.

Dust your work surface with a little icing sugar and roll out your marzipan to a 4mm (¼in) thickness, aiming for a large square that's around 20cm (8in) wide. Brush the marzipan liberally with your now slightly cooled raspberry jam, reserving a little for later.

Place one of each colour strip into the middle of the marzipan (browned bottom facing up) and brush the tops with jam. Brush between the two coloured strips with more jam and then push them together. Place the other two sponges on top (browned bottom facing up again) but this time reverse the order of the colours to create a chequerboard effect, brushing between the strips with jam before pushing them together.

Carefully bring the marzipan up and over your assembled strips, keeping it as tight to the cake as possible to reduce any gaps. Trim any excess marzipan to create a seam right in the middle – this will be underneath so no need to be too neat.

Carefully flip the cake over and trim the cake at each end to remove the excess marzipan, revealing your beautiful chequerboard pattern. Finish with fresh raspberries and lemon zest.

Pictured on page 38.

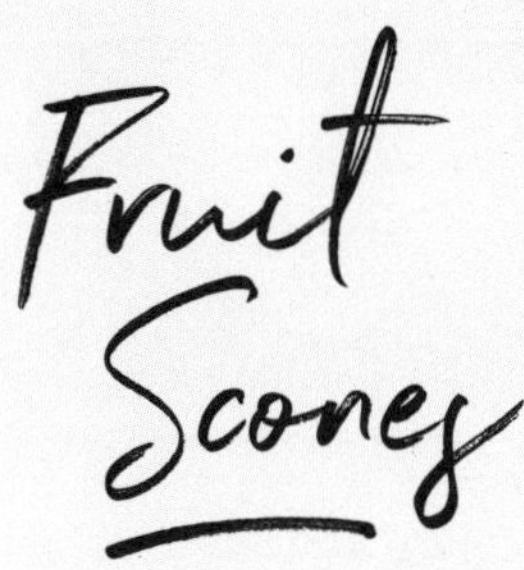

use dairy-free milk and a (hard) dairy-free butter alternative

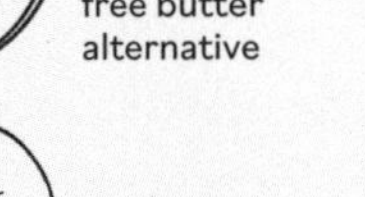

use lactose-free milk

use dairy-free milk (also for brushing the tops in place of egg) and a (hard) dairy-free butter alternative

MAKES · 7–8 SCONES

TAKES · 30 MINUTES

- 340g (2½ cups) gluten-free self-raising (self-rising) flour, plus extra for dusting
- 1 tsp gluten-free baking powder
- ¼ tsp xanthan gum
- 85g (⅓ cup plus 2 tsp) cold butter, cubed
- 4 tbsp caster (superfine) sugar
- 75g (2½oz) sultanas (golden raisins) or chopped glacé cherries
- 175ml (¾ cup) milk
- 3 tsp lemon juice
- 1½ tsp vanilla extract
- 1 large egg, beaten

When *the* Nigella Lawson recommended my gluten-free scones on Twitter, I absolutely knew I had to pop them in this book. So here's a spin on that recipe which incorporates dried fruit. If it's good enough for Nigella, it's certainly good enough for me!

Preheat your oven to 200°C fan / 220°C / 425°F. Line a baking sheet with non-stick baking parchment and place in the oven to heat up.

In a large mixing bowl, mix your flour, baking powder and xanthan gum. Add your cold, cubed butter and rub it in with your fingertips until you achieve a breadcrumb-like consistency, then stir in the sugar and sultanas or cherries.

Gently warm your milk in a jug (pitcher). I do this in the microwave at full power for about 35 seconds, but ensure that it doesn't get hot – it needs to be lukewarm. Add your lemon juice to the milk and allow to stand for 1–2 minutes – it will look slightly curdled and lumpy when it's ready. Add the vanilla extract to the milk and beat until well combined.

Make a well in the middle of your dry mixture. Pour in the wet mixture and work it in using a metal fork or knife. Keep working it till it forms a slightly sticky dough.

Lightly dust your work surface and hands with a little flour. Turn the dough out of your bowl and fold it a few times to bring it together. Then shape the dough into a round that's about 4cm (1½in) thick. The taller, the better! Ensure you don't work the dough too much or it will be tough once baked.

Using a 5cm (2in) round or fluted cookie cutter, push down into the dough and lift out your scone with the cutter. Gently push the dough out of the cutter and put to one side until you have used up all the dough. Instead of re-rolling the dough, keep gently re-rounding the dough back into a ball using your hands and continue to cut out your scones.

Brush the tops of the scones with beaten egg, transfer to the hot baking sheet and bake for about 12–15 minutes until golden on top.

Allow to cool briefly before enjoying warm, or allow to cool completely, then serve with jam and cream. Once cooled, store in an airtight container or freeze for up to 3 months.

Making it low FODMAP?
Use lactose-free milk and add sultanas rather than glacé cherries, but no more than 50g (1¾oz) of them (or leave out the dried fruit entirely.). One scone is a safe low-FODMAP serving size.

Pictured on pages 2 and 38.

Manor House FRUIT CAKE

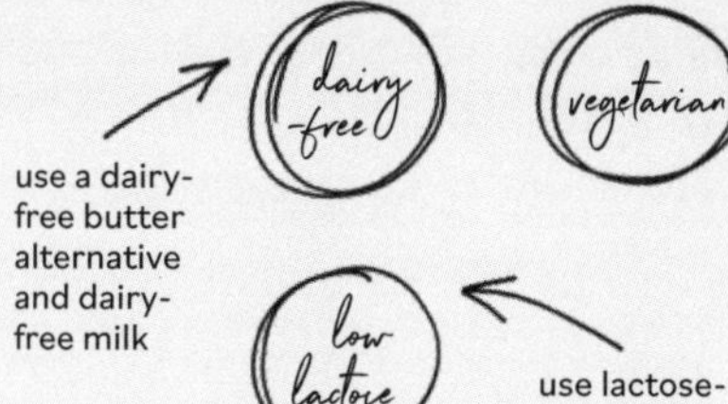
dairy-free
vegetarian
use a dairy-free butter alternative and dairy-free milk
low lactose
use lactose-free milk

MAKES · 10 SLICES

TAKES · 2¼ HOURS + 1 HOUR SOAKING

- 525g (1lb 3oz) dried fruit (I like to use a mix of raisins, currants, sultanas/golden raisins and chopped glacé cherries)
- 150ml (⅝ cup) hot strong English breakfast tea, made using 2 tea bags
- 300g (1⅓ cups) butter, softened, plus extra for greasing
- 300g (1½ cups) caster (superfine) sugar
- 4 medium eggs
- 450g (3½ cups minus 2 tsp) gluten-free self-raising (self-rising) flour, plus 1 tbsp for the fruit
- 1 tsp xanthan gum
- 1½ tsp ground ginger
- 1 tsp ground cinnamon
- 285ml (1 cup plus 3 tbsp) milk
- 2 tbsp demerara (turbinado) sugar

More often than not, the inspiration behind my recipes can be found on supermarket shelves, wrapped in plastic, in a cardboard box. Ok – it doesn't sound all that inspiring to most, but as soon as you're told you can't eat them ever again, it's almost impossible to fight the urge to recreate them at home. But not surprisingly, you'll find that when you make your own, it's always a million miles better than what you used to buy in the supermarket anyway!

Place the dried fruit in a large mixing bowl and pour over the hot, strong tea. Mix, then allow to sit for at least an hour so the fruit has time to hydrate. When you are ready to use the fruit, drain off the tea.

Preheat your oven to 140°C fan / 160°C / 325°F. Grease a deep 20cm (8in) round, loose-bottomed or springform cake tin (pan) and line with non-stick baking parchment.

In a large mixing bowl, cream together your butter and caster sugar until light and fluffy (I prefer to use an electric hand whisk or a stand mixer for this). Add your eggs one at a time, mixing between each addition.

In a separate, medium mixing bowl, stir together your flour, xanthan gum, ginger and cinnamon. Add half your flour mixture to the large mixing bowl and mix in. Follow this by mixing in half the milk, then repeat with the remaining flour and milk until everything is combined.

Coat the dried fruit in the tablespoon of flour to prevent it from sinking in the cake, before carefully folding the fruit into your cake mixture. Spoon into the prepared tin, ensuring that it's nice and level. Sprinkle it with the demerara sugar and bake in the oven for 90 minutes.

Check the cake after this time, and if the top is starting to brown too much, then cover with some foil. Bake for a further 30 minutes until cooked through: check by poking a skewer into the middle – if it comes out clean, then it's done. Allow to cool in the tin for about 15 minutes before removing to a wire rack and allowing to cool completely.

Maple
Pecan

APPLE CAKE

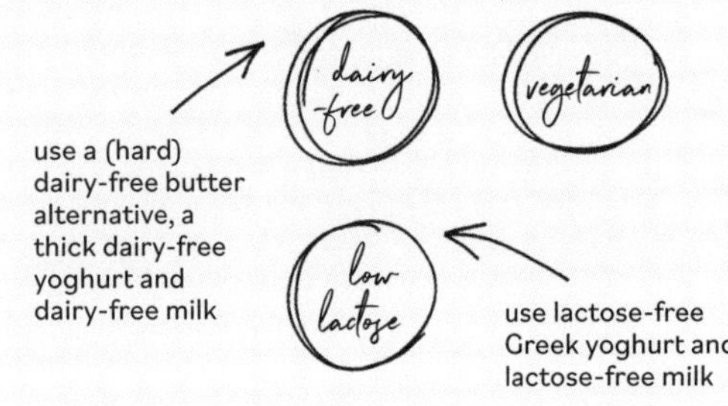
dairy-free
vegetarian
low lactose
use a (hard) dairy-free butter alternative, a thick dairy-free yoghurt and dairy-free milk
use lactose-free Greek yoghurt and lactose-free milk

MAKES · 12 SLICES

TAKES · 1¼ HOURS + COOLING

- 200g (1½ cups) gluten-free plain (all-purpose) flour
- ¼ tsp xanthan gum
- 2 tsp gluten-free baking powder
- ½ tsp bicarbonate of soda (baking soda)
- 1 tsp ground cinnamon
- 140g (¾ cup) light brown sugar
- 200g (7oz) cooking apples, such as Bramley, peeled, cored and chopped
- 75g (2½oz) pecans, toasted and finely chopped, plus 50g (1¾oz) for the top
- 2 large eggs
- 1 tsp vanilla extract
- 115ml (scant ½ cup) vegetable oil, plus extra for greasing
- 115ml (scant ½ cup) Greek yoghurt or sour cream

For the topping

- 20g (¾oz) butter, melted and cooled
- 1 tsp ground cinnamon
- 45g (¼ cup) caster (superfine) sugar

For the maple drizzle

- 200g (1½ cups) icing (confectioners') sugar, sifted
- 30ml (2 tbsp) maple syrup
- 30ml (2 tbsp) milk

Maple pecan is a flavour sensation on its own, but pairing it with my incredibly moist, cinnamon-spiced, apple cake, then topping it with sweet, crisp topping? It's a match made in gluten-free heaven, or as it's now more commonly known, your own kitchen!

Preheat your oven to 160°C fan / 180°C / 350°F. Grease a deep 20cm (8in) round loose-bottomed or springform cake tin (pan) and line with non-stick baking parchment.

Start by making the topping. Mix together the cooled, melted butter, cinnamon and sugar so that it forms an almost sandy, clumpy mixture, then place to one side.

In a large mixing bowl, put your flour, xanthan gum, baking powder, bicarb, cinnamon and sugar. Stir in your chopped apple so it is evenly dispersed, followed by your chopped pecans.

In a medium mixing bowl, mix together your eggs, vanilla extract, oil and yoghurt or sour cream until combined.

Add your wet mixture to your dry ingredients and carefully mix together using a spatula or wooden spoon until combined – definitely don't overmix this one! Spoon the batter into your tin, making sure it's nice and level. Sprinkle over the topping you prepared earlier, ensuring a full coverage.

Bake in the oven for 45 minutes until golden brown and cooked through – check by poking a skewer into the middle – if it comes out clean, it's done. Allow to cool in the tin for about 15 minutes before transferring to a wire rack to cool completely.

While the cake is cooling, make the drizzle by mixing the ingredients together in a bowl until smooth and of a pourable consistency.

Sprinkle half of your 50g (1¾oz) toasted chopped pecans over the top of the cake, then drizzle your maple glaze on top, followed by the remaining pecans.

use dairy-free milk, and a (hard) dairy-free butter alternative

use lactose-free milk

MAKES · 15 SLICES

TAKES · 1 HOUR 50 MINUTES + AT LEAST 30 MINUTES CHILLING

For 3 sponge cake layers (i.e half the total)

- 225g (1 cup) butter, softened, plus extra for greasing
- 225g (1 cup plus 2 tbsp) caster (superfine) sugar
- 4 large eggs
- 1 tsp vanilla extract
- 225g (1¾ cups) gluten-free self-raising (self-rising) flour
- 1 tsp gluten-free baking powder
- ¼ tsp xanthan gum
- Food colouring pastes (red, orange, yellow, green, blue, purple)

For the vanilla buttercream

- 500g (scant 2¼ cups) butter, softened
- 1kg (7 cups) icing (confectioners') sugar, sifted
- 2 tsp vanilla extract
- 1–3 tsp milk, if needed

To finish

- Gluten-free multi-coloured sprinkles

This cake is made of six sponges, but to get the job done perfectly, we'll be making three at a time. Please ensure you have double of all the ingredients required for the sponge before you start!

The sight of a gluten-free rainbow cake never fails to fill me with glee – it's everything I thought gluten-free baking could never be! Please tag me in your photos on Instagram if you bake this because I love seeing them!

Preheat your oven to 160°C fan / 180°C / 350°F. Grease three 20cm (8in) round cake tins (pans) and line with non-stick baking parchment.

In a mixing bowl, cream the butter and sugar until fluffy (I use an electric hand whisk or a stand mixer). Add the eggs one by one, mixing between each, then mix in the vanilla extract. Mix in your flour, baking powder and xanthan gum until combined. Divide the mixture equally into three bowls and add red, orange and yellow food colouring, one to each bowl – just enough to achieve a vibrant colour. Don't overmix the batter. Pour each mixture into a prepared tin and bake for 20–25 minutes. Check they're done by poking a skewer into the middle; if it comes out clean, they're ready. Leave the sponges in their tins for 5 minutes before turning out onto a wire rack to cool.

Clean your tins and then make three more sponges the same way, using green, blue and purple food colouring this time.

Once cooled, use a cake leveller (or sharp knife) to trim the risen tops of all six sponges to create level tops.

To make the buttercream, place the butter into the bowl of a stand mixer (or use an electric hand whisk) and mix on a medium speed for 5 minutes until fluffy. Add the icing sugar in three stages, beating for 3 minutes between each addition. Start your mixer slowly to avoid an icing sugar explosion, but then increase the speed to medium-high each time. Finally, mix in the vanilla extract. If the icing seems too thick, add a little milk (dairy-free or lactose-free if needed) to loosen.

To assemble your cake, place the purple sponge on a serving plate and spread a small layer of buttercream on top. Repeat, layering your sponges and buttercream in the following order: blue, green, yellow, orange and, finally, red on top. Next, apply a crumb coat. This means applying a thin coating of buttercream all over the cake, so use a small, cranked palette knife to do just that. You should be able to see all the sponges through the crumb coat. Place the cake in the fridge for 30–60 minutes to allow it to set. Cover the remaining buttercream to stop it drying out.

Now ice your cake for real. Use a palette knife to apply a 5mm (¼in) coating of buttercream to the entire cake. To smooth the sides, simply touch the icing with a cake scraper and rotate the plate until you achieve a smooth finish – an icing turntable comes in handy here. For the top of the cake, smooth the buttercream inwards with your cake scraper to create sharp edges and a smooth top. Pipe any leftover buttercream on top and finish with gluten-free sprinkles.

Angel Cake Slice

use a (hard) dairy-free butter alternative → dairy-free

low fodmap

low lactose

vegetarian

MAKE · 8 SLICES

TAKES · 1 HOUR + COOLING

For the génoise sponges

- Oil, for greasing
- 115g (¾ cup plus 2 tbsp) gluten-free plain (all-purpose) flour
- ½ tsp gluten-free baking powder
- 4 large eggs, separated
- 125g (⅔ cup minus 2 tsp) caster (superfine) sugar

For the vanilla sponge

- ½ tsp vanilla extract

For the raspberry sponge

- ½ tsp raspberry extract
- Pink or red food colouring paste

For the yellow sponge

- Grated zest of 1 lemon (or ½ tsp lemon extract)
- Yellow food colouring paste

For the Italian meringue buttercream

- 100g (½ cup) caster (superfine) sugar
- 4 tbsp water
- 1 large egg white
- 85g (⅓ cup plus 2 tsp) butter, cubed and softened

For the icing

- 200g (1½ cups) icing (confectioners') sugar, sifted
- 30ml (2 tbsp) water
- Pink or red food colouring paste

Who could resist an angelic slice of gluten-free heaven? Each génoise sponge is as light as a cloud, flavoured with vanilla, raspberry and lemon – separated by sweet and fluffy Italian meringue buttercream. The pink and white feathered icing on top is, quite literally, the icing on the cake! Make sure you use food colouring paste for this one as liquid food colouring can dilute your mixture (not good!) while still failing to provide a vibrant colour.

Preheat your oven to 170°C fan / 190°C / 375°F. Grease three 900g (2lb) loaf tins (pans) with a little oil and line with non-stick baking parchment. Alternatively, if you don't have this many tins to hand, you can always use a large rectangular baking tin. In that case, you'd need to use three loaf tin liners and place three of those in your rectangular baking tin for an easy option.

In a small bowl, combine the flour and baking powder and set aside.

In the bowl of a stand mixer, add the egg whites and whisk on a medium-high speed. Once soft peaks form, add the sugar in two batches, mixing in between each addition. Once all the sugar has been added, turn the speed up to high until stiff peaks form, if they haven't already.

Lower the speed of the mixer back to medium and, still mixing, add the egg yolks. Once incorporated, stop the mixer and add your dry mixture. Mix until smooth and consistent. At this point, it's important to work quickly! Spoon your mixture evenly into three small mixing bowls.

Gently fold the vanilla extract into one bowl, using a silicone spatula. To another bowl, fold in the raspberry extract and enough pink or red food colouring to achieve a pastel pink colour. To the final bowl, fold in the lemon zest or extract and enough yellow food-colouring paste to achieve a vibrant yellow colour.

Pour each mixture into each of your prepared baking tins (or each section of your prepared rectangular tin) and spread out using a silicone spatula. Gently shake from side to side to create a smooth, even finish.

Bake in the oven for 12 minutes. They will initially rise a lot and sink down once removed from the oven – that's fine! Turn all three sponges onto a wire rack and allow to cool completely.

While the sponges are cooling, make the Italian meringue buttercream. Put the sugar and water in a small saucepan and place over a low heat. Put the egg white in a stand mixer and whisk on a high speed until you achieve soft peaks, then stop. (If your stand mixer struggles to whisk this small quantity of egg white, you can always achieve the same result using an electric hand whisk.)

Continued overleaf...

Meanwhile, keep an eye on your syrup. Once all the sugar has dissolved, increase the heat to medium and bring to the boil until the mixture reaches 120°C (240°F). At this point, there's no need to stir the mixture. If you don't have a digital cooking thermometer, pay close attention to the middle of the mixture: once it starts bubbling, wait around 30 seconds to 1 minute and it should be ready.

Once your egg white has achieved soft peaks, pour in all of your sugar syrup with the mixer still running, trying not to let the sugar syrup touch the side of the bowl as it will instantly harden.

Continue mixing until the meringue is wonderfully thick and glossy, then allow to cool for around 20 minutes until room temperature (or the butter will melt when you add it).

Once cooled, start the mixer up again at a medium speed and add your softened butter cubes, two at a time, ensuring it is completely incorporated before adding the next two cubes. Once all your butter has been added, it should be fairly thick and fluffy. Definitely don't overmix this otherwise it'll turn into something which resembles scrambled eggs!

Place the buttercream in a small bowl and chill in the fridge until completely cooled and firm. Once cooled, you can start making the icing for the top of the cake.

Place your icing sugar and water in a small bowl and mix with a metal spoon until you achieve a thick, spreadable consistency. Transfer 2 tablespoons of this mixture to another small bowl and add a tiny amount of pink or red food colouring paste to achieve a pale pink colour. Place the pink icing in a piping bag.

To construct the angel cake, trim the edges off all the sponges for the neatest finish - this exposes all the beautiful colour hidden underneath, but is totally optional of course!

Place your vanilla sponge on a serving plate. Generously spread your chilled Italian meringue buttercream onto the sponge, then place the raspberry sponge on top. Add more Italian meringue buttercream and then place the final, yellow, layer on top.

Spoon the white icing on top, a tablespoon at a time, then use a palette knife to spread a lovely, thick layer. Try to avoid letting the icing drip off the edges! Snip off the end of your piping bag, leaving a 3mm (⅛in) hole. Pipe three lines of your pink icing down the length of the cake, roughly 1cm (½in) apart.

Using a cocktail stick, feather the icing in alternate directions to create a beautiful feathered pattern. Allow the icing to set for 30 minutes, then slice and enjoy.

TIP:
To clean the saucepan you made your sugar syrup in, simply fill with boiling water. Add in any utensils used too. Bring it to a simmer for 5–10 minutes and all the sugar will magically dissolve into the water. If you use cold water to clean your pan, the sugar syrup will harden and be near impossible to remove!

Want to make a simpler, quicker version? Make the sponges and allow to cool. Instead of making Italian meringue buttercream, simply double the icing quantities, mix it up and spread it between the layers and on top. Job done!

Zebra CAKE

use dairy-free milk and chocolate, and a (hard) dairy-free butter alternative

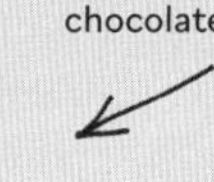

use lactose-free milk and chocolate

MAKES · 12 SLICES

TAKES · 1 HOUR + COOLING

- 225g (1 cup) butter, softened, plus extra for greasing
- 225g (1 cup plus 2 tbsp) caster (superfine) sugar
- 4 large eggs
- 1 tsp vanilla extract
- 220g (1¾ cups) gluten-free self-raising (self-rising) flour
- 1 tsp gluten-free baking powder
- ¼ tsp xanthan gum
- 3 tbsp unsweetened cocoa powder, sifted
- 2 tbsp milk
- 50g (1¾oz) white chocolate, grated, to finish

For the chocolate buttercream

- 55g (2oz) dark chocolate
- 125g (½ cup plus 1 tbsp) butter, softened
- 90g (⅔ cup) icing (confectioners') sugar
- 25g (¼ cup) unsweetened cocoa powder
- 1–3 tsp milk, if needed

I think we can all agree that 'fun' and 'gluten-free' don't often go hand in hand, but my chocolate and vanilla zebra cake disagrees. Despite its bold design, it's actually incredibly simple to achieve that eye-catching, striped effect; plus when every slice is chocolatey, sweet and moist, topped with an indulgent chocolate buttercream, this cake most definitely earns its stripes (sorry, I couldn't resist).

Preheat your oven to 160°C fan / 180°C / 350°F. Grease a deep 20cm (8in) round, loose-bottomed or springform tin (pan) and line it with non-stick baking parchment.

In a large mixing bowl, cream together your butter and sugar until light and fluffy (I prefer to use an electric hand whisk or a stand mixer for this). Add your eggs one at a time, mixing in between each addition, then add your vanilla extract and mix that in too. Add your flour, baking powder and xanthan gum and mix until well combined, then split your mixture equally into two bowls.

In a separate, small mixing bowl, mix together your cocoa powder and milk to form a smooth paste, then add this to one of the cake batters and mix in until well combined – don't overmix though.

Spoon about 2 tablespoons of the vanilla mixture into the middle of the cake tin, followed by 2 tablespoons of the chocolate mixture, again into the middle. Repeat this process, alternating the mixtures and creating a bullseye-like effect as the mixture spreads out and reaches the edges of the tin.

Bake in the oven for 30–35 minutes until cooked through. Check that it's cooked by sticking a skewer into the middle – if it comes out clean, then it's done.

Allow to cool briefly in the tin before transferring to a wire rack to cool completely.

While the cake is cooling, make your buttercream. Firstly, melt your dark chocolate (I do this in the microwave, mixing in between short bursts until melted), then put to one side to cool slightly while you make the rest of the buttercream.

Place your butter into the bowl of a stand mixer (an electric hand whisk will do the job just fine too, or you can do it by hand) and mix on a medium speed for about 5 minutes until fluffy and paler in colour. Sift in your icing sugar and mix until incorporated, then sift in your cocoa powder, mixing once more until fully combined.

Mix in your slightly cooled, melted chocolate until fully incorporated. If the icing seems too thick, just add a teaspoon or so of milk (dairy-free or lactose-free if needed) to loosen it.

Spread a thin layer of the buttercream all over the top and sides of your cooled zebra cake. Finish with some grated white chocolate.

PIÑATA

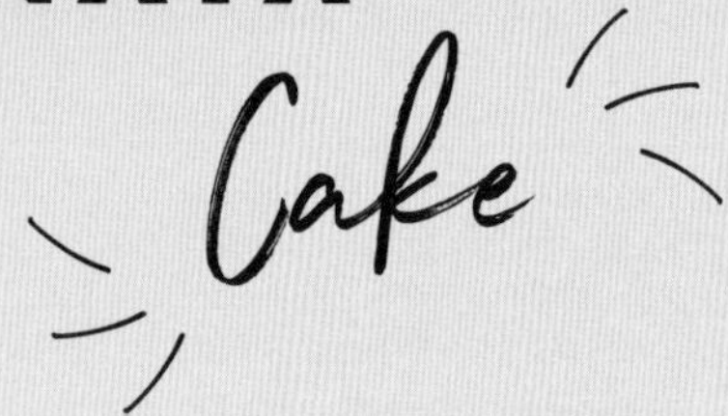

use dairy-free milk, a (hard) dairy-free butter alternative and ensure any treats used are dairy-free

vegetarian

use lactose-free milk and ensure treats used are FODMAP-friendly

use lactose-free milk and ensure any treats used are lactose-free

MAKES · 15 SLICES

TAKES · 1 HOUR 50 MINUTES + AT LEAST 30 MINUTES CHILLING

- 390g (1¾ cups plus 1 tbsp) butter, softened, plus extra for greasing
- 390g (2 cups minus 1 tbsp) caster (superfine) sugar
- 7 large eggs
- 2 tsp vanilla extract
- 390g (3 cups minus 1 tbsp) gluten-free self-raising (self-rising) flour
- 1 tsp gluten-free baking powder
- ½ tsp xanthan gum
- 200g (7oz) gluten-free funfetti sprinkles, must be bake-stable (optional)

For the piñata filling

- 400g (14oz) selection of mini gluten-free chocolate treats (I use either gluten-free M&Ms or jellybeans)

For the vanilla buttercream

- 500g (scant 2¼ cups) butter, softened
- 1kg (7 cups) icing (confectioners') sugar, sifted
- 2 tsp vanilla extract
- Blue food colouring paste (optional)
- 1–3 tsp milk, if needed

It doesn't matter what age you are – when you see all those treats pour out of the middle of this cake, you can't help but smile (or weep with joy when it's gluten-free)!

Preheat your oven to 160°C fan / 180°C / 350°F. Grease three 20cm (8in) round cake tins (pans) and line with non-stick baking parchment.

In a large bowl, cream the butter and sugar until light and fluffy (I use an electric hand whisk or a stand mixer). Add your eggs one by one, mixing between each addition, then mix in the vanilla extract. Mix in your flour, baking powder, xanthan gum and funfetti, if using, until combined.

Divide the mixture evenly between the three prepared tins and bake for 35 minutes until risen and cooked through. Check by poking a skewer into the middle – if it comes out clean they're done. Leave in the tins for 5 minutes before turning out onto a wire rack to cool completely.

Once cooled, use a cake leveller or sharp knife to trim the risen tops of your three sponges to create level tops. Ensure that you don't tear through the cake as you do this. Remove the middle of two of the three sponges using a 6cm (2¼in) cookie cutter. Make sure the cut-out is in the exact same place on both.

To make the buttercream, place the butter in the bowl of a stand mixer (or use electric hand whisk) and mix on a medium speed for 5 minutes until fluffy and pale. Add your icing sugar in two or three stages, beating for 3 minutes between each addition. Start your mixer slowly to avoid an icing sugar explosion, then increase the speed to medium-high for each of your 3-minute mixing intervals. Finally, mix in the vanilla extract and enough blue food colouring (if using) to achieve a sky-blue colour. If the icing is too thick, just add a little milk (dairy-free or lactose-free if needed) to loosen it.

To assemble the cake, place one of your cut-out sponges on a serving plate and spread a modest layer of the buttercream all over it, right to the edges. Then put the second cut-out layer on top, ensuring the hole is perfectly aligned with the first. Again, spread this with a layer of buttercream. Fill the hole to the top with your chocolates and sweets then place the final sponge layer (the one without the hole) on top.

Next, we need to apply a crumb coat. This means applying a thin coating of buttercream all over the cake, so use a small, cranked palette knife to do exactly that. You should be able to see all the sponges through the crumb coat. Place the cake in the fridge for 30–60 minutes to allow the crumb coat to set. Cover the remaining buttercream to stop it from drying out.

Now it's time to ice your cake for real. Use a large palette knife to apply a 5mm (¼in) coating of buttercream to the entire cake. To smooth the sides, simply touch the icing with your cake scraper and rotate the serving plate until you achieve a smooth finish – an icing turntable comes in handy here. For the top of the cake, smooth the buttercream inwards towards the middle with your cake scraper to create nice, sharp edges and a smooth top. Finish with more funfetti!

SALTED CARAMEL Cake

use dairy-free double (heavy) cream (minimum 30% fat) for the salted caramel, and a (hard) dairy-free butter alternative

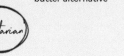

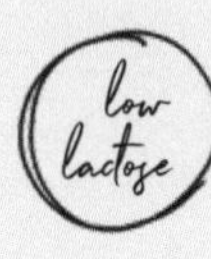

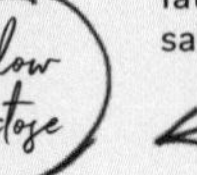

use lactose-free whipping cream (minimum 30% fat) for the salted caramel

MAKES · 12 SLICES

TAKES · 1 HOUR + COOLING

- 225g (1 cup) butter, softened, plus extra for greasing
- 225g (1 cup plus 2 tbsp) light brown sugar
- 4 large eggs
- 1 tsp vanilla extract
- 225g (1¾ cups) gluten-free self-raising (self-rising) flour
- 1 tsp gluten-free baking powder
- ¼ tsp xanthan gum

For the salted caramel

- 125ml (½ cup) double (heavy) cream
- ½ tsp vanilla extract
- 125g (scant ⅔ cup) caster (superfine) sugar
- 75ml (5 tbsp) water
- Sea salt

For the salted caramel buttercream

- 200g (¾ cup plus 2 tbsp) butter, softened
- 430g (3 cups) icing (confectioners') sugar, sifted
- 120g (4oz) salted caramel (see above), plus 80g (3oz) for drizzling

Does it get any better than this? The buttercream is infused with salted caramel and a little more of it (or a lot more if you're me) drizzled on top goes a long way!

Preheat your oven to 160°C fan / 180°C / 350°F. Grease two 20cm (8in) round cake tins (pans) and line with non-stick baking parchment.

In a large mixing bowl, cream the butter and sugar until light and fluffy (I use an electric hand whisk or stand mixer for this). Add your eggs one at a time, mixing between each addition. Add your vanilla extract and mix that in too. Add your flour, baking powder, xanthan gum and mix until well combined.

Divide the mixture evenly between the two prepared tins and bake for 25–30 minutes until golden and cooked through – check by poking a skewer into the middle – if it comes out clean, then they're done.

Remove from the oven and leave the sponges in their tins for about 5 minutes before turning them out onto a wire rack to cool completely.

Meanwhile, make the salted caramel. Mix the cream and vanilla extract together in a jug (pitcher). Put the sugar and water into a large saucepan, ensuring the sugar is evenly spread across the base. Place over a medium heat and allow the sugar to dissolve and the mixture to bubble: under no circumstances must you stir it! Keep a careful watch over it, and when the mixture reaches an amber colour, which should take about 10 minutes, remove from the heat and slowly pour the cream into the pan, stirring constantly until well combined. Pour into a heatproof bowl and allow to cool completely, before stirring in a little sea salt to taste.

For the buttercream, I use a stand mixer, but an electric hand whisk will do the job just fine too. If making by hand, ensure you mix for longer, until everything is well combined.

Mix your butter on a medium speed for 5 minutes until it has turned a lot paler in colour. Add your icing sugar in two or three stages, beating for 3 minutes between each addition. Start your mixer slowly to avoid creating a mini icing sugar explosion, but then increase the speed to medium-high for each of your 3-minute mixing intervals. Add in 120g (4oz) of your cooled salted caramel and mix until fully combined.

To assemble your cake, place one sponge on a serving plate and spread over half the buttercream. Drizzle a couple of tablespoons of salted caramel on top of the buttercream. Place the other sponge on top and finish with a final layer of buttercream. Drizzle with more salted caramel, allowing some to drip down the sides too.

TIP:
If you want to speed things up a bit, you can always use store-bought caramel that comes in 397g (14oz) cans instead of making your own – just add a little salt to taste.

CHOCOLATE Courgette CAKE

use dairy-free chocolate, choc chips and yoghurt, and a (hard) dairy-free butter alternative

use lactose-free chocolate, choc chips and yoghurt

MAKES · 12 SLICES

TAKES · 1 HOUR 10 MINUTES + COOLING

- 150g (¾ cup) caster (superfine) sugar
- 150g (¾ cup) light brown sugar
- 3 large eggs
- 80g (¼ cup) yoghurt
- 1 tsp vanilla extract (optional)
- 240ml (1 cup) vegetable oil, plus extra for greasing
- 350–400g (10½ -14oz) grated courgette (zucchini) – about 2 medium courgettes
- 240g (1¾ cups) gluten-free plain (all-purpose) flour
- ½ tsp xanthan gum
- 60g (½ cup plus 1½ tbsp) unsweetened cocoa powder, sifted
- 2 tsp bicarbonate of soda (baking soda)
- ½ tsp gluten-free baking powder
- 150g (5oz) dark chocolate chips (optional)

For the buttercream

- 220g (7oz) dark chocolate, broken into pieces
- 500g (2 cups) butter, softened
- 370g (2½ cups) icing (confectioners') sugar, sifted
- 110g (1 cup) unsweetened cocoa powder, sifted
- 1–3 tsp milk, if needed

I just wanted to begin by saying: no, this cake doesn't taste like courgette (zucchini), nor does it incorporate a vegetable in order to be healthier! The courgette plays a similar role to carrot in carrot cake, making the sponges *incredibly* moist and fudgy. Note that the weight of the courgettes is *after* grating. If you don't intend to ice the outside of the cake (just the middle and top), then simply halve the buttercream quantities, or use the chocolate frosting recipe on page 211 instead.

Preheat your oven to 160°C fan / 180°C / 350°F. Grease two 20cm (8in) round cake tins (pans) and line with non-stick baking parchment.

In a large mixing bowl, add both sugars, the eggs, yogurt, vanilla extract (if using) and oil, and mix well (I use an electric hand whisk or a stand mixer). Add the courgette and mix once more until combined.

In a separate bowl, mix together the flour, xanthan gum, cocoa powder, bicarb and baking powder. Mix your dry ingredients into the wet mixture, making sure that you don't overmix, but also ensuring all the dry mixture is well combined, without any lumps.

Fold in the chocolate chips, if using. Divide evenly between the two tins and bake for 35–40 minutes until risen and cooked through. Check by poking a skewer into the middle – if it comes out clean, then they're done. Leave the sponges in their tins for 5 minutes before turning out onto a wire rack to cool completely. These sponges are fudgy, making them more delicate than your average sponge cake, so handle with care.

While the sponges are cooling, make your buttercream. Firstly, melt your chocolate (I do this in the microwave mixing in between short bursts), then allow to cool slightly.

Place the butter in the bowl of a stand mixer (or use electric hand whisk). Mix on a medium speed for about 5 minutes until fluffy and paler in colour. Add your icing sugar in three stages, beating for 3 minutes between each addition. Start your mixer slowly (to avoid creating a mini icing sugar explosion) then increase the speed to medium-high for each of your 3-minute mixing intervals. Sift in your cocoa powder and mix again until fully combined.

Mix in your slightly cooled, melted chocolate until fully incorporated. If the icing seems too thick, just add a teaspoon or so of milk (dairy-free or lactose-free if needed) to loosen.

Carefully place one of your sponges on a cake stand or serving plate – I use a cake lifter to move this one due to it being a little delicate. Spread an even layer of buttercream on top, then add your second sponge on top of that and use the remaining icing to simply coat the outside of the cake.

Or, if you want a fancy finish like mine, coat the entire cake in a thin layer of buttercream, then transfer the remaining icing to a piping bag fitted with a star nozzle and pipe rosettes all over the cake.

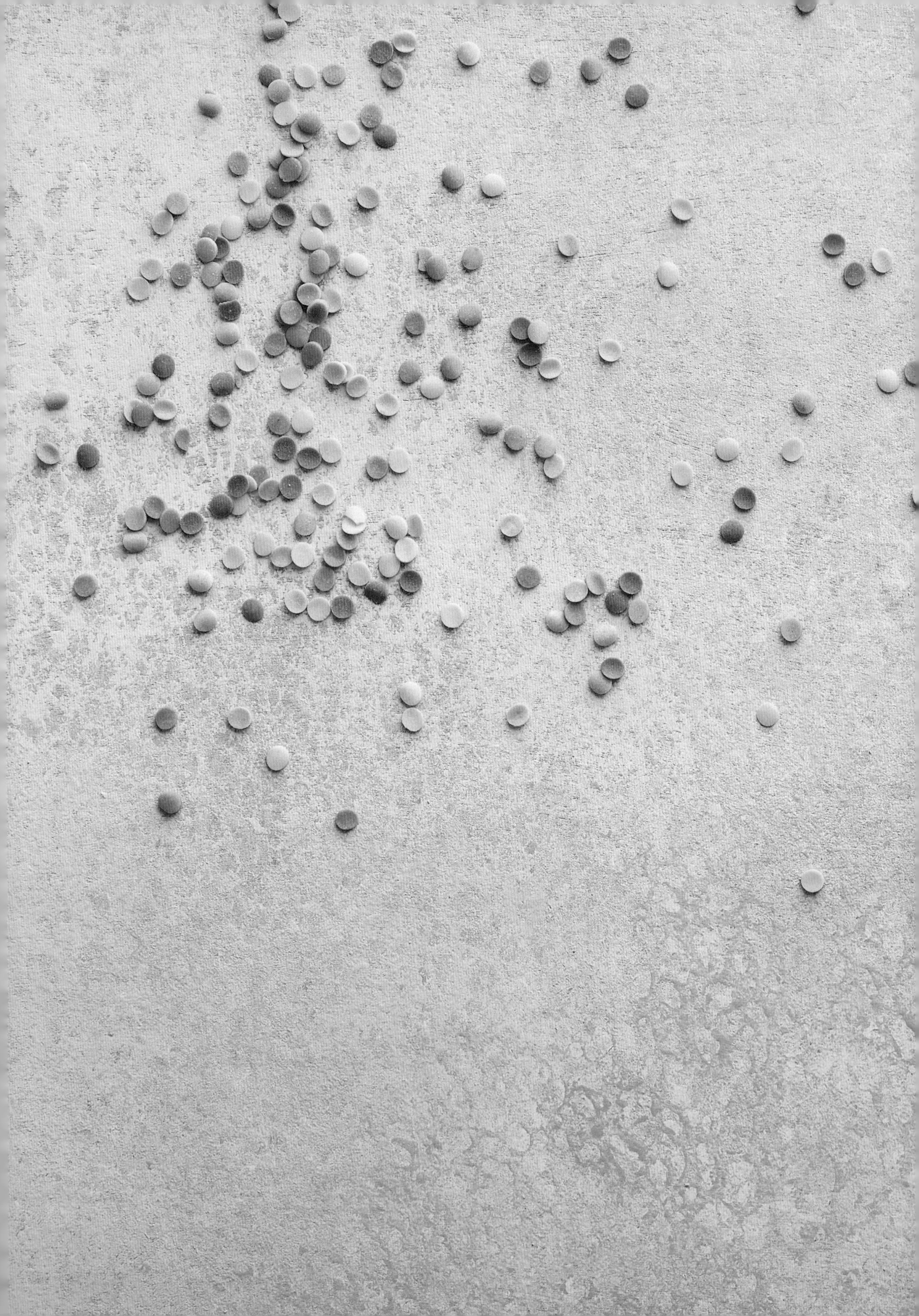

Traybakes and Cupcakes

Why did I group these two beautiful creations together? Good question... well, to be honest, it's mostly because it rhymed!

But in all seriousness, this chapter demonstrates just how many game-changing bakes you can easily make in a 23cm (9in) square baking tin or a 12-hole cupcake tin. Think smores brownies, baked cheesecake bars, flapjacks and millionaire's shortbread, alongside carrot cake cupcakes, red velvet cupcakes and a boatload more.

Baked Raspberry Cheesecake Bars

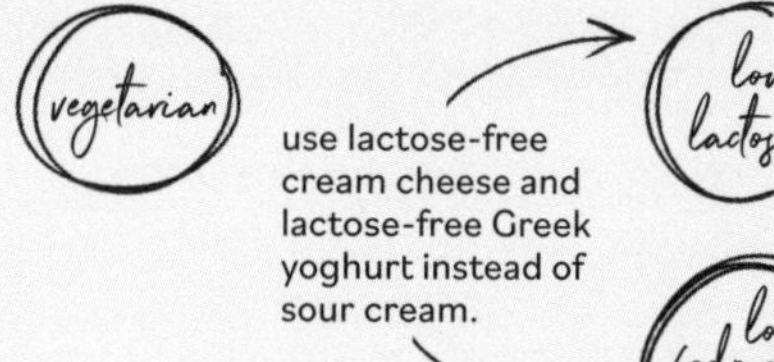

use lactose-free cream cheese and lactose-free Greek yoghurt instead of sour cream.

MAKES · 18 BARS

TAKES · 1¼ HOURS + 3 HOURS CHILLING

- 230g (8oz) fresh or frozen raspberries, plus extra for the top
- 220g (8oz) gluten-free digestive biscuits (graham crackers)
- 90g (⅓ cup plus 1 tbsp) butter, melted
- 500g (1lb 2oz) mascarpone
- 100g (3½oz) sour cream
- 125g (⅔ cup minus 2 tsp) caster (superfine) sugar
- 15g (1½ tbsp) cornflour (cornstarch)
- 2 large eggs
- Grated zest of 1 lemon and 1½ tsp juice
- 1 tsp vanilla extract

First of all, yes, they do taste as good as they look! Each slice has a crisp, buttery biscuit base, topped with a delightfully creamy filling that's packed with gooey raspberries and cut with sweet and sharp raspberry sauce. If you're still reading this, that's probably a good sign that you should go and make them now!

Preheat your oven to 160°C fan / 180°C / 350°F. Line a 23cm (9in) square baking tin (pan) with non-stick baking parchment.

Place a small saucepan over a medium heat, add the raspberries and allow to completely break down. Sieve them into a bowl, then place just the liquid back in the saucepan and discard the rest. Continue to heat until the mixture reduces and thickens slightly. Remove from the heat and allow to cool completely.

Next, make your base. In a food processor, blitz your biscuits into a crumb-like consistency – not into a fine dust! Alternatively, pop the biscuits into a zip-lock bag and bash them with a rolling pin. Transfer the crushed biscuits to a large mixing bowl, add the melted butter and mix well until combined. Spoon your crushed biscuit mixture into the lined tin and compact it into a nice, even layer. Bake in the oven for about 10 minutes, then remove and allow to cool. Reduce the oven temperature to 120°C fan / 140°C / 285°F.

Meanwhile, for the filling, mix together the mascarpone and sour cream in a large mixing bowl until smooth. Add your sugar and cornflour and mix until combined. Crack your eggs in one at a time, mixing between each addition. Finally, add the lemon zest, juice and vanilla extract, and mix once more.

Mix 2 tablespoons of the cheesecake filling with the cooled raspberry reduction until lovely and smooth. Spoon the rest of the cheesecake mixture on top of the cooled base, then spoon the raspberry mixture on top of that. Use a skewer to create a swirly pattern, and press extra raspberries into the top.

Bake in the oven for 40–45 minutes until slightly wobbly and a little brown around the edges. Instead of removing the tin from the oven, leave it in and turn the oven off, leaving the door ajar. Allow to completely cool. Once cooled, place in the fridge to chill for at least 3 hours, but ideally overnight, then cut into bars to serve.

Store in an airtight container or freeze for 2–3 months.

DIY Flapjacks

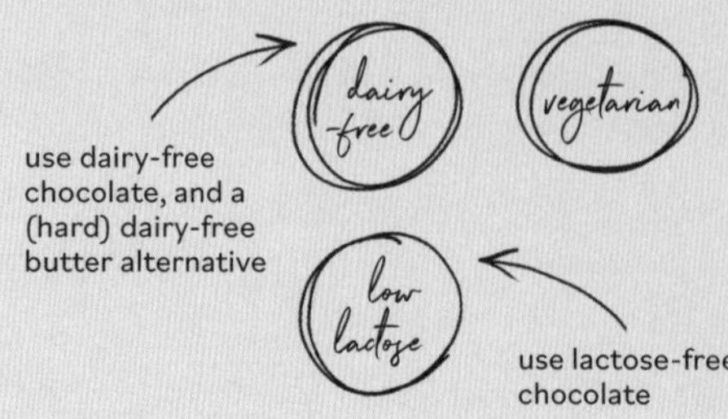
dairy free
vegetarian
low lactose
use dairy-free chocolate, and a (hard) dairy-free butter alternative
use lactose-free chocolate

MAKES · 9 LARGE OR 16 SMALL FLAPJACKS

TAKES · 40 MINUTES

- 160g (¾ cup minus 2 tsp) butter, plus extra for greasing
- 115g (⅓ cup) golden syrup
- 115g (½ cup plus 1 tbsp) light brown sugar
- 300g (3 cups) gluten-free oats
- 100g (3½oz) dried fruit, frozen berries, chopped roasted nuts or chocolate chips (see variations, right)

For the chocolate drizzle (optional)

- 100g (3½oz) white, dark or milk chocolate

I am a massive fan of sharing recipes with you guys that you can completely customize and make your own. So feel free to use my sweet, buttery flapjack base to create whatever your heart desires – I often use this to make white chocolate and cranberry/raspberry flapjacks, triple chocolate flapjacks, blueberry flapjacks or fruity flapjacks. See the variations for which added extras you'll need to create all of the above combos, but of course, feel free to mix things up however you like.

Preheat your oven to 160°C fan / 180°C / 350°F. Grease a 20cm (8in) square baking tin (pan) and line it with non-stick baking parchment, leaving a little overhang as this will help you remove the flapjacks from the tin.

Place a small saucepan over a low heat, add the butter, golden syrup and sugar, and melt until smooth, stirring occasionally. Add your oats and stir until the oats are well coated and incorporated. Mix in your choice of dried fruit, frozen berries, chopped roasted nuts or chocolate chips – unless you wish to enjoy them without, of course!

Press your mixture into your prepared tin. If using frozen berries or choc chips, push a few extra into the flapjack mixture, so they're flush with the surface. Bake in the oven for 25 minutes until golden. Remove from the oven and allow to cool in the tin briefly, then carefully lift out onto a wire rack to cool completely.

Melt your chocolate, if using. You can do this in the microwave (mixing in between short bursts) or in a heatproof bowl set over a saucepan of boiling water, making sure the water isn't touching the bowl, and stirring until melted.

Drizzle zig-zag lines of melted chocolate on top of the flapjack. Allow to set briefly, then slice into 9 large or 16 smaller squares. Store in an airtight container or freeze for 2–3 months.

VARIATIONS

Pair your fillings with different types of chocolate to create a ton of different flavour combos! Here are a few of my faves to get you started:

- **White Chocolate and Cranberry Flapjacks:** use 70g (2½oz) dried cranberries, 30g (1oz) white choc chips, and white chocolate for drizzling.
- **Triple Chocolate Flapjacks:** use 50g (1¾oz) milk choc chips, 50g (1¾oz) white choc chips, and dark chocolate for drizzling.
- **White Chocolate and Raspberry Flapjacks:** use 70g (2½oz) frozen raspberries, 30g (1oz) white choc chips, and white chocolate for drizzling.
- **Blueberry Flapjacks:** use 100g (3½oz) frozen blueberries and dark chocolate for drizzling.
- **Fruity Flapjacks:** Use 70g (2½oz) sultanas (golden raisins), 30g (1oz) dried apricots (chopped), and milk chocolate for drizzling.

TIP:

This recipe contains gluten-free oats – if you can't find them, check page 14 for more details on them.

White Chocolate & Raspberry BLONDIES

use dairy-free white choc chips and a (hard) dairy-free butter alternative

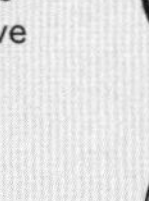

low lactose

use lactose-free white choc chips

MAKES · 9 LARGE OR 16 SMALLER BLONDIES

TAKES · 55 MINUTES

- 250g (1 cup plus 2 tbsp) butter, melted and cooled, plus extra for greasing
- 130g (⅔ cup) light brown sugar
- 130g (⅔ cup) caster (superfine) sugar
- 2 large eggs
- 1 tsp vanilla extract
- 285g (2 cups plus 2½ tbsp) gluten-free plain (all-purpose) flour
- ¼ tsp xanthan gum
- 1 tbsp cornflour (cornstarch)
- 180g (6½oz) white chocolate chips
- 180g (6½oz) fresh raspberries

White chocolate and raspberry is one of my favourite flavour combos when it comes to baking and this is the perfect flavour ambassador. It has the crisp, paper-like top and fudgy middle you'd expect to find in a brownie, but with a sweet vanilla flavour and, of course, fresh raspberries and creamy, chunky white choc chips. If you've never made or eaten a blondie before, here's the place to start!

Preheat your oven to 160°C fan / 180°C / 350°F. Grease a 23cm (9in) square baking tin (pan) and line it with non-stick baking parchment, leaving a little overhang as this will help you remove the blondies from the tin.

In a large mixing bowl, mix together your cooled, melted butter and both sugars until you can no longer see the yellow of the liquid butter. Allow the mixture to rest for 5–10 minutes to thicken up, then add your eggs and vanilla extract, mixing until well combined.

Add your flour, xanthan gum and cornflour. Briefly mix until just combined and the mixture is smooth, with no visible lumps or pockets of flour. Gently fold in your chocolate chips, followed by your raspberries, being careful not to break them up.

Spoon the mixture into the prepared tin, smoothing it over to create a nice, even layer. Bake in the oven for about 35 minutes until lightly golden – the very middle might still seem a little wobbly but the outer edges should be cooked through. Don't overbake this one or you'll lose all the lovely fudgy texture!

Allow to cool in the tin briefly then carefully lift onto a wire rack to cool completely, before cutting into 9 big or 16 smaller squares. Store in an airtight container or freeze for 2–3 months.

TIP:
Don't like raspberries? Try blueberries, strawberries, nuts or just more chocolate chips!

MILLIONAIRE'S Shortbread

MAKES · 9 LARGE OR 16 SMALL

TAKES · 55 MINUTES, + 4 HOURS CHILLING

For the shortbread base

- 200g (¾ cup plus 2 tbsp) butter, softened, plus extra for greasing
- 100g (½ cup) caster (superfine) sugar
- 300g (2¼ cups) gluten-free plain (all-purpose) flour
- ¼ tsp xanthan gum

For the caramel layer

- 185g (¾ cup plus 1 tbsp) butter
- 35g (3 tbsp) golden caster (superfine) sugar
- 65g (3 tbsp) golden syrup
- 1 x 397g (14oz) can of condensed milk

For the chocolate topping

- 200g (7oz) milk chocolate
- 80g (3oz) white chocolate

If I had my own bakery, gluten-free millionaire's shortbread would most definitely be on sale all day, every day... unless I accidentally ate all of the stock myself, which is a possibility. This is a reader favourite from the blog that so many of you have tried, tested and loved, so it certainly earned its place here in my second book. Feel free to blind taste test this one on muggles – nobody would ever notice the difference!

Preheat your oven to 160°C fan / 180°C / 350°F. Grease a 23cm (9in) square baking tin (pan) and line it with non-stick baking parchment, leaving a little overhang to help you remove them from the tin later.

In a large mixing bowl, cream together your butter and sugar until light and pale (I prefer to use an electric hand whisk or a stand mixer for this). Mix in the flour and xanthan gum, then use your hands to bring the dough together into a ball – it might be slightly crumbly at this point, but that's fine.

Press your dough into your prepared tin, pushing it right into the corners and trying to make it flat and even. Prick the top all over with a fork and bake in the oven for 20–22 minutes until slightly golden on top. Set aside to cool.

For your caramel layer, place all the ingredients in a small saucepan over a low-medium heat. Allow the butter to melt and the sugar to dissolve, then mix well to ensure it doesn't stick to the bottom and is all well combined. Turn the heat up so the mixture starts to bubble a little, and keep stirring continuously for about 5–8 minutes or until the mixture has thickened and developed into a dark, golden colour.

Pour your caramel on top of your cooled shortbread layer, spreading it so that it's level and even. Place in the fridge to set for at least 2 hours. Once chilled, remove from the fridge, ready to add the final layer.

In two separate small bowls, melt both chocolates. You can do this in the microwave (mixing in between short bursts) or in a heatproof bowl over a saucepan of boiling water, without letting the water touch the bowl, and stirring until melted.

First, pour the milk chocolate all over the top of the set caramel layer. Spread it out in an even layer, right to the edges. Quickly spoon big dollops of white chocolate on top and use a skewer to create a swirly pattern. It's important to work quickly with the white chocolate as the milk chocolate will begin to set as soon as it hits the cold caramel.

Place back in the fridge for around 1 hour and 30 minutes, until the chocolate has fully set.

Remove the millionaires from the fridge about 30 minutes before you want to cut it (to prevent the chocolate top from cracking). Remove it from the tin and, using a large knife warmed in hot water, cut into 9 large or 16 smaller squares.

Store in an airtight container or freeze for 2–3 months.

Making it lactose-free, dairy-free or vegan?
Visit my blog (glutenfreecuppatea.co.uk), search for 'vegan millionaire's shortbread recipe' and your prayers shall be answered!

SMORES Brownies

use dairy-free chocolate, choc chips and biscuits, and a (hard) dairy-free butter alternative

use lactose-free chocolate, choc chips and low FODMAP biscuits

use lactose-free chocolate, choc chips and biscuits

MAKES · 12 BROWNIES

TAKES · 55 MINUTES

For the base

- 200g (7oz) digestive biscuits (graham crackers)
- 80g (⅓ cup) butter, melted, plus extra for greasing

For the brownie layer

- 125g (4½oz) chocolate (I use half dark, half milk), broken into pieces
- 125g (½ cup plus 1 tbsp) butter
- 140g (¾ cup minus 1 tbsp) caster (superfine) sugar
- 2 medium eggs
- 50g (6 tbsp) gluten-free plain (all-purpose) flour
- 25g (¼ cup) unsweetened cocoa powder, sifted

For the topping

- 100g (3½ oz) chocolate chips
- 2 digestive biscuits (graham crackers), broken up into chunks
- 70g (2½oz) mini white marshmallows

This isn't just any gluten-free brownie! Each slice has a crisp, crunchy, buttery biscuit base and gooey, fudgy, intensely chocolatey brownie on top – but that's not all! It's finished with melty choc chips, smashed biscuit chunks and toasted marshmallows. If I'm ever having a bad day, these never fail to put a smile back on my face.

Preheat your oven to 160°C fan / 180°C / 350°F. Grease a 23cm (9in) square baking tin (pan) and line it with non-stick baking parchment, leaving a little overhang as this will help you remove the brownies from the tin.

Next, make your base. In a food processor, blitz your biscuits into a crumb-like consistency. Alternatively, pop the biscuits into a zip-lock bag and bash them with a rolling pin. Transfer the crushed biscuits to a large mixing bowl, add the melted butter and mix well until combined. Spoon your crushed biscuit mixture into the lined tin and compact it into a nice, even layer, then bake in the oven for 10 minutes. Remove and allow to cool.

In a large heatproof bowl, add your chocolate and butter. Place the bowl over a saucepan of gently boiling water, making sure the water isn't touching the base of the bowl. Keep stirring until everything has melted and mixed together, then allow to cool to near room temperature.

In a large mixing bowl, whisk together your sugar and eggs until fluffy and frothy. Next, fold in your melted chocolate and butter and mix until combined. Lastly, fold in your flour and cocoa powder until fully combined. Pour the batter over your biscuit base and bake in the oven for about 22 minutes, until it develops a shiny, paper-like crust on top.

Remove from the oven and switch your oven to a medium grill (broiler) setting.

Cover the top of your brownies with the chocolate chips, biscuit chunks and a layer of marshmallows. Place under the grill for a minute or two just until the marshmallows start to colour a little. Remove from the grill and allow to cool completely in the tin. Once cooled, remove from the tin and, using a sharp knife warmed in hot water, cut into 12 squares.

Once cooled, store in an airtight container or freeze for 2–3 months.

TRIPLE CHOC CHIP
Bakery-Style
MUFFINS

use dairy-free milk and choc chips

use lactose-free milk and choc chips

MAKES · 8

TAKES · 40 MINUTES

- 175g (1⅓ cups) gluten-free plain (all-purpose) flour
- ¼ tsp xanthan gum
- 50g (¼ cup) unsweetened cocoa powder, sifted
- 125g (⅔ cup minus 2 tsp) caster (superfine) sugar
- 2 tsp gluten-free baking powder
- ¼ tsp salt
- 235ml (1 cup minus 1 tsp) whole milk
- 120ml (½ cup) vegetable oil
- 1 large egg
- 1 tsp vanilla extract
- 170g (6oz) white and milk chocolate chips

I never thought I'd struggle to find a gluten-free chocolate muffin that matched the ones I used to enjoy in coffee shops, or picked up in one of the many mind-blowing bakeries in London (those were the days). But I've found that so many gluten-free muffins just taste like chocolate cupcakes, or a big hunk of chocolate sponge. A muffin should be super-moist, incredibly soft, light and chocolatey and packed with chocolate chips… which is exactly what you'll find here!

Preheat your oven to 200°C fan / 220°C / 425°F. Line a cupcake/ muffin tin (pan) with tulip muffin liners.

In a large mixing bowl, mix together your dry ingredients. In a separate bowl, whisk together your wet ingredients.

Pour your wet ingredients into your dry ingredients and very carefully mix together using a silicone spatula. Only mix around ten times or the muffins will become tough and dense. Briefly stir in 150g (5oz) of your chocolate chips.

Spoon your mixture equally between your muffin liners and evenly add the rest of the chocolate chips to the tops. Bake in the oven for 10 minutes, then reduce the oven temperature to 160°C fan / 180°C / 350°F and bake for a further 8 minutes.

Remove from the oven and allow to cool completely. Although… they do taste amazing warm too!

Making it vegan?
Follow the advice to make the muffins dairy-free, then replace the egg with 3 tbsp aquafaba (whisked until frothy).

Pictured on page 67.

Carrot Cake CUPCAKES

use dairy-free buttercream (page 209) instead of the cream cheese frosting

use lactose-free cream cheese

MAKES · 12

TAKES · 45 MINUTES

- 3 medium eggs
- 175g (¾ cup plus 2 tbsp) light brown sugar
- 150ml (⅝ cup) vegetable oil
- 195g (1½ cups minus 2 tsp) gluten-free self-raising (self-rising) flour
- ½ tsp bicarbonate of soda (baking soda)
- 1½ tsp ground cinnamon, plus extra to finish
- ½ tsp ground ginger
- Grated zest of ½ orange
- 185g (6½oz) carrots, grated
- 45g (1½oz) pecans, finely chopped, plus extra to finish (optional)
- Edible carrot decorations (optional)

For the cream cheese frosting

- 150g (⅔ cup) butter, softened
- 150g (1 cup) icing (confectioners') sugar, sifted
- 300g (1⅓ cups) full-fat cream cheese
- 1 tsp vanilla extract

Imagine all the awesomeness of a full-sized carrot cake, compacted into a cupcake. Ok, you can stop drooling now! They have a lovely, distinctively moist texture and a sweet, warming flavour. They're packed with crunchy pecans and topped with creamy, whipped cream cheese frosting on top. Optionally tell people that it's one of your five a day…

Preheat your oven to 160°C fan / 180°C / 350°F. Line a 12-hole cupcake tin (pan) with cupcake cases. (I like to sprinkle a few grains of uncooked rice beneath each case as it helps to absorb unwanted moisture.)

In a large mixing bowl, crack in your eggs, then add the sugar and your oil. Mix together until well combined (I prefer to use an electric hand whisk or a stand mixer for this part).

In a medium mixing bowl, add your flour, bicarb, cinnamon and ginger. Add the dry mixture to the wet mixture and gently fold in. Add your orange zest, grated carrots and chopped pecans, if using. Fold into the mixture so that everything is evenly dispersed, then spoon your mixture evenly into the cupcake cases. Bake in the oven for 20–25 minutes until golden and cooked through. Check by poking a skewer into the middle of a cupcake – if it comes out clean, then they're done. Remove the cupcakes from the tin and transfer to a wire rack to cool completely.

While your cupcakes cool, make your cream cheese frosting. Place your butter into the bowl of a stand mixer (an electric hand whisk will do the job just fine too) and mix on a medium speed for about 5 minutes until the butter has turned a lot paler. If making by hand, ensure you mix for longer until everything is well-combined and consistent.

Add your icing sugar in two to three stages, beating for about 3 minutes between each addition. Start your mixer slowly (to avoid creating a mini icing sugar explosion) but then increase the speed to medium-high for each of your 3-minute mixing intervals.

Add your cream cheese and vanilla extract then mix for 2–3 more minutes until well combined, and the icing is light and fluffy, without lumps.

You can then either use a piping bag with an open star nozzle to pipe the icing on, or simply spoon the cream cheese frosting onto the cooled cupcakes. Finish each cupcake with a dusting of cinnamon, some chopped up pecan nuts and a couple of little edible carrot decorations, if you like.

Pictured on pages 38 and 66.

RED VELVET *Cupcakes*

use dairy-free buttercream (page 209) instead of the cream cheese frosting

use lactose-free milk and cream cheese

MAKES · 12–18

TAKES · 45 MINUTES

- 225ml (1 cup minus 1 tbsp) milk
- 2 tbsp lemon juice
- 115g (½ cup) butter, softened
- 240g (1¼ cups) caster (superfine) sugar
- 3 large eggs
- 30g (4 tbsp) unsweetened cocoa powder
- ¼ tsp xanthan gum
- 1½ tsp vanilla extract
- Red food colouring paste
- 270g (2 cups) gluten-free plain (all-purpose) flour
- 1 tsp bicarbonate of soda (baking soda)
- 2 tsp white wine vinegar or cider vinegar

For the cream cheese frosting

- 150g (⅔ cup) butter, softened
- 150g (1 cup) icing (confectioners') sugar, sifted
- 300g (1⅓ cups) full-fat cream cheese
- 1 tsp vanilla extract

To me, love at first sight is roughly on par with the sight of a gluten-free red velvet cupcake – of course, both are bested by actually eating one! Getting that vibrant red colour is incredibly simple with a smidge of red food colouring paste.

In a jug (pitcher), mix your milk and lemon juice and allow to stand for 10 minutes until it curdles a little.

Preheat your oven to 160°C fan / 180°C / 350°F. Line a 12-hole cupcake tin (pan) with cupcake cases. (I sprinkle a few grains of uncooked rice beneath each case as it helps to absorb unwanted moisture.)

In a large mixing bowl, cream together your butter and sugar until light and pale (I prefer to use an electric hand whisk or a stand mixer for this).

Crack in the eggs, one at a time, mixing in between each addition, until well combined. Sift in your cocoa powder and xanthan gum and mix in. In a small dish, combine the vanilla extract and a pea-sized amount of red food colouring paste together. Add to your mixing bowl and mix well.

Add half your flour, followed by half your milk mixture. Mix it together thoroughly, but only briefly, before adding in your second half of flour and milk mixture. Mix in until well combined and smooth, but make sure you don't mix this too much either. Finally, mix together your bicarb and vinegar in a small dish, then add to the cake batter and mix in immediately. But remember, don't overmix!

If your cake batter isn't a vibrant red colour at this point, add a little more food colouring paste and mix briefly to evenly distribute.

Spoon your mixture evenly into the cupcake cases (don't overfill – if you have any extra batter you can bake a few extra cupcakes after you've baked the first 12). Bake in the oven for 20–25 minutes until cooked through. Check by poking a skewer into the middle of a cupcake – if it comes out clean, then they're done. Remove the cupcakes from the tin and transfer to a wire rack to cool.

While your cupcakes cool, make your cream cheese frosting. Place your butter into the bowl of a stand mixer (an electric hand whisk will do the job just fine too) and mix on a medium speed for about 5 minutes until the butter has turned a lot paler. If making by hand, ensure you mix for longer, until everything is well-combined.

Add your icing sugar in two to three stages, beating for about 3 minutes between each addition. Start your mixer slowly (to avoid creating a mini icing sugar explosion) but then increase the speed to medium-high for each of your 3-minute mixing intervals.

Add your cream cheese and vanilla extract and mix for 2–3 more minutes until well combined, and the icing is light and fluffy, without lumps.

You can then either use a piping bag with a round nozzle to pipe the icing on, or simply spoon the cream cheese frosting onto the completely cooled cupcakes.

Pictured on page 66.

CHOCOLATE Peanut Butter CUPCAKES

use dairy-free milk, choc chips, chocolate and omit peanut butter cups

use lactose-free milk, choc chips, chocolate and omit peanut butter cups

MAKES · 12–16

TAKES · 1 HOUR

- 90ml (6 tbsp) milk
- 1 tbsp lemon juice
- 200g (1½ cups) gluten-free plain (all-purpose) flour
- 50g (½ cup) unsweetened cocoa powder
- 160g (¾ cup plus 1 tbsp) caster (superfine) sugar
- 150g (¾ cup) light brown sugar
- 1 tsp gluten-free baking powder
- 1 tsp bicarbonate of soda (baking soda)
- ½ tsp xanthan gum
- 2 medium eggs
- 80ml (5 tbsp plus 1 tsp) melted butter, cooled (or use oil)
- 1 tbsp vanilla extract
- 1 tbsp instant coffee powder
- 190ml (¾ cup plus 1 tbsp) boiling water

For the filling

- 45g (3 tbsp) butter
- 110g (4oz) smooth peanut butter
- 110g (generous ¾ cup) icing (confectioners') sugar, sifted

For the buttercream

- 200g (¾ cup plus 2 tbsp) butter, softened
- 100g (scant ½ cup) smooth peanut butter
- 400g (3 cups) icing (confectioners') sugar
- 2–3 tbsp milk

To finish

- Gluten-free mini peanut butter cups
- A little melted chocolate, for drizzling (optional)

Meet my favourite peanut butter cups... but in cupcake form! Each cupcake has a moist, chocolatey sponge, filled with a peanut-butter-cup-style filling, finished with a peanut buttercream. These never last long in our house!

Preheat your oven to 160°C fan / 180°C / 350°F. Line a 12-hole cupcake tin (pan) with cupcake cases. (I sprinkle a few grains of uncooked rice beneath each case as it helps to absorb unwanted moisture.)

In a jug (pitcher), mix your milk and lemon juice and allow to stand for 10 minutes until it curdles a little.

In a large mixing bowl, add all the dry ingredients, sifting in the flour and cocoa powder. Mix well.

Crack the eggs into the curdled milk, then add the melted butter or oil, and vanilla extract. Beat until smooth. Mix the wet mixture into the dry ingredients until well combined.

Next, dissolve the coffee in the boiling water and mix into the cake mixture until it has a nice shine. Divide among the cupcake cases and bake for 22 minutes until cooked through. Check by poking a skewer into the middle of a cupcake – if it comes out clean, they're done.

Remove the cupcakes from the tin and transfer to a wire rack to cool.

While your cupcakes cool, make the filling. Place the butter and peanut butter into a large mixing bowl and combine with an electric mixer until smooth. Add the icing sugar and mix once more. Use your hands to bring the mixture together into a ball, then cover and set aside.

To make the buttercream, place the butter into the bowl of a stand mixer and mix on a medium speed for 5 minutes until pale. Add the peanut butter and mix until combined. Add your icing sugar in three stages, beating for 3 minutes between each addition. Start your mixer slowly (to avoid an icing sugar explosion) then increase to medium-high for each 3-minute mixing interval. Peanut buttercream can be quite stiff, so I often add a little milk to loosen it. Add a small amount at a time until you're at the right consistency – I aim for pipeable and smooth.

Once the cupcakes are cool, remove the middle of each one – just make sure you don't go too deep! I use the wide end of a piping nozzle to plug and then lift out the core. Take a small piece of the peanut filling, roll it into a ball, roughly the size of the hole you've just created, then press it into the middle of the cupcake. Next, either use a piping bag with an open star nozzle to pipe the icing on, or simply spoon the buttercream onto the cupcakes. Finish with some mini peanut butter cups and a drizzle of melted chocolate, if you like.

Pictured on page 67.

COOKIES AND BISCUITS

It's concerning that I could create an entire recipe book filled with gluten-free cookies and biscuits, yet whenever I head to a bakery, there's a 99% chance that there's zero gluten-free cookies or biscuits to be found.

And so often people then leave, assuming that bakeries don't sell them because they're impossible to bake gluten-free. But, in reality, they're no harder to make than muggle cookies or biscuits, and they look and taste exactly the same. Don't believe me? Give them a try for yourself!

EMPIRE Biscuits

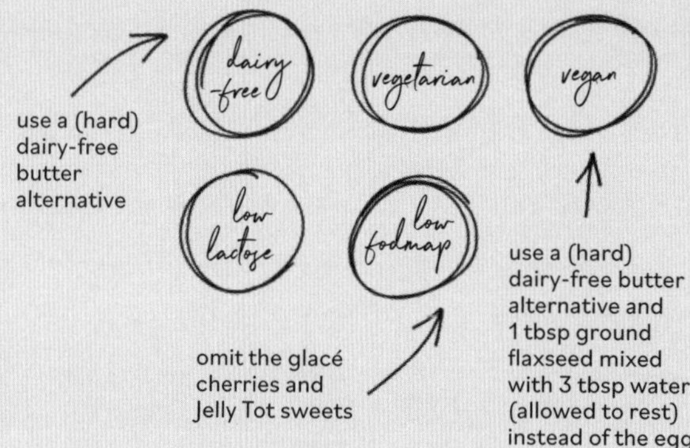
dairy-free
vegetarian
vegan
low lactose
low fodmap
use a (hard) dairy-free butter alternative
omit the glacé cherries and Jelly Tot sweets
use a (hard) dairy-free butter alternative and 1 tbsp ground flaxseed mixed with 3 tbsp water (allowed to rest) instead of the egg

MAKES · 8

TAKES · 40 MINUTES + COOLING

- 220g (¾ cup plus 2 tbsp) butter, softened
- 125g (⅔ cup minus 2 tsp) caster (superfine) sugar
- 1 medium egg, beaten
- 325g (2½ cups minus 1½ tbsp) gluten-free plain (all-purpose) flour, plus extra for dusting
- ½ tsp xanthan gum

For the filling and icing

- Strawberry or raspberry jam
- 200g (scant 1½ cups) icing (confectioners') sugar, sifted
- 30ml (2 tbsp) water
- Glacé cherries, halved, or Jelly Tot sweets (candies)

It's hard to express just how good this humble sandwich biscuit tastes, but that won't stop me from trying. Imagine melt-in-the-mouth, buttery shortbread with fruity jam sandwiched in the middle, topped with a sweet icing, finished with a classic Jelly Tot sweet (candy) or glacé cherry. Then stop imagining/drooling and make it a reality!

Preheat your oven to 160°C fan / 180°C / 350°F. Line two large baking sheets with non-stick baking parchment.

In a large mixing bowl, cream together your butter and sugar until light and fluffy (I prefer to use an electric hand whisk or a stand mixer for this). Add in your beaten egg and briefly mix it in. Next, add your flour and xanthan gum. Mix until all the flour is combined and it starts to come together as a dough.

Lightly flour a large sheet of non-stick baking parchment (and your rolling pin) and roll out your dough to a 6mm (¼in) thickness. Use a 7cm (2¾in) round cutter to stamp out rounds. Re-roll the dough as necessary to cut out as many as possible (you should get 16).

Transfer to your prepared sheets, ideally using a small palette knife, and bake for 12–14 minutes until the edges are slightly golden. Allow the biscuits to cool briefly on the sheets before transferring to a wire rack to cool completely.

Once cool, spread half the biscuits with a thin layer of jam and then sandwich the remaining biscuits on top.

Place your icing sugar in a small bowl and add the water gradually until you have a thick, smooth, spreadable icing. You basically want it thick enough so that it won't drip off your biscuits! Dip your biscuits in the icing (or spread the icing on top). Place a glacé cherry half or a jelly tot in the middle to finish. Allow to set briefly, then enjoy.

TIP:
Swap the jam for lemon curd and use lemon juice instead of water for the icing if you fancy a citrus twist. Or sprinkle desiccated coconut on top of your icing instead. Remix them however you like! You don't need to chill this dough but if it's a hot day or your dough feels a little too soft and sticky to work with, you definitely can.

VIENNESE *Fingers & Whirls*

low lactose

use lactose-free milk and chocolate

use dairy-free milk, chocolate and a hard dairy-free alternative to butter

MAKES · 12 DOUBLE WHIRLS OR 20 FINGERS

TAKES · 30 MINUTES + 30 MINUTES CHILLING

- 230g (1 cup plus 1 tsp) butter, softened
- 75g (½ cup plus ½ tbsp) icing (confectioners') sugar, sifted, plus extra for dusting
- ½ tsp almond extract
- 1 tsp vanilla extract
- 270g (2 cups) gluten-free plain (all-purpose) flour
- ¼ tsp xanthan gum
- 30g (¼ cup) cornflour (cornstarch)
- 2 tbsp milk

For the whirls

- ½ quantity of buttercream (page 209)
- 200g (7oz) strawberry or raspberry jam

For the fingers

- 200g (7oz) milk or dark chocolate of your choice, melted

I couldn't choose between buttery, melt-in-the-mouth Viennese fingers or wondrous whirls, sandwiched with buttercream and jam. So, being the painfully indecisive person that I am, I'm now writing both down and leaving the decision-making to you!

Line 2 large baking sheets with non-stick baking parchment.

In a large mixing bowl, cream together the butter and icing sugar until light and fluffy (I recommend using an electric hand whisk or stand mixer for this). Mix in your almond and vanilla extracts.

Combine your flour, xanthan gum and cornflour in a medium mixing bowl and add it to the mixture in three stages, mixing in between each addition. Add the milk, which will now make the dough loose enough to pipe.

Transfer the mixture to a piping bag fitted with a large star nozzle, then pipe either 24 round whirls 4cm (1½in) across, or 20 fingers 10cm (4in) long onto your prepared baking sheets, ensuring there are gaps between each for slight spreading. Piping biscuit dough isn't the most fun thing, it's a bit of a workout I find, but the results are worth it! Place in the fridge to chill and firm up for a good 30 minutes.

Preheat your oven to 160°C fan / 180°C / 350°F.

Bake for 12–15 minutes until the edges are starting to turn golden. Remove from the oven and allow to cool for about 10 minutes on the baking sheets before transferring to a wire rack to cool completely.

For whirls, place your buttercream in a piping bag fitted with your (clean) star nozzle. Spread a scant teaspoon of jam on the flat side of half the biscuits. Pipe a small amount of buttercream on the flat side of the remaining biscuits. Sandwich the whirls together and finish with a dusting of icing sugar.

For fingers, dip the fingers less than halfway into the melted chocolate. Transfer back to the wire rack and allow to set completely before tucking in.

Pictured on page 73.

CHOCOLATE DIPPED Anzac Biscuits

use lactose-free chocolate – one biscuit is a FODMAP-friendly serving size

use lactose-free chocolate

vegan

use a (hard) dairy-free butter alternative and dairy-free chocolate

MAKES · 15

TAKES · 45 MINUTES

- 125g (1 cup minus 1 tbsp) gluten-free plain (all-purpose) flour
- 150g (¾ cup) caster (superfine) sugar
- 180g (1¾ cups) gluten-free oats
- 55g (2oz) desiccated (dried shredded) coconut
- ¼ tsp salt
- 110g (½ cup minus ¼ tbsp) butter
- 75ml (3½ tbsp) golden syrup
- 1 tsp bicarbonate of soda (baking soda)
- 30ml (2 tbsp) boiling water
- 200g (7oz) dark or milk chocolate of choice, melted, to coat

This classic Aussie/Kiwi biscuit is something that everyone needs to be familiar with. The combination of buttery oats and coconut works harmoniously together, and dipping the biscuits in chocolate is pure gluten-free perfection. Having a strictly 'gluten-free only' biscuit jar of these is always a good idea.

Preheat your oven to 160°C fan / 180°C / 350°F. Line two large baking sheets with non-stick baking parchment.

In a large mixing bowl, mix together your flour, sugar, oats, coconut and salt. Create a well in the middle and set aside.

Place a small saucepan over a low heat and melt the butter and syrup together.

In a small dish, mix together the bicarb with the boiling water, then stir it into the melted butter and syrup – it should turn nice and frothy. Pour the contents of the pan into the well in the dry ingredients and mix until well combined.

Using your hands, form small, evenly sized balls of dough (you should get 15) on your lined baking sheet, spacing them out so that they have room to spread. Bake in the oven for about 15 minutes until flattened and golden.

Leave to cool briefly on the sheets before transferring to a wire rack to cool completely.

Melt your chocolate (I do this in the microwave, mixing in between short bursts until melted) then half-dip each of your biscuits into it. Transfer back to the wire rack and allow to set completely before tucking in!

TIPS:

You can stir 50g (1¾oz) dried fruit or chocolate chips into the mixture too if you like!

This recipe contains gluten-free oats – if you can't find them, check page 14 for more details.

GIANT Birthday Cookie

use dairy-free chocolate chips and a (hard) dairy-free butter alternative

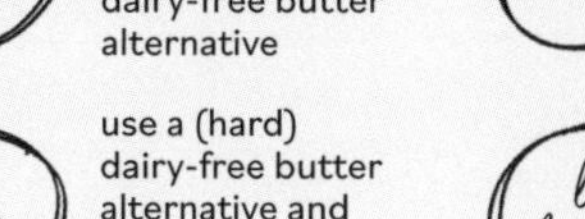

use a (hard) dairy-free butter alternative and 60ml (¼ cup) dairy-free milk instead of the egg

use lactose-free chocolate chips

SERVES · 7–8

TAKES · 55 MINUTES + COOLING

- 130g (½ cup plus 1 tbsp) butter, softened, plus extra for greasing
- 50g (¼ cup) caster (superfine) sugar
- 150g (¾ cup) light brown sugar
- 1 large egg
- 1 tsp vanilla extract
- 280g (2 cups plus 2 tbsp) gluten-free plain (all-purpose) flour
- ¼ tsp xanthan gum
- 1 tsp bicarbonate of soda (baking soda)
- ½ tsp salt
- 1 tbsp cornflour (cornstarch)
- 220g (8oz) chocolate chips (a mixture of milk, dark and white)
- 80g (3oz) gluten-free funfetti sprinkles (must be bake-stable), (optional)
- Sprinkles (ensure gluten-free), to decorate

For the buttercream

- 100g (½ cup minus 1 tbsp) butter, softened
- 200g (scant 1½ cups) icing (confectioners') sugar, sifted
- ½ tsp vanilla extract
- Food colouring paste (optional)

Nothing says 'happy birthday' like an enormous, chunky cookie, packed with chocolate chips, colourful sprinkles and the decoration or personalized message of your choice iced on top. Especially when you're gluten-free! Plus, it's even easier to make than a batch of cookies and an actual birthday cake. If you're ever baking this for me, please just write 'this is gluten-free' on it in huge letters, thanks!

Preheat your oven to 160°C fan / 180°C / 350°F. Grease a 23cm (9in) round springform tin (pan) and line with non-stick baking parchment.

In a large bowl, add the softened butter and both sugars and mix together until combined (I prefer to use an electric hand whisk for this but you can do it by hand). Next, add the egg and vanilla extract, then mix again until fully combined. Add your flour, xanthan gum, bicarb, salt and cornflour, and mix until you have the perfect cookie dough. Reserve 20g (¾oz) of your chocolate chips, then mix in the remaining choc chips so that they're well distributed, then mix in your funfetti sprinkles.

Spoon your mixture into your prepared tin and, using your hands, press in to create a nice, even layer. Sprinkle your reserved chocolate chips evenly on top and gently press in so they're level with the dough.

Bake in the oven for about 30 minutes until golden and the cookie barely has a wobble. If it is undercooked it might sink a little in the middle, but don't worry, it still tastes just as good! Allow to cool completely in the tin before removing to decorate.

Meanwhile, make your buttercream. Place your butter into the bowl of a stand mixer (an electric hand whisk will do the job just fine too) and mix on a medium speed for about 5 minutes until fluffy and a lot paler in colour. If making by hand, ensure you mix for longer until everything is well-combined and consistent.

Add your icing sugar in three stages, beating for about 3 minutes between each addition. Start your mixer slowly (to avoid creating a mini icing sugar explosion), then increase the speed to medium-high for each of your 3-minute mixing intervals. Add the vanilla extract, food colouring paste, if using, and mix once more.

Place in a piping bag with an open star nozzle and pipe around the edge of the cookie. You can also add a message or any design you like to the middle of your cookie! Add lots of sprinkles to finish.

TIP:
You can bake this in a smaller, 20cm (8in) tin to make a cookie pie; just increase the baking time by 5 minutes. Or, if you like a gooey middle, bake for 25–30 minutes.

Vanilla BISCUITS

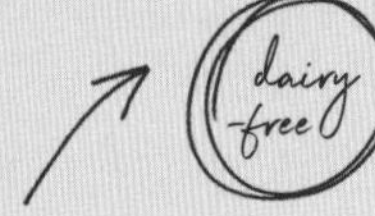

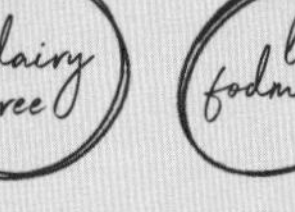

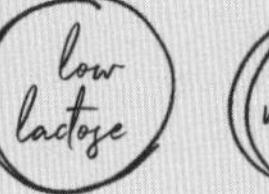

use a (hard) dairy-free butter alternative

use a (hard) dairy-free butter alternative and 60ml (¼ cup) dairy-free milk instead of the egg

MAKES · 20 (USING A 5CM/2IN COOKIE CUTTER)

TAKES · 35 MINUTES

- 100g (½ cup minus 1 tbsp) butter, softened
- 100g (½ cup) caster (superfine) sugar
- 1 large egg, beaten
- 1½ tsp vanilla extract
- 270g (2 cups) gluten-free plain (all-purpose) flour, plus extra for dusting
- ½ tsp xanthan gum
- 1 x quantity of royal icing (page 214)

Sometimes you just need a simple, reliable, yet delicious biscuit/cookie recipe to act as a blank canvas for a spontaneous icing session. And this recipe is exactly that! Pair this recipe with my royal icing recipe and there's no limit to the wild and wonderful decorations you can create.

Preheat your oven to 170°C fan / 190°C / 375°F. Line a large baking sheet with non-stick baking parchment.

In a large mixing bowl, cream together the butter and sugar until light and fluffy (I prefer to use an electric hand whisk or a stand mixer for this). Add your beaten egg and vanilla extract, and briefly mix in. Next, add your flour and xanthan gum. Mix until all the flour is combined and the mixture starts to come together as a dough.

Lightly flour a large sheet of non-stick baking parchment (and your rolling pin) and roll out your dough to a 6mm (¼in) thickness. Cut out your shapes with whatever cookie cutters you have.

Transfer the shapes to your prepared sheet, ideally using a small palette knife, then bake in the oven for 8–10 minutes until the edges are very, very slightly golden. Bear in mind that larger cookies may need a little longer and smaller ones a little less.

Allow to cool briefly on the sheet before transferring to a wire rack to cool completely.

Meanwhile, make the royal icing, using the recipe on page 214.

Use the royal icing to create either simple, white line decorations, or go the extra mile to incorporate multiple colours. You can also use line and flood icing to create more intricate designs of your choice that suit the shape of your biscuits. The sky's the limit!

CHOC CHIP Biscotti

use a (hard) dairy-free butter alternative and dairy-free choc chips

low lactose

use lactose-free choc chips

MAKES · 16–20

TAKES · 1 HOUR 20 MINUTES

- 265g (2 cups) gluten-free plain (all-purpose) flour, plus extra for dusting
- ¼ tsp xanthan gum
- 150g (¾ cup) caster (superfine) sugar
- 25g (¼ cup) ground almonds (almond flour)
- 2 tsp gluten-free baking powder
- Pinch of salt
- 2 large eggs
- 55g (¼ cup) butter, melted
- ½ tsp almond extract
- ½ tsp vanilla extract
- 60g (2oz) milk or dark chocolate chips

When we went to Rome and visited some of their amazing gluten-free bakeries, gluten-free biscotti were literally everywhere. When I got home, however, I would sooner find a unicorn hiding in my back garden. Fortunately, I created my own at home which captures all the magic that those crunchy, almond-flavoured biscuits made me feel every day of my trip.

Preheat your oven to 160°C fan / 180°C / 350°F. Line a baking sheet with non-stick baking parchment.

Place your flour, xanthan gum, sugar, ground almonds, baking powder and salt in a large mixing bowl and mix together.

Add your eggs, melted butter, and almond and vanilla extracts, then mix once more (I prefer to use an electric hand whisk or a stand mixer for this). Add your chocolate chips and mix until just combined.

Turn your dough out onto a lightly floured surface. Briefly knead so it comes together and is fairly smooth, then cut in half.

Shape each half with your hands to form a rectangle about 7 x 13cm (2¾ x 5in) and 3cm (1¼in) thick. Place on your prepared baking sheet, leaving a little space between them as they will spread a little.

Bake in the oven for about 30 minutes – at this point the dough should be lightly browned and have a few cracks on the outside. Remove from the oven and allow to cool. Reduce the oven temperature to 140°C fan / 160°C / 325°F.

Once cooled, cut each rectangle into slices 2cm (¾in) thick, using a sharp knife. Place on the baking sheet, cut-side up, and bake for a further 20–25 minutes until dry and golden.

Allow to cool completely on a wire rack before tucking in.

TIP:
You can dip the ends of these in melted chocolate if you fancy too! Feel free to swap out the chocolate chips for the chopped nuts of your choice – almonds work particularly well.

Pinwheel COOKIES

use a (hard) dairy-free butter alternative

use a (hard) dairy-free butter alternative and 60ml (¼ cup) dairy-free milk instead of the egg

MAKES · 18

TAKES · 40 MINUTES + 1¾ HOURS CHILLING

- 220g (1 cup minus 1 tsp) butter, softened
- 220g (1 cup plus 1½ tbsp) caster (superfine) sugar
- 1 medium egg, beaten
- 300g (2¼ cups) gluten-free plain (all-purpose) flour
- ½ tsp xanthan gum
- 20g (¾oz) unsweetened cocoa powder, sifted
- 2 tsp water
- 1 tsp vanilla extract

Inspired by a trip to Disneyland, here's another treat that I was sadly never able to eat. But fortunately, they're incredibly simple to make at home, thus reinforcing that my own kitchen is, in fact, the real 'happiest place on Earth'. Sorry Disneyland.

In a large mixing bowl, cream together the butter and sugar until light and fluffy (I prefer to use an electric hand whisk or a stand mixer for this). Add your beaten egg, and briefly mix it in. Next, add your flour and xanthan gum. Mix until all the flour is combined and it starts to come together into a dough.

Halve the dough and place one half in a separate bowl. Mix your cocoa powder into the dough in one of the bowls, then add the water and mix it in. Add vanilla extract to the other bowl and mix into the dough. Wrap both pieces of dough separately in cling film (plastic wrap) and place in the fridge to chill for about 45 minutes.

Place a large sheet of non-stick baking parchment on a flat surface, then place your vanilla dough on it and cover with a second sheet of non-stick baking parchment. Roll out the dough to a large rectangular shape, around 25 x 30cm (10 x 12in). Repeat this with the chocolate dough, rolling out between two more sheets of baking parchment.

Peel the top layer of baking parchment off both rolled out doughs. Next, carefully place the chocolate dough sheet on top of the vanilla, with the baking parchment sheet facing up. Use your rolling pin to gently roll over the top of them so that they stick together well, then remove the top sheet of baking parchment.

With one of the short sides closest to you, roll up the two layers of dough nice and tightly, using the baking parchment to help you to roll it forwards. Make sure you don't roll the paper into the dough! Wrap the log of dough in cling film and chill in the fridge for 2 hours, or the freezer for 1 hour.

Preheat your oven to 160°C fan / 180°C / 350°F and line a large baking sheet with non-stick baking parchment.

Using a sharp knife, trim the ends off the chilled dough log and cut into 1cm (½in) slices. Place on your lined baking sheet, leaving a slight gap between them to allow room for them to spread.

Bake in the oven for 15–17 minutes until slightly spread, with a crisp exterior. Allow to cool briefly on the baking sheet before transferring to a wire rack to cool completely.

Pictured on page 82.

Caramelized White Chocolate & HAZELNUT COOKIES

use a hard dairy-free butter alternative, and dairy-free white choc chips instead of the caramelized white chocolate

low fodmap

use lactose-free white choc chips instead of the caramelized white chocolate

MAKES · 12

TAKES · 40 MINUTES + 40 MINUTES CHILLING

- 100g (3½oz) hazelnuts
- 125g (½ cup plus 1 tbsp) butter, softened
- 100g (½ cup) light brown sugar
- 100g (½ cup) caster (superfine) sugar
- 1 large egg
- 1 tsp vanilla extract
- 295g (2¼cups) gluten-free self-raising (self-rising) flour
- ½ tsp bicarbonate of soda (baking soda)
- 180g (6½oz) caramelized white chocolate (see below)

For the caramelized white chocolate

- 225g (8oz) white chocolate (minimum 30% cocoa butter)

I cannot emphasize just how much I adore these bakery-style cookies. They're crisp on the outside, chewy in the middle, and the combination of sweet, creamy caramelized white chocolate with hazelnut is an underrated joy. Making your own caramelized white chocolate is incredibly easy and only takes 10 minutes, plus cooling time. It tastes like a Caramac chocolate bar, which isn't actually gluten-free, so take this chance to remind yourself of what it tastes like!

Line one large and one small baking sheet with non-stick baking parchment.

First, make your caramelized white chocolate. In a heatproof bowl, melt your white chocolate in the microwave, mixing between short bursts until it's completely melted and smooth.

Once melted, return to the microwave for 15-second blasts at a time, stirring after each. Repeat this process until the white chocolate turns to more of a golden caramel colour. This will take longer than you think – it might seem like it's never going to turn, but it definitely will, so be patient! Once golden, pour onto the large prepared baking sheet and allow to solidify completely.

Preheat your oven to 160°C fan / 180°C / 350°F. Spread your hazelnuts out on the small prepared baking sheet and toast in the oven for about 10 minutes until they smell amazing and look lightly golden. Allow to cool, then chop into smaller pieces and put to one side.

Line two more large baking sheets with non-stick baking parchment.

In a large mixing bowl, cream together your softened butter and both sugars until light, fluffy and well combined. Then add your egg and vanilla extract, and mix until combined. Add your flour and bicarb, mixing well to ensure there are no pockets of flour.

Break up your caramelized white chocolate into 1.5cm (⅔in) chunks. Reserve a handful, then mix in the rest so that it's well distributed, then mix in your chopped hazelnuts.

Divide your dough into 12 evenly sized pieces and roll each into a ball (mine weighed around 60g/2oz each). Place on an unlined baking sheet (not your lined sheets) and push a few of your reserved pieces of caramelized white chocolate into the top of each ball. Chill on the sheet for about 40 minutes in the freezer, or over an hour in the fridge.

Preheat your oven to 180°C fan / 200°C / 400°F. Place your 2 lined baking sheets in the oven to heat up.

Remove the hot baking sheets from the oven and place the chilled balls on the sheets, ensuring you leave adequate space between them to allow them to spread. Bake for 10–12 minutes until golden.

Leave to cool on the sheets for 15–20 minutes before transferring to a wire rack. You can enjoy them warm or completely cooled.

TIP:
You can always just use standard white chocolate and switch out the nuts for dried cranberries. Remix it however you like!

Pictured on page 83.

·NYC·
Triple Chocolate Cookies

use dairy-free choc chips and a (hard) dairy-free butter alternative

use a hard dairy-free butter alternative, dairy-free choc chips, and 60ml (¼ cup) dairy-free milk instead of the egg

use lactose-free chocolate chips

MAKES · 8 CHUNKY COOKIES

TAKES · 35 MINUTES + 40 MINUTES CHILLING

- 125g (½ cup plus 1 tbsp) butter, softened
- 100g (½ cup) light brown sugar
- 100g (½ cup) caster (superfine) sugar
- 1 large egg
- 1 tsp vanilla extract
- 255g (1¾ cups) gluten-free self-raising (self-rising) flour
- ¼ tsp xanthan gum
- 25g (¼ cup) unsweetened cocoa powder, sifted
- ½ tsp bicarbonate of soda (baking soda)
- 300g (10½oz) mixture of milk, dark and white chocolate chips

A 'New York City' cookie is like no other – they're crisp on the outside but thick and chunky with lots of melty choc chips and soft cookie dough in the middle. They're also never gluten-free, but that changes now!

Line a large baking sheet with non-stick baking parchment.

In a large mixing bowl, cream together the butter and both sugars until light and fluffy (I prefer to use an electric hand whisk or a stand mixer for this). Crack in your egg and add the vanilla extract, then mix in. Add in your flour, xanthan gum, cocoa powder and bicarb, then mix well so that there are no pockets of flour. Fold in your chocolate chips so that they're well distributed.

Using your hands, divide your dough into 9 balls, each weighing around 110g (4oz). Roll them roughly into balls so they are a little messy and rustic – *not* neat, smooth balls – and place on the lined baking sheet. Also, if there are no chocolate chips visible once rolled, feel free to push a few spare into the top.

Chill your dough balls on the sheet for about 40 minutes in the freezer, or longer in the fridge. This step is important as it prevents them from spreading so much in the oven, allowing them to become extra chunky and thick.

Preheat your oven to 180°C fan / 200°C / 400°F. Line two large baking sheets with non-stick baking parchment and place them in the oven to heat up.

Remove the sheets from the oven and quickly place the chilled balls on the sheets, generously spaced apart. Bake for about 11–12 minutes until the cookies are a little gooey still, with a hump in the middle. Remember – you want the hump in the middle, you don't want them to be totally flat!

Allow to cool for 15 minutes on the sheet before transferring to a wire rack to cool completely.

TIP:
Replace the cocoa powder with an equal quantity of gluten-free self-raising (self-rising) flour for classic NYC choc chip cookies.

Pictured on page 83.

Fudgy BROWNIE COOKIES

use dairy-free chocolate/choc chips and a (hard) dairy-free butter alternative

use lactose-free chocolate/choc chips

MAKES · 18

TAKES · 40 MINUTES

For the dry mixture

- 190g (1½ cups minus 1 tbsp) gluten-free plain (all-purpose) flour
- 40g (½ cup minus 1 tbsp) unsweetened cocoa powder
- 1½ tsp gluten-free baking powder
- ¼ tsp xanthan gum
- ¼ tsp salt

For the wet mixture

- 300g (10½oz) dark chocolate, broken into pieces
- 185g (¾ cup plus 1 tbsp) butter
- 225g (1 cup plus 2 tbsp) caster (superfine) sugar
- 150g (¾ cup) light brown sugar
- 3 large eggs
- 100g (3½oz) milk chocolate chips
- 2–3 tsp milk (optional)
- Flaky sea salt, to sprinkle on top (optional)

What do you get when you cross a fudgy brownie with a cookie? Sorry if you thought there was going to be a punchline here – the answer is a brownie cookie! With a fudgy, super-chocolatey middle, this is certainly a crossover that can't be beat.

Preheat your oven to 160°C fan / 180°C / 350°F. Line two large baking sheets with non-stick baking parchment.

In a medium mixing bowl, combine your dry ingredients.

Put your chocolate and butter in a large heatproof bowl and place over a saucepan of gently boiling water, making sure the base of the bowl isn't touching the water. Keep stirring until everything has melted and mixed together, then remove from the heat.

In a large mixing bowl, whisk together both sugars with the eggs for 5–6 minutes (I prefer to use an electric hand whisk or a stand mixer on a high speed for this) until it starts to become paler and almost shiny. Immediately pour in your melted chocolate mixture and mix on a low speed for around a minute until well combined.

Mix your dry ingredients into the chocolate mixture. Don't overmix but do ensure it is well combined, without any lumps or pockets of flour. Lastly, mix in your chocolate chips. If the mixture feels too thick, add a couple of teaspoons of milk to loosen it slightly. It should have more of a batter-like consistency, rather than that of a dough.

The quicker you get these cookies in the oven the better they will be. I know that sounds weird, but trust me! The sooner they go in, the more shiny the top of each cookie will be.

As the mixture should be quite sticky, use an ice-cream scoop to transfer balls of wet dough to the prepared sheets, leaving space between each one so that they have room to spread. If your cookie balls aren't smooth on top, wet your finger and dab the top of each to smooth them over. Sprinkle with a few flakes of salt, if you like, then bake in the oven for 12 minutes.

Remove from the oven and allow to cool for about 25 minutes before moving them to a wire rack to cool completely.

Pictured on page 82.

Doughnuts

When you're told you can't eat something, for some reason that only makes you crave it ten times more. And that's how we've ended up with an entire chapter dedicated to gluten-free doughnuts!

To me, a gluten-free doughnut should be exactly like a muggle doughnut – golden on the outside, with a light and fluffy, sometimes chewy middle and definitely *not* dense or heavy. So that's exactly what I created, in all variations under the sun.

For the 'real deal' experience start with my authentic jam, custard or apple doughnuts, ring doughnuts (inspired by everyone's favourite doughnut brand...), or my jam and custard finger doughnuts, all of which are proved and fried, for an authentic doughnut taste and texture.

If you're in a hurry, make my mini ricotta fried doughnuts or no-yeast glazed ring doughnuts. Or, if you don't fancy frying at all, there's easy baked options to hand, such as my cinnamon sugar apple cider doughnuts, custard-filled choux rings or jam, custard or apple duffins.

Whatever you do, just make sure you enjoy some gluten-free doughnuts for me!

KOPYKAT RING Doughnuts

use dairy-free milk and a (hard) dairy-free butter alternative

use lactose-free milk

use lactose-free milk and raspberry jam for the filling

use dairy-free milk, a (hard) dairy-free butter alternative and 3 tbsp aquafaba (whisked until frothy) instead of the egg

MAKES · 10–12

TAKES · 1 HOUR + 4 HOURS PROVING

- Vegetable oil, for deep-frying

For the yeast mixture

- 165ml (⅔ cup) warm milk
- 10g (2½ tsp) caster (superfine) sugar
- 7g (¼oz) dried active yeast (ensure gluten-free)

For the dough

- 150g (1 cup plus 2 tbsp) gluten-free self-raising (self-rising) flour
- 80g (½ cup) tapioca starch (ensure gluten-free), plus extra for dusting
- 1 tsp gluten-free baking powder
- 50g (¼ cup) caster (superfine) sugar
- ½ tsp xanthan gum
- 10g (⅓oz) psyllium husk powder (ensure gluten-free)
- 1 tsp apple cider vinegar
- 1 large egg
- 40g (3 tbsp) butter, melted

For a powdered finish

- 150g (1 cup) icing (confectioners') sugar, sifted

For a glazed finish

- 250g (1¾ cups) icing (confectioners') sugar, sifted
- 50ml (3½ tbsp) milk
- 1 tsp vanilla extract

For a chocolate glaze finish

- 170g (scant 1¼ cups) icing (confectioners') sugar, sifted
- 25g (¼ cup) unsweetened cocoa powder, sifted
- 30ml (2 tbsp) milk
- 1 tsp vanilla extract
- Gluten-free sprinkles

Whenever I ask you guys, 'what would you eat if you could eat gluten again?', a certain American doughnut brand beginning with 'K' pops up *a lot*. So here are three classic variations!

In a jug (pitcher), stir together your warm milk, sugar and yeast. Allow to stand for 10 minutes until frothy. Line a large baking sheet with non-stick baking parchment.

In a large mixing bowl, mix together the flour, tapioca starch, baking powder, sugar, xanthan gum and psyllium husk powder. Add the vinegar, egg, melted butter and yeast mixture and mix well (I use an electric hand whisk). Transfer to a clean bowl, cover with cling film (plastic wrap) and leave to prove in a warm place for 2 hours until risen.

Flour your work surface with tapioca starch and divide the dough into 70g (2½oz) balls. Using a rolling pin (or your hands), flatten each ball to 1cm (½in) thick. Use a 9cm (3½in) round cutter to cut out your doughnuts and a 3cm (1¼in) round cutter to remove the middle of each. Place on the lined baking sheet, cover with cling film and prove for another 2 hours (or cover and place in the fridge overnight to cold-prove).

Half-fill a large, heavy-based saucepan with oil and place over a medium heat for 15 minutes or until it reaches 170°C (340°F). If you don't have a digital thermometer, check the temperature using the wooden spoon test (page 21).

Carefully remove your doughnuts from the parchment and lower them, in batches of 2, into the hot oil – they should gently sizzle. Fry for 2–2½ minutes on each side until golden. Don't let the oil get too hot or the doughnuts will darken before the middle is cooked. Remove from the oil using a slotted spoon, then place on a plate lined with kitchen paper. Transfer to a wire rack to cool.

POWDERED FINISH:
After resting on a wire rack for 5 minutes, roll the doughnuts on both sides on a plate of icing sugar.

GLAZED FINISH:
Mix the ingredients to form a glaze. Dip each doughnut in the glaze on both sides, then place on a wire rack set over baking parchment to set.

CHOCOLATE GLAZE FINISH:
Mix the icing sugar, cocoa powder, milk and vanilla to form a glaze. Dip each doughnut in the glaze on one side, then place on a wire rack. Cover with sprinkles and allow to set.

NO-YEAST *Glazed* RING DOUGHNUTS

use a (hard) dairy-free butter alternative, a thick dairy-free yoghurt instead of sour cream, and dairy-free milk

vegetarian

low fodmap

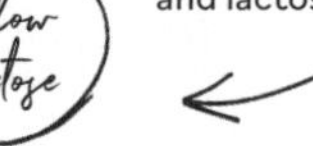

use lactose-free Greek yoghurt instead of sour cream and lactose-free milk

MAKES · 6-7

TAKES · 45 MINUTES + 1 HOUR CHILLING

- 45g (3 tbsp) butter, softened
- 40g (3¼ tbsp) caster (superfine) sugar
- 60g (5 tbsp) light brown sugar
- 2 large egg yolks
- 1 tsp vanilla extract
- 160g (¾ cup) sour cream
- 260g (2 cups) gluten-free self-raising (self-rising) flour
- ¼ tsp xanthan gum
- 1 tbsp cornflour (cornstarch)
- ¼ tsp ground nutmeg (optional)
- Vegetable oil, for deep-frying

For the glaze

- 60g (¼ cup) butter, melted
- 185g (1¼ cups) icing (confectioners') sugar, sifted
- ½ tsp vanilla extract
- 2 tbsp milk

These beautiful, fried golden rings, drenched in a crisp, sweet glaze were the first doughnuts I created for this chapter. And I almost just called it a day right there, because I was so pleased with how they turned out! Thanks to the sour cream, the dough was just so easy to work with (which is rare in gluten-free baking) and it also made the doughnuts wonderfully light once fried. No yeast or proving required!

In a large mixing bowl, cream together the butter and sugars until light and fluffy (I prefer to use an electric hand whisk or a stand mixer for this). Next, add your egg yolks and vanilla extract and mix in until combined. Then stir in your sour cream, ensuring it's fully incorporated.

In a medium mixing bowl, mix together the flour, xanthan gum, cornflour and nutmeg, if using, then add them to your bowl of wet ingredients. Mix by hand with a spatula so you don't overmix. Cover your bowl with cling film (plastic wrap) and chill in the fridge for about 1 hour until the dough has firmed up a little.

Once chilled, remove the dough from the fridge and roll it out on a lightly floured sheet of non-stick baking parchment to a 2cm (¾in) thickness. Then use a 9cm (3½in) round cutter to cut out your doughnut shapes and a 3cm (1¼in) round cutter for the hole to remove the middle of each.

Lift your doughnut shapes onto a baking sheet (using the parchment to lift them) and place in the fridge to chill while you heat your oil.

Half-fill a large, deep, heavy-based saucepan with vegetable oil and place over a medium heat for 15 minutes or until it reaches 170°C (340°F). If you don't have a digital food thermometer, check the temperature of the oil using the wooden spoon test (page 21).

Remove the chilled doughnut shapes from the fridge, then lift them from the baking parchment using a palette knife and gently lower them, in batches of 3, into your hot oil – they should gently sizzle. Fry for around 90 seconds to 2 minutes on each side until golden, then remove from the oil using a slotted spoon and place on a plate lined with kitchen paper to absorb excess oil. Repeat with the rest of your doughnuts.

Make your glaze by combining the melted butter, icing sugar, vanilla extract and milk in a medium mixing bowl and mixing until smooth.

Dip each doughnut into the glaze on both sides, then place on a wire rack set over a sheet of baking parchment (to catch any drips) to completely set. These are best enjoyed warm on the day they are fried.

TIP:
Fry the doughnut 'holes' like you would the doughnuts, but for only 1 minute at most on each side, until golden.

Pictured on pages 96–97.

No-Yeast Banoffee BEIGNETS

make my salted caramel sauce dairy-free

make my salted caramel sauce lactose-free

serve with blueberries instead of banana and make my salted caramel sauce low FODMAP

SERVES · 4–5

TAKES · 45 MINUTES

- 1 quantity of gluten-free choux pastry (page 208)
- Vegetable oil, for deep-frying

To finish and serve

- Icing (confectioners') sugar, sifted, for dusting
- 2 ripe bananas, sliced
- Salted caramel sauce (see page 50 for homemade, or use store-bought)

If you're not familiar with a beignet (bonus points if you even know how to pronounce it) then allow me to enlighten you. Think puffy choux pastry meets fried doughnut. They're crisp on the outside and stupidly light and airy in the middle and often dusted with icing (confectioners') sugar for a sweet finish. Serve up for dessert or a sweet brunch with ripe banana and a drizzling of salted caramel sauce.

Make the choux as directed on page 208.

Half-fill a large, deep, heavy-based saucepan with vegetable oil and place over a medium heat for 15 minutes, or until it reaches 170°C (340°F). If you don't have a digital food thermometer, check the temperature of the oil using the wooden spoon test (page 21).

Pipe your choux into an ice cream scoop (or a tablespoon will do, at a pinch) then gently turn it into the oil – it should gently sizzle as you lower them in. Add as many as will comfortably fit into your pan without touching each other and fry for 2–2½ minutes, turning halfway through, until fully puffed up and golden on all sides. Remove from the oil using a slotted spoon and transfer to a plate lined with kitchen paper, to absorb any excess oil.

Transfer to serving plates and dust with icing sugar. Top with slices of ripe banana and drizzle with salted caramel sauce.

TIP:
You can also enjoy these with maple syrup and bacon, or simply with Nutella (briefly heated in the microwave) as a dip.

Pictured on page 96.

MINI RICOTTA

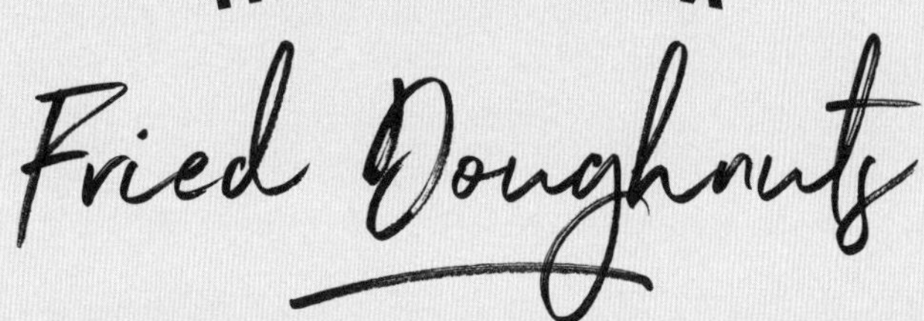

MAKES · 10–15 MINI DOUGHNUTS

TAKES · 45 MINUTES

- 250g (1 cup plus 2 tbsp) ricotta
- 2 large eggs
- 1 tsp vanilla extract
- 45g (¼ cup minus 1 tsp) caster (superfine) sugar
- 105g (¾ cup plus 2 tsp) gluten-free plain (all-purpose) flour
- ¼ tsp xanthan gum
- 2 tsp gluten-free baking powder
- Vegetable oil, for deep-frying

To finish and serve

- Granulated sugar, for coating
- Raspberry or strawberry jam, for dipping

This is, by far, my easiest and quickest fried doughnut recipe – simply mix up the batter, fry and enjoy, no yeast, proving or dough shaping necessary. Also no, these don't taste like cheese! The ricotta gives these a pillowy soft, light and springy middle, yet with a golden, crisp exterior thanks to the frying process. Roll in granulated sugar for that distinctive doughnut-like finish and serve with jam for dipping.

In a large mixing bowl, mix your ricotta, eggs, vanilla and sugar together until combined and smooth (I use an electric hand whisk for this).

In a medium mixing bowl, mix the flour, xanthan gum and baking powder, then add it to the main bowl. Mix until well combined, then chill the batter in the fridge while you heat your oil.

Half-fill a large, deep, heavy-based saucepan with vegetable oil and place over a medium heat for 15 minutes or until it reaches 170°C (340°F). If you don't have a digital food thermometer, check the temperature of the oil using the wooden spoon test (page 21).

Cover a large plate with granulated sugar and set aside.

Remove the doughnut batter from the fridge. Use an ice cream scoop to transfer a portion of the batter straight into the hot oil – it should gently sizzle. Scoop in as many portions of batter as will comfortably fit into your pan without them touching, and fry for 2–4 minutes, turning regularly until golden and puffy on both sides.

Remove from the oil using a slotted spoon and place on the plate of sugar to coat all over, then transfer to a wire rack to cool briefly. Repeat with the rest of your batter. Serve with strawberry or raspberry jam as a dip.

Making it lactose-free? Or low FODMAP?

Make your own lactose-free ricotta cheese! Simply take 2 litres (8½ cups) of lactose-free whole milk and bring to the boil in a large pan. Once bubbling, add 80ml (⅓ cup) of white wine vinegar and 1 tsp of salt and stir in, then remove from the heat. Allow to stand for 15 minutes. Use a slotted spoon to remove all the solid parts from the pan, transfer them to a colander and allow to drain for 30 minutes. Use in this recipe as directed.

Real deal JAM, CUSTARD OR APPLE DOUGHNUTS

use dairy-free milk and a (hard) dairy-free butter alternative

use lactose-free milk

use lactose-free milk; for the filling, use either raspberry jam or low FODMAP crème pâtissière

use dairy-free milk, a (hard) dairy-free butter alternative, jam or apple for the filling and 3 tbsp aquafaba (whisked until frothy) instead of the egg

MAKES · 10–12

TAKES · 1 HOUR + 4 HOURS PROVING

- Vegetable oil, for deep-frying
- Granulated sugar, for coating

For the yeast mixture

- 165ml (⅔ cup) warm milk
- 10g (2½ tsp) caster (superfine) sugar
- 7g (¼oz) dried active yeast (ensure gluten-free)

For the dough

- 150g (1 cup plus 2 tbsp) gluten-free self-raising (self-rising) flour
- 80g (½ cup) tapioca starch, plus extra for dusting
- 1 tsp gluten-free baking powder
- 50g (¼ cup) caster (superfine) sugar
- ½ tsp xanthan gum
- 10g (⅓oz) psyllium husk powder (ensure gluten-free)
- 1 tsp apple cider vinegar
- 1 large egg
- 40g (3 tbsp) butter, melted

For the filling

- Seedless raspberry jam

OR

- 1 quantity of crème pâtissière (page 213)

OR

- Apple filling (see recipe opposite)

If you miss eating those golden-on-the-outside, fluffy-in-the-middle doughnuts, bursting with jam, custard or apple filling, then this recipe was made for you. Like when baking 'real' doughnuts, you'll need to exercise a little patience while waiting for them to prove, but trust me – good things come to those who wait!

In a jug (pitcher), stir together your warm milk, sugar and yeast. Allow to stand for 10 minutes until nice and frothy. Line a large baking sheet with non-stick baking parchment.

In a large mixing bowl, mix together your flour, tapioca starch, baking powder, sugar, xanthan gum and psyllium husk powder. Add your vinegar, egg, melted butter and frothy yeast mixture and mix until well combined (I prefer to use an electric hand whisk for this).

Transfer to a clean mixing bowl, cover with cling film (plastic wrap) and leave to prove in a warm place for about 2 hours until risen.

Lightly flour your work surface with tapioca starch and divide your dough into balls that weigh 55–60g (2oz) each. Using a rolling pin (or just the palms of your hands), flatten each portion of dough to be around 1cm (½in) thick. Place on the lined baking sheet, cover with cling film and place in a warm place to prove for another 2 hours, until slightly risen (or cover and place in the fridge overnight to cold-prove).

Half-fill a large, deep, heavy-based saucepan with vegetable oil and place over a medium heat for 15 minutes or until it reaches 170°C (340°F). If you don't have a digital food thermometer, use the wooden spoon test (page 21).

Cover a large plate with granulated sugar and set aside.

Carefully remove your doughnut shapes from the parchment and gently lower them, in batches of 2 or 3, into the hot oil – they should gently sizzle. Fry for 2–2½ minutes on each side until golden. Don't let the oil get too hot, or the doughnuts will darken before the middle is cooked properly. Once golden on both sides, remove from the oil using a slotted spoon, place on the plate of granulated sugar to coat, then transfer to a wire rack to cool.

Attach a round 1cm (½in) nozzle to a piping bag and fill it with your chosen filling. Push a skewer or chopstick into the middle of your doughnut and wiggle it around to create a pocket. Pipe your filling into the middle of each doughnut until it feels a little heavier – the more filling the better! These are best enjoyed fresh on the day they are fried.

Pictured on page 97.

JAM, CUSTARD OR APPLE *Duffins*

use a (hard) dairy-free butter alternative and dairy-free milk

use lactose-free milk; for the filling, use either raspberry jam or low FODMAP crème pâtissière

use lactose-free milk

MAKES · 12 (OR 14–16 SMALL)

TAKES · 1 HOUR

- 150ml (⅝ cup) milk
- 1 tbsp lemon juice
- 345g (2½ cups) gluten-free self-raising (self-rising) flour
- ¼ tsp xanthan gum
- 175g (¾ cup plus 2 tbsp) caster (superfine) sugar
- ½ tsp ground cinnamon (optional)
- 75g (⅓ cup) butter, melted and cooled, plus extra for greasing
- 50ml (3½ tbsp) vegetable oil
- 2 large eggs
- 1 tsp vanilla extract

For coating

- 100g (½ cup) granulated sugar
- 50g (3½ tbsp) butter, melted

For the filling

- Seedless raspberry jam

OR

- 1 quantity of crème pâtissière (page 213)

OR

- 1 quantity apple filling (see right)

In case you didn't know, a 'duffin' is a cross between a doughnut and a muffin (I guess 'muffnut' sounded too ambiguous?). Since they're baked, they're slightly closer to a muffin in terms of a light, moist texture, but once you add the sugared coating and jam, custard or apple filling, they're easily halfway between the two!

Preheat your oven to 160°C fan / 180°C / 350°F. Grease a 12-hole cupcake tin (pan) with butter or a little spray of oil, spreading it around each hole.

In a jug (pitcher), briefly mix your milk and lemon juice together. Allow to stand for 10–15 minutes until it becomes thicker and a little lumpy.

In a large mixing bowl, mix the flour, xanthan gum, sugar and cinnamon, if using, until combined.

In a medium mixing bowl, mix the cooled, melted butter, oil, eggs, vanilla extract, and milk mixture, then whisk until combined. Pour your wet ingredients into your dry ingredients and mix together until just combined – definitely don't overmix this one!

Spoon your mixture into the cupcake holes, filling them up as high as you like: if you want a better doughnut shape, about halfway works; if you want a bigger muffin/doughnut shape, fill them to the top. Bake in the oven for 18–20 minutes or until golden and cooked through (or 16–18 minutes if you only half-filled the holes). Check by poking a skewer into the middle – if it comes out clean, then they're done. Allow to cool for 5 minutes in the tin before gently easing them out.

Spread the granulated sugar out onto a large plate and place the melted butter in a small bowl. While still warm, carefully roll each duffin in the melted butter bowl and then roll in the sugar until well coated. Transfer to a wire rack and allow to cool completely.

Attach a round 1cm (½in) nozzle to a piping bag and fill it with your chosen filling. Push a skewer or chopstick into the top of each duffin and wiggle it around to create space in the middle. Pipe your filling into the middle until it feels a little heavier – the more filling the better!

FOR AN APPLE FILLING

- 400g (14oz) cooking apples, such as Bramley, cored, peeled and chopped
- 15g (1 tbsp) butter
- 120g (⅔ cup minus 2 tsp) caster (superfine) sugar
- ½ tsp ground cinnamon

Put your chopped apples in a large saucepan with the butter and sugar. Cook over a low heat for 15 minutes, then stir in the cinnamon. Cook for a further 15 minutes or so until lovely and thick, any excess water has evaporated and the apples are super-soft. Use a stick blender to blend to a smooth paste, then allow to cool before piping into your doughnuts.

JAM & CUSTARD Finger Doughnuts

use dairy-free milk and a (hard) dairy-free butter alternative

use lactose-free milk

MAKES · 10

TAKES · 1 HOUR + 4 HOURS PROVING

- Vegetable oil, for deep-frying
- Granulated sugar, for coating

For the yeast mixture

- 165ml (⅔ cup) warm milk
- 10g (2½ tsp) caster (superfine) sugar
- 7g (¼oz) dried active yeast (ensure gluten-free)

For the dough

- 150g (1 cup plus 2 tbsp) gluten-free self-raising (self-rising) flour
- 80g (½ cup) tapioca starch (ensure gluten-free), plus extra for dusting
- 1 tsp gluten-free baking powder
- 50g (¼ cup) caster (superfine) sugar
- ½ tsp xanthan gum
- 10g (⅓oz) psyllium husk powder (ensure gluten-free)
- 1 tsp apple cider vinegar
- 1 large egg
- 40g (3 tbsp) butter, melted

For filling and to finish

- Granulated sugar
- 1 quantity of crème pâtissière (page 213)
- Seedless raspberry jam

Pictured on page 96.

Just looking at one of these instantly takes me back to my childhood. But since being gluten-free, looking at them was all I was allowed to do! I didn't realize just how much I missed them until I successfully made them myself. These sugared doughnut fingers are super-soft and light, filled with a thick custard and a little jam for good measure.

In a jug (pitcher), stir together your warm milk, sugar and yeast. Allow to stand for 10 minutes until nice and frothy. Line a large baking sheet with non-stick baking parchment.

In a large mixing bowl, mix together the flour, tapioca starch, baking powder, sugar, xanthan gum and psyllium husk powder. Add the vinegar, egg, melted butter and yeast mixture and mix well (I use an electric hand whisk for this). Transfer to a clean mixing bowl, cover with cling film (plastic wrap) and leave to prove in a warm place for about 2 hours until risen.

Lightly flour your work surface with tapioca starch and divide your risen dough into balls that weigh 60–65g (2oz) each. Roll each into a sausage shape that is 15cm (6in) long. Place on the lined baking sheet, cover with cling film and place in a warm spot to prove for another 2 hours until slightly risen (or cover and place in the fridge overnight to cold-prove).

Half-fill a large, deep, heavy-based saucepan with vegetable oil and place over a medium heat for 15 minutes or until it reaches 170°C (340°F). If you don't have a digital food thermometer, check the temperature of the oil using the wooden spoon test (page 21).

Cover a large plate with granulated sugar and set aside.

Carefully remove your doughnut shapes from the baking parchment and lower them into the hot oil, in batches of 2 – they should gently sizzle. Fry for about 2½ minutes on each side until golden. Don't let the oil get too hot or the doughnuts will darken too much before the middle is cooked properly. Once golden on both sides, remove from the oil using a slotted spoon, place on the plate of granulated sugar to coat, then transfer to a wire rack to cool.

Once cooled, use a serrated knife to create a deep cut lengthwise in your doughnut fingers (without accidentally cutting them in half!).

Fill a piping bag (open star nozzle attached) with the crème pâtissière and pipe a line down the middle of each doughnut. Fill another piping bag with jam, snip off the end to create a 3mm (⅛in) opening and pipe a line of jam down the middle of the crème pâtissière filling. (If you don't have piping bags to hand and/or don't mind a more rough and ready finish, simply spoon the filling and jam into the middle. These are best enjoyed fresh on the day they are fried.

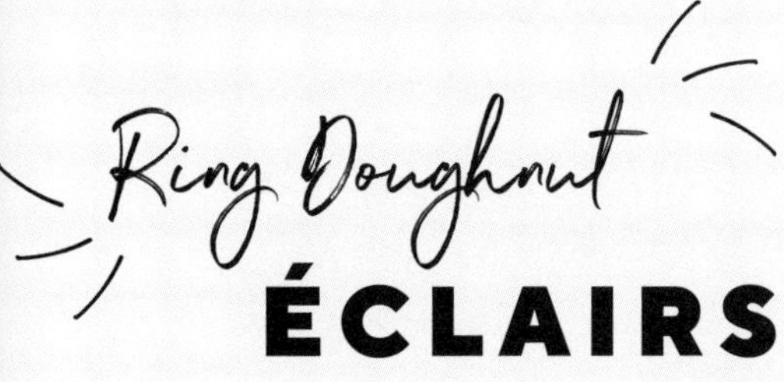

Ring Doughnut ÉCLAIRS

use dairy-free milk

use lactose-free milk

MAKES · 6

TAKES · 45 MINUTES

- 1 quantity of crème pâtissière (page 213)
- 1 quantity of gluten-free choux pastry (page 208)

For the glaze and to finish

- 85g (generous ½ cup) icing (confectioners') sugar, sifted
- 3 tbsp milk
- 1 tsp vanilla extract
- Pink food colouring paste (or any colour you like)
- Gluten-free sprinkles

Whether you like to call them 'doughclairs' or 'éclairnuts' is completely up to you, but one thing is for certain: this is a crossover that we all need in our lives. With light, crisp choux pastry, pumped full of custard and topped with a vanilla glaze and sprinkles, you could call them whatever you like and I'd still eat them!

Make and chill your crème pâtissière as directed on page 213.

Preheat your oven to 190°C fan / 210°C / 410°F. Line a large baking sheet with non-stick baking parchment.

Make the choux pastry as directed on page 208, then transfer to a piping bag fitted with an open star or round nozzle. Pipe thick rings, 7.5cm (3in) diameter, onto your baking sheet, allowing 2.5cm (1in) of space between them as they will puff up when baked.

Bake in the oven for 25–30 minutes until puffy and golden. Quickly remove the sheet from the oven and flip all the choux doughnuts over. Pierce the base of each one a couple of times using a skewer and pop them back in the oven for a further 5 minutes to finish crisping up and drying out.

Switch off the oven but leave the doughnuts in, with the door ajar, for a further 20 minutes. Transfer to a wire rack to cool completely.

Fill a piping bag with small open star nozzle attached with crème pâtissière. Pipe into each choux pastry ring through one of the steam holes (you may have to wiggle a skewer around in the hole first to make it a little larger) until it feels a little heavier. Place them back on the wire rack. Alternatively, you can carefully slice each choux ring in half, then spoon (or pipe) the crème pâtissière inside and sandwich the halves back together.

For the glaze, grab a medium mixing bowl and add your icing sugar, milk and vanilla extract. Mix until it reaches a smooth, slightly thick, yet still pourable consistency. Add a tiny amount of the food colouring paste of your choice until you achieve a vibrant colour. Dip each of your doughnuts into the glaze on one side (or spoon it on top), then place on a wire rack. Cover with sprinkles and allow to set.

TIP:
You can always used whipped cream instead of crème pâtissière if you're in a hurry.

Pictured on pages 86 and 97.

BAKED CINNAMON SUGAR *Apple Cider* DOUGHNUTS

use dairy-free milk and a (hard) dairy-free butter alternative

use lactose-free milk/ chocolate

MAKES · 12

TAKES · 50 MINUTES

- 120ml (½ cup) milk
- 1 tbsp lemon juice
- 250ml (1 cup) cider (hard cider)

For the dry mixture

- 240g (1¾ cups) gluten-free plain (all-purpose) flour
- 1 tbsp cornflour (cornstarch)
- ¼ xanthan gum
- 1 tsp bicarbonate of soda (baking soda)
- ½ tsp gluten-free baking powder
- 1½ tsp ground cinnamon
- ½ tsp ground nutmeg
- Pinch of salt

For the wet mixture

- 1 large egg
- 30g (2 tbsp) butter, melted and cooled
- 100g (½ cup) light brown sugar
- 100g (½ cup) caster (superfine) or granulated sugar
- 1 tsp vanilla extract

For coating

- 100g (scant ½ cup) butter, melted
- 150g (¾ cup) granulated sugar
- 1½ tsp ground cinnamon
- ½ tsp ground nutmeg

If you fancy all the awesomeness of doughnuts with none of the frying, then my baked ring doughnuts were made especially for you! Thanks to the cider, they're incredibly fluffy, with a satisfying cinnamon sugar crunch on the outside. Get your 6-hole doughnut trays at the ready!

Preheat your oven to 160°C fan / 180°C / 350°F and lightly grease two 6-hole doughnut trays.

In a jug (pitcher), briefly mix your milk and lemon juice together. Allow to stand for 10–15 minutes until it becomes thicker and a little lumpy.

Heat the cider in a small saucepan over a low heat for 15 minutes, until reduced down by half. Ideally, measure it to ensure it's done – you should have around 120ml (½ cup) left. Set aside to cool.

Place all the dry ingredients in a large mixing bowl and mix together. Put the wet ingredients in a medium-sized mixing bowl, add your milk and lemon mixture, and mix together. Pour your wet mixture into your dry mixture along with your cooled cider, mixing to a thick, smooth batter. Ensure you don't overmix this one!

Spoon your mixture into the doughnut rings, filling them two-thirds full. Bake in the oven for 10 minutes until risen and golden. Leave to cool for a couple of minutes in the trays, then transfer to a wire rack to cool slightly.

Grab two small bowls, put your melted butter in one of them, and mix the granulated sugar, cinnamon and nutmeg in the other.

Dip each doughnut in the melted butter on both sides, then transfer to the cinnamon sugar and toss until well coated.

Serve immediately. Once cooled, store in an airtight container or freeze for up to 3 months.

TIP:
If you don't have doughnut trays you can simply use the batter in a muffin tin (pan) to create 'duffins'. They will likely need longer in the oven, so bake them for around 18 minutes.

MAPLE PECAN CRULLER

use dairy-free milk

vegetarian

use lactose-free milk

MAKES · 10–12

TAKES · 45 MINUTES + 30 MINUTES CHILLING

- 1 quantity of gluten-free choux pastry (page 208)
- Vegetable oil, for greasing and deep-frying

For the maple pecan glaze

- 200g (scant 1½ cups) icing (confectioners') sugar, sifted
- 30ml (2 tbsp) maple syrup
- 30ml (2 tbsp) milk
- 50g (1¾oz) pecans, toasted and finely chopped

This chapter feels like an encyclopaedia of doughnuts and I'm most definitely ok with that. After all, how often do you get this kind of choice when you're gluten-free? A cruller doughnut is made from choux pastry that's piped into a ring and fried for a crisp, puffy golden finish, with a fried doughnut flavour. When drizzled with maple pecan glaze, they're a thing of beauty.

Make the choux pastry as directed on page 208, transferring it to a piping bag (fitted with a large open star nozzle) and chilling it in the fridge for around 30 minutes before using.

Half-fill a large, deep, heavy-based saucepan with vegetable oil and place over a medium heat for 15 minutes or until it reaches 170°C (340°F). If you don't have a digital food thermometer, check the temperature of the oil using the wooden spoon test (page 21).

Cut out 10–12 squares of non-stick baking parchment, each 7.5cm (3in), lightly grease them and pipe a thick ring of choux pastry onto each of them.

Lower one of your choux rings on the paper into the hot oil – it should gently sizzle. Fry for 2½–3 minutes on each side until a deep golden brown, removing the paper from the back of the choux using a pair of tongs after 1 minute.

It should have puffed up quite a bit and feel somewhat lighter in weight once fully cooked. Once golden on both sides, remove from the oil using a slotted spoon and place on a plate lined with kitchen paper to absorb excess oil. Repeat to make the remaining doughnuts. Transfer to a wire rack set over a sheet of non-stick baking parchment and allow to cool completely before glazing.

To make your glaze, mix together the icing sugar, maple syrup and milk in a medium mixing bowl, until smooth and of a drizzling consistency. Drizzle the glaze on top of each choux ring, followed by your chopped pecans, and allow to set.

DESSERTS

When you flick through this chapter, can you believe that so many restaurants still think that fruit salad is an acceptable gluten-free dessert?

I promise you now, none of these desserts are any more complicated than making their gluten-containing equivalent – nor do they look or taste any different. So I think it's time we banished fruit salad from gluten-free dessert menus for good!

Welcome to my dream dessert menu, starring everything from lemon meringue pie, black forest gateaux and a show-stopping apple pie to strawberry cheesecake, key lime pie and tons more. Take your pick!

. BEST EVER .
Lemon Meringue Pie

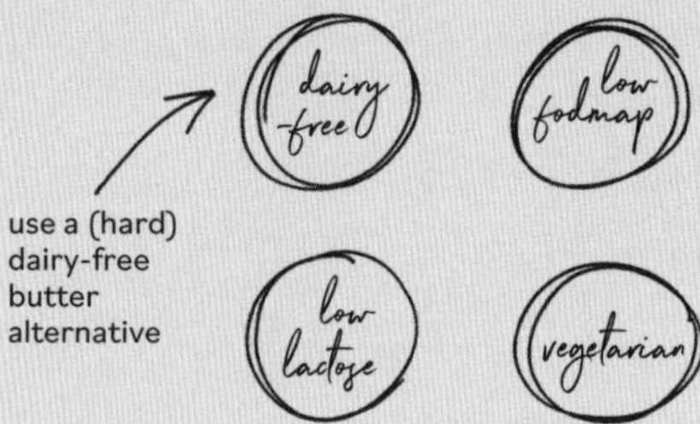

SERVES · 12

TAKES · 1 HOUR + 3–4 HOURS CHILLING

- 1 quantity of ultimate gluten-free shortcrust pastry (page 206)
- Gluten-free plain (all-purpose) flour, for dusting
- 1 medium egg white, beaten

For the filling

- 5 large egg yolks
- 55g (½ cup minus ½ tbsp) cornflour (cornstarch)
- 250g (1¼ cups) caster (superfine) sugar
- Grated zest of 4 lemons
- 180ml (¾ cup) lemon juice
- 290ml (1¼ cups minus 2 tsp) water
- 55g (¼ cup minus 1 tsp) butter, softened

For the Italian meringue

- 100g (3½oz) egg whites (3–4 eggs)
- 200g (1 cup) caster (superfine) sugar
- 45ml (3 tbsp) water
- ¼ tsp cream of tartar

Where do I start? Every bite contains buttery pastry, topped with a sweet, sharp and zesty lemon filling with a mountain of sticky, fluffy meringue proudly sitting on top. You'll need either a sugar thermometer or a digital cooking thermometer, as precision is everything when it comes to Italian meringue. A kitchen blowtorch also helps to achieve the ultimate finish, but a few minutes under the grill (broiler) will do the job just fine too.

If your chilled pastry dough is quite firm, leaving it out at room temperature ahead of time is definitely advised.

Lightly flour your rolling pin and a large sheet of non-stick baking parchment, then roll out the dough to a 2mm (1⁄16) thickness. Aim to roll out a large circular shape, but remember not to handle your dough excessively as it will warm it up and make it more fragile.

Transfer the pastry to a 23cm (9in) loose-bottomed fluted tart tin (pan). I do this by supporting and flipping the pastry and parchment in one gentle movement. Peel off the baking parchment. Next, use your fingers to carefully ease the pastry into place, so that it neatly lines the tin. Lift the overhanging pastry and, using your thumb, squash 2mm (1⁄16in) of pastry back into the tin. This will result in slightly thicker sides which will prevent your pastry from shrinking when baked. Allow the remaining overhang to do its thing – we'll trim it after chilling. Lightly prick the base of the pastry case several times with a fork, then place in the fridge for 15 minutes.

Preheat your oven to 180°C fan / 200°C / 400°F. Place a baking sheet inside to heat up.

Remove the pastry case from the fridge and use a rolling pin to roll over the top of the tin, removing the overhang and flattening the pastry rim. Loosely line the base with a piece of scrunched up baking parchment and fill with baking beans (or uncooked rice if you don't have any). Place on the hot baking sheet in the oven and bake for 15 minutes, then remove the baking parchment and baking beans and bake for a further 5 minutes.

Brush the base with the beaten egg white and pop back in the oven for a couple of minutes (the egg wash helps to seal the pastry when filled to prevent it from becoming soggy). Allow to cool completely.

For your filling, place your egg yolks in a medium mixing bowl and whisk together to break them up, then place to one side.

Continued overleaf...

Put your sugar and cornflour in a medium saucepan and whisk together until combined. Whisk in your lemon zest, juice and water, then place over a medium heat, whisking until thickened. Pour one-third of the mixture into your egg yolks, whisking constantly to combine. Follow with another third of your mixture, whisking once more until well incorporated.

Pour the contents of your mixing bowl back into your saucepan with the remaining third of the lemon mixture. Whisk constantly over a medium heat for 2–3 minutes until it combines and thickens further. Remove from the heat and stir in your butter until smooth and well incorporated. Allow the filling to cool down briefly before pouring it into the pastry case, then place in the fridge to chill and set for at least 3–4 hours, but ideally overnight.

To make the meringue, place your egg whites in the bowl of a stand mixer with a whisk attachment in place, ready to whisk.

In a medium saucepan, add your sugar and water, then mix together so it's combined and gloopy – try to avoid getting any sugar up the sides of the pan. Place over a medium heat and work quickly from this point onwards.

Add the cream of tartar to the egg whites and whisk on a medium speed until soft peaks form.

Once the sugar syrup reaches 120°C (248°F), remove from the heat and carefully drizzle it into the egg whites, with the mixer still running. Try not to get the sugar syrup on the sides of the bowl as it will instantly harden and crystallize. Continue to whisk until the meringue is stiff, glossy and cooled.

Top your chilled lemon filling with the Italian meringue, leaving a small amount of the lemon filling exposed around the edges. Create some fancy peaks using a silicone spatula, then add the ultimate finish by using a kitchen blowtorch to toast some of the meringue.

TIP:
To clean the saucepan you made your sugar syrup in, simply fill with boiling water. Add any utensils used too. Bring it to a simmer for 5–10 minutes and all the sugar will magically dissolve into the water. If you use cold water to clean your pan, the sugar syrup will harden and be near impossible to remove!

Tiramisu CRÊPE CAKE

use lactose-free milk/cream cheese/whipping cream (minimum 30% fat)

use dairy-free milk and cream cheese (minimum 23% fat), plus a dairy-free equivalent to double cream (minimum 30% fat)

use lactose-free milk/cream cheese/ whipping cream (minimum 30% fat) and omit the alcohol

MAKES · 8–10 SLICES

TAKES · 45 MINUTES + 2 HOURS CHILLING

- 3 large eggs
- 420ml (1¾ cups) milk
- 150g (1 cup plus 2 tbsp) gluten-free plain (all-purpose) flour
- 2 tbsp unsweetened cocoa powder, plus extra for dusting
- 2 tbsp caster (superfine) sugar
- ½ tsp instant coffee mixed with 30ml (2 tbsp) boiling water, cooled
- 1 tbsp coffee liqueur, brandy or Marsala (optional)
- Vegetable oil, for frying

For the filling

- 300ml (1¼ cups) double (heavy) cream
- 140g (1 cup) icing (confectioners') sugar, sifted
- 2 tsp vanilla extract
- 2 tbsp coffee liqueur, brandy or Marsala (optional)
- 500g (2¼ cups) mascarpone

I think we can all agree that a stack of gluten-free crêpes is a heavenly sight. So take that feeling, multiply it by a billion and that's exactly what you'll get with my tiramisu crêpe cake. The crêpes are super-chocolatey with a hint of coffee and a boozy hit of liqueur, brandy or Marsala. Couple that with several layers of fluffy, creamy filling and you've got an indulgent, decadent tiramisu in crêpe cake form. No need to even switch the oven on!

In a jug (pitcher), whisk the eggs and milk together.

Sift in the flour and cocoa powder into a large mixing bowl, then stir in the sugar. Pour in half of the milk and egg mixture to the bowl and whisk until well combined. Pour in the remaining milk and egg, and whisk once again until smooth.

Add your cooled coffee, and liqueur, if using. The batter should be a slightly thicker consistency than water. Allow to rest for 10 minutes, then whisk once more before using.

Place a 20cm (8in) frying pan or crêpe pan over a low heat. Add 1 teaspoon of vegetable oil and brush over the base of the pan. Once heated, add a ladle's worth of the batter to the middle of your pan. Lift the pan and use a circular tilting motion to help the batter spread as much as possible. Aim to make the crêpes as thin as you can so that your batter goes further! Flip after 45 seconds, then cook for a further 20 seconds.

Repeat until you've used up the batter, adding 1 teaspoon of oil per crêpe, and ensuring that you stir the batter occasionally to stop the flour from sinking to the bottom. You should end up with 16–18 crêpes – the more, the better! Allow to completely cool on a wire rack.

For the filling, put the cream, icing sugar, vanilla extract, and liqueur, if using, in a large mixing bowl. Whisk until soft peaks form (I prefer to use an electric hand whisk for this). Add your mascarpone and beat together until combined and the mixture is thick and fluffy. Stop once it reaches this point as the mixture can split!

Grab a 20cm (8in) springform cake tin (pan) (a loose-bottomed cake tin works too) and, ideally, a small, angled palette knife. Remove the base from your springform tin and set the other part aside.

To construct the cake, place one of your crêpes on top of the base of the tin. Spoon a generous, heaped tablespoon of the filling on top.

Continued overleaf...

Using the palette knife, spread it into a nice, thin layer, right to the edges. Lay the next crêpe on top and repeat the process until you've used up all of your crêpes. Reserve 1 heaped tablespoon of filling to finish the cake later (keep it covered in the fridge) and spread any more leftover filling around all of the edges of the cake, using your palette knife.

Carefully place the springform ring part of the tin over your crêpe cake and close the clips so that it locks to the base. Cover with cling film (plastic wrap) and allow to set in the fridge for at least 2 hours, but ideally overnight.

Once chilled, remove from the fridge and place a plate or cake stand upside-down on top of the springform tin. Quickly invert it and open the springform ring, then remove it, and lift off the base.

To finish, spread your reserved filling over the top, then sift over some cocoa powder in a nice, even layer. Cover and store in the fridge, or slice up and freeze for 2–3 months.

TIP:
If you fancy yourself as a multi-tasking pancake master and have two 20cm (8in) pans, you can massively speed things up by making two crêpes at once! Of course, you can always just make the crêpes and serve them rolled up with the filling inside, too.

MARK'S JAPANESE-STYLE Cotton Cheesecake

use lactose-free milk and lactose-free cream cheese

SERVES · 12

TAKES · 1½ HOURS + COOLING AND CHILLING

- Vegetable oil, for greasing
- 5 large eggs
- 340g (1½ cups) mascarpone
- 50ml (3½ tbsp) milk
- 40g (4¾ tbsp) gluten-free plain (all-purpose) flour
- 1½ tbsp lemon juice
- 2 tsp vanilla extract
- 100g (½ cup) caster (superfine) sugar
- 2 tbsp apricot jam
- 1 tbsp water

In our house, Mark is the master of all East Asian-style cakes – they've always been his favourites, after all! So, not surprisingly, his Japanese-style cheesecake is like taking a direct bite out of a cloud. He's perfected that lovely, creamy taste and even made it gluten-free for me… and now for you too!

Grease a 20cm (8in) round baking tin (pan), at least 6cm (2¼in) deep (don't use a loose-bottomed or springform tin). Line the base and sides with non-stick baking parchment so that it comes above the sides of the tin a little. You will also need an ovenproof dish that is 5cm (2in) deep and will fit your baking tin inside for the water bath.

Preheat your oven to 160°C fan / 180°C / 350°F. Grab two small bowls and separate the eggs – you should have about 200g (7oz) whites and 85g (3oz) yolks.

Place a small saucepan over a low heat. Add the mascarpone and heat until it starts to melt, then add the milk. Once the mascarpone has softened and the mixture looks slightly thick and lumpy, whisk until smooth. Remove from the heat and pour into a large bowl. Allow to cool for 5–10 minutes. Add the egg yolks and whisk until well combined. Add the flour and whisk until no lumps are visible. Whisk in the lemon juice and vanilla, and set aside.

Place the egg whites and sugar in the bowl of a stand mixer and mix on a medium speed for 1 minute until frothy, then increase the speed to high and whisk until just before stiff peaks. (You can of course do this in a mixing bowl with an electric hand mixer. It's possible to do it by hand, but you'll need a little elbow grease!)

Next, add your meringue mixture to the mixing bowl, a third at a time, folding it in slowly using a silicone spatula – keep folding until there are no lumps of meringue visible. Repeat until all of the meringue mixture is folded in, but do not overmix!

Boil a full kettle of water. Pour the cheesecake mixture into your prepared tin – it will be very full. Gently shake the tin from side to side to obtain a smooth surface on top. Place the baking tin inside the larger ovenproof dish. Place on the bottom shelf of your oven and immediately add boiling water to the larger dish, to come just under halfway up the cheesecake tin. Reduce the oven temperature to 140°C fan / 160°C / 325°F and bake for 40 minutes, then reduce the heat down further to 120°C fan / 140°C / 285°F and bake for a final 30 minutes until risen in the middle.

Leave the cheesecake in the oven with the door slightly ajar and the oven switched off, for 15 minutes, then remove from the oven and remove from the ovenproof dish. Allow to cool for a further 20 minutes. By this point, the cheesecake will have sunk back below the top of the tin.

Line a plate with non-stick baking parchment and gently invert the cheesecake onto it. Remove the parchment stuck to the base and sides. Place a serving plate on top of it (upside down) and quickly invert once again, then remove the plate and baking paper on top.

In a small dish, mix the jam and water together and heat in the microwave for 30 seconds. Give it a stir, then brush on top of the cheesecake. Allow to cool completely, then cover with cling film (plastic wrap) and chill in the fridge overnight. Don't be tempted to dig into this as soon as it's cooled – it will have a strong taste of egg! Chilling it removes this taste completely.

Mum's Lemon SURPRISE PUDDING

use dairy-free milk and a (hard) dairy-free alternative to butter

use lactose-free milk

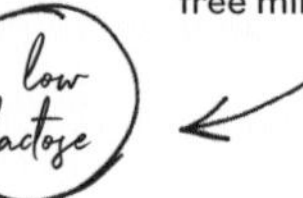

vegetarian

SERVES · 5–6

TAKES · 1 HOUR

- 65g (¼ cup plus 1 tsp) butter, softened, plus extra for greasing
- 250g (1¼ cups) caster (superfine) sugar
- Grated zest of 3 lemons
- 130ml (½ cup plus 2 tsp) lemon juice
- 4 large eggs, separated
- 65g (7½ tbsp) gluten-free plain (all-purpose) flour
- 320ml (1⅓ cups) milk
- Icing (confectioners') sugar, sifted, for dusting

My mum is certainly no stranger to entertaining a crowd, and this all-in-one lemon pudding is her secret weapon – it only takes 15 minutes of effort, yet serves 5–6 lucky people. Each guest gets a portion of sweet, zesty warm sponge and, of course, the 'surprise': a layer of sticky lemon curd hiding underneath. Obviously, she always makes it gluten-free for me, but nobody ever even notices – thanks Mum!

Preheat your oven to 160°C fan / 180°C / 350°F. Lightly grease a rectangular baking dish, about 20 x 25cm (8 x 10in). Boil a kettle's worth of water.

In a large mixing bowl, cream your butter to properly soften it, then mix in your sugar. You can do this by hand or with an electric mixer.

Mix in the lemon zest, then add the lemon juice and egg yolks, and mix to combine. Follow this with your flour and then milk. The mixture doesn't look great but as long as it's well combined you're doing it right!

In a separate bowl, whisk your egg whites to soft peaks (I prefer to use an electric hand whisk for this part), then carefully fold them into your main mixture. Pour the mixture into the baking dish, then place the dish inside a roasting tin that comfortably fits the baking dish inside it. Fill the tin halfway up with hot water and place in the oven. Bake for 45–50 minutes until golden, set but still lovely and soft.

Dust with icing sugar and serve straight away, or warm up just before serving.

TIP:
Fancy making individual puddings? Pop the mixture into individual ramekins and bake for around 20 minutes instead.

KEY LIME PIE

SERVES · 12

TAKES · 1 HOUR + 1 HOUR CHILLING

- 300g (10½oz) gluten-free ginger biscuits (cookies)
- 100g (½ cup minus 1 tbsp) butter, melted
- 3 large egg yolks
- 1 x 397g (14oz) can of condensed milk
- Grated zest and juice of 4 limes, plus extra zest to finish

To finish

- 300ml (1¼ cups) double (heavy) cream
- 2 tbsp icing (confectioners') sugar, sifted

A good key lime pie is never a bad idea, but a gluten-free key lime pie is always a good idea. Say hello to three layers of pure joy: a buttery, gluten-free biscuit base, topped with sweet, rich filling with lots of lime-y kick to it, adorned with fluffy whipped cream. If I could only eat one dessert for all eternity, I'd be just fine with this one, thank you very much.

Preheat your oven to 160°C fan / 180°C / 350°F.

Firstly, make your base. Blitz your biscuits to a crumb-like texture in a food processor - not into a fine dust! Alternatively, you can pop the biscuits into a zip-lock bag and bash them with a rolling pin. In a large mixing bowl, put your blitzed biscuits and pour in your melted butter. Mix until well combined.

Spoon the mixture into a 23cm (9in) loose-bottomed fluted tart tin (pan). Compact it into the base and up the sides of the tin, using the back of a spoon. Next, use a small jar or a measuring cup to tightly compact the base and the sides, ensuring the sides are a consistent thickness. It should look deceptively similar to a pastry case. Place on a baking sheet and bake in the oven for 15 minutes. Remove from the oven and allow to cool completely.

To make your filling, place your egg yolks in a large mixing bowl and whisk for a solid minute. Add your condensed milk and mix once more, then add the lime zest and juice and mix for a further 2–3 minutes until combined and thick.

Pour the mixture into your cooled biscuit case, ensuring that you have a smooth, even top. Bake in the oven for 15 minutes until the filling is firm with a very slight wobble.

Allow to cool to room temperature before placing in the fridge to firm up for at least an hour.

When ready to serve, whip the cream and icing sugar to soft peaks. Then either spoon the cream onto the top of the pie or pipe the cream around the edge of the pie using a piping bag with an open star nozzle attached.

Finish off with a sprinkling of lime zest and enjoy!

TIP:

Instead of finishing with whipped cream, you can always use your leftover egg whites to make Italian meringue for the top using the recipe over on page 106.

BLACK FOREST

use dairy-free cream (minimum 30% fat) and dairy-free chocolate

use lactose-free whipping cream (minimum 30% fat) and lactose-free chocolate

SERVES · 12
TAKES · 1 HOUR + COOLING

- Oil, for greasing
- 145g (1 cup plus 1½ tbsp) gluten-free plain (all-purpose) flour
- 60g (½ cup plus 1½ tbsp) unsweetened cocoa powder
- ½ tsp xanthan gum
- 1½ tsp gluten-free baking powder
- 7 large eggs, separated
- 200g (1 cup) caster (superfine) sugar

For the filling

- 340g (12oz) black cherry jam
- 15 cherries in Kirsch
- 10 tbsp Kirsch syrup (taken from the jar of cherries in Kirsch)
- 900ml (3¾ cups) double (heavy) cream
- 120g (generous ¾ cup) icing (confectioners') sugar, sifted

To finish

- 9 tbsp Kirsch syrup (taken from the jar of cherries in Kirsch)
- 12 fresh cherries
- 150g (5oz) dark chocolate, grated and chilled

This retro boozy bake is back, and this time we can actually eat it! Each chocolate sponge is incredibly light and moist, with layers of sweet, Kirsch-infused cherry jam and wondrous whipped cream. You can find a jar of cherries in Kirsch in most supermarkets – simply take the Kirsch syrup straight from the jar.

Preheat your oven to 180°C fan / 200°C / 400°F. Grease three 20cm (8in) round baking tins (pans) and line the bases with non-stick baking parchment.

In a mixing bowl, combine the flour, cocoa powder, xanthan gum and baking powder, then set aside.

Add the egg whites to the bowl of a stand mixer (or use an electric hand whisk – by hand is achievable, but it will take longer). Mix on a medium-high speed to soft peaks, then add the sugar in two batches, mixing in between each addition. Once all the sugar has been added, turn the speed up to high and mix until stiff peaks form, if they haven't already.

Reduce the speed to medium and, while still mixing, add the egg yolks. Once incorporated, stop the mixer and add your dry ingredient mixture. Return to a medium speed until the mixture is smooth, combined and glossy.

Evenly divide the mixture among the three prepared tins and spread out using a silicone spatula, then gently shake from side to side to create a smooth, even finish. Bake in the oven for 15 minutes until lovely and risen. Invert onto a wire rack, remove the baking parchment and then carefully flip them over (the tops of the sponges will stick to the rack if you don't flip them!). Allow to cool completely.

Prepare the filling. In a small mixing bowl, mix the cherry jam, cherries and 4 tablespoons of the Kirsch syrup until well combined, then set aside. Pour the cream into a large mixing bowl and whisk until it reaches soft peaks. Add the icing sugar and mix until well combined, then add the remaining 6 tablespoons of Kirsch syrup and mix once more.

To construct the cake, place one sponge on a serving plate. Drizzle 3 tablespoons of the Kirsch syrup all over the top, then spread on a layer of your cherry jam mixture right up to the edges. Spread a 1cm (½in) thick layer of cream on top. Place the next sponge on top and repeat. Finally, place the last sponge on top, with the flat side facing up. Drizzle the final 3 tablespoons of syrup on top, then cover the entire cake with cream, using a small palette knife.

Transfer the remaining cream to a piping bag with an open star nozzle. Pipe on 12 swirls of cream around the top edge of the cake and place a fresh cherry on each swirl. Finish by sprinkling your chilled, grated chocolate on top and all up the sides of the cake. (Chilling the chocolate and applying with cold hands means it won't immediately melt when handled.)

Keep chilled or slice and freeze for up to 3 months.

TIP:

For a simpler finish, halve the ingredients required for the cream. Continue with the recipe up until you place your final sponge on top, then simply spread the remaining cream on top. Grate the chocolate on top of the cake (no need to chill it) and omit the fresh cherries. Job done!

COFFEE & CREAM *Éclairs*

MAKES · 14

TAKES · 50 MINUTES + COOLING

- 1 quantity of gluten-free choux pastry (page 208)
- 1 quantity of crème pâtissière (page 213) made with 1 tbsp instant coffee granules in place of vanilla extract
- 200g (scant 1½ cups) icing (confectioners') sugar, sifted
- 1–2 tbsp strong black coffee

As a non-coffee-drinker (judge me as you wish) I can't really tell you why this is an exception to that rule. It's probably because the combo of crisp choux filled with an indulgent coffee cream works so well against that deep, rich coffee-flavoured topping. Who knows – these may even convert me to a coffee drinker yet!

Make and chill your crème pâtissière, using instant coffee granules instead of vanilla extract, as directed on page 213.

Preheat your oven to 190°C fan / 210°C / 410°F. Line a large baking sheet with non-stick baking parchment.

Make the choux pastry as directed on page 208, then transfer to a piping bag fitted with a medium/large open star or round nozzle. If you don't have a piping bag, you can simply spoon the pastry onto the baking sheet instead. Pipe thick, straight lines, 10cm (4in) long, onto your baking sheet, leaving 2.5cm (1in) of space between them as they will puff up when baked.

Bake in the oven for 25–30 minutes until puffy and golden. Quickly remove the sheet from the oven and flip all the éclairs over. Pierce the base of each one using a skewer, then pop them back in the oven for a further 5 minutes to finish crisping up and drying out.

Switch off the oven but leave the éclairs in, with the door ajar, for a further 20 minutes. Transfer to a wire rack to cool completely.

Once the éclairs are cooled and your coffee crème pâtissière is prepared, you have two choices of how to fill them. Firstly, you can carefully slice the éclairs in half and spoon (or pipe) the crème pâtissière on as though you were assembling a sandwich. Alternatively, you can place your crème pâtissière in a piping bag fitted with a small, open star nozzle and pipe inside from the bottom of the éclair until it starts to feel heavier and full.

For the icing, grab a small bowl and mix the icing sugar with enough coffee to create a spreadable consistency. It shouldn't be too thick or too runny, just somewhere in between. Dip the tops of your éclairs into the icing and allow to set briefly.

Enjoy immediately before the pastry starts to lose its crisp exterior, or store in the fridge for 1–2 hours before serving.

XL Profiterole Buns

use dairy-free cream (minimum 30% fat) and dairy-free chocolate

use lactose-free whipping cream (minimum 30% fat) and lactose-free chocolate

MAKES 8–10

TAKES: 1 HOUR + COOLING

- 1 quantity of gluten-free choux pastry (page 208)
- 1 quantity of crème pâtissière (page 213)
- 175ml (¾ cup) double (heavy) cream
- 175g (6oz) dark or milk chocolate, finely chopped

No, I didn't name this after myself! (Well, I suppose I accidentally did?) This was inspired by a trip to Rome where so many of the gluten-free bakeries would serve these oversized choux buns, packed with custard, finished with a variety of toppings. Ever since I got home, I've wanted to make oversized profiteroles and yes, it was a great idea!

Make and chill your crème pâtissière as directed on page 213.

Preheat your oven to 190°C fan / 210°C / 410°F. Line a large baking sheet with non-stick baking parchment.

Make the choux pastry as directed on page 208, then transfer to a piping bag fitted with an open star or round nozzle. If you don't have a piping bag, you can simply spoon the pastry onto the baking sheet instead. Spoon or pipe large balls of choux onto your baking sheet (around 5cm/2in in diameter), leaving 2.5cm (1in) of space between them as they will puff up when baked. They should be bigger than a standard profiterole!

Bake in the oven for 35 minutes until puffy and golden. Quickly remove the sheet from the oven and flip all the buns over. Pierce the base of each one using a skewer, then pop them back in the oven for a further 5 minutes to finish crisping up and drying out.

Switch off the oven but leave the buns in, with the door ajar, for a further 20 minutes. Transfer to a wire rack to cool completely.

Once your choux buns are cool and your crème pâtissière is prepared, you have two choices of how to fill them. Firstly, you can carefully slice the choux buns in half and spoon (or pipe) the crème pâtissière in as though you were assembling a sandwich. Alternatively, you can place your crème pâtissière in a piping bag fitted with a small, open star nozzle and pipe it in from the bottom of the profiterole until it starts to feel heavier and full.

For your chocolate ganache top, pour your cream into a small saucepan and place over a low heat until just before it begins to boil. Add your chopped chocolate to a heatproof bowl and pour the hot cream onto the chocolate. Leave to stand for a few minutes before mixing together until smooth. Briefly cool and then either dip the top of your choux buns into the ganache or drizzle the ganache over them using a spoon.

Enjoy immediately before the pastry starts to lose its crisp exterior, or store in the fridge for 1–2 hours before serving.

PEACH & RASPBERRY Cobbler

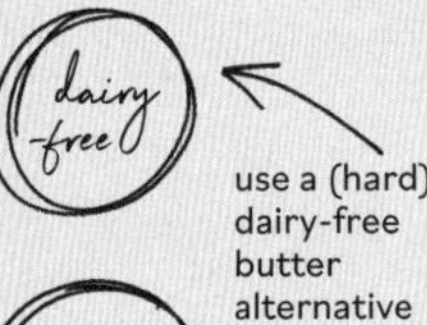

use a (hard) dairy-free butter alternative

SERVES 5–6

TAKES: 1 HOUR

- 6–8 ripe peaches
- 100g (3½oz) raspberries
- 40g (3¼ tbsp) caster (superfine) sugar

For the cobbler

- 115g (½ cup) butter, melted and cooled, plus extra for greasing
- 150g (¾ cup) caster (superfine) sugar
- 150g (1 cup plus 2 tbsp) self-raising (self-rising) flour
- 1 tsp vanilla extract
- 1 tsp ground cinnamon
- Pinch of salt

So often when I make a dessert like this, it's all about the apple crumble, apple cobbler, apple crisp – apple everything! But trust me, nothing beats a peach and raspberry cobbler for totally obliterating that cycle. With a crisp, chunky, crunchy topping with a hint of cinnamon concealing slices of caramelized, perfectly ripe peach and gooey raspberries, there's most definitely a new contender for best dessert in town.

Preheat your oven to 160°C fan / 180°C / 350°F and lightly grease a 23 x 30cm (9 x 12in) rectangular baking dish.

Halve your peaches, remove the stone (pit) and thinly slice. Place in the baking dish along with your raspberries. Add the sugar and mix it into the fruit, ensuring you have an even layer.

To make your cobbler, put your melted butter, sugar, flour, vanilla, cinnamon and salt in a large mixing bowl and mix together until a cookie-dough-like texture is formed.

Crumble your dough in lumps over the fruit – it doesn't need to be fully covered, the peaches and raspberries should be somewhat visible through it.

Bake for about 40 minutes, until the fruit is bubbling and the top is golden and crisp.

Remove from the oven and allow to cool a little before serving with vanilla ice cream, custard or cream.

TIP:
You can happily use other fruit with this cobbler topping, such as apples and pears. You can also use frozen or canned peaches – the texture might be slightly different but it will definitely be just as delicious.

BANANA *Upside Down* CAKE

use dairy-free choc chips and a (hard) dairy-free butter alternative

use lactose-free choc chips

use dairy-free choc chips, a (hard) dairy-free butter alternative and 6 tbsp aquafaba (whisked until frothy) instead of the eggs

SERVES 8–10

TAKES: 45 MINUTES

For the topping

- 50g (3½ tbsp) butter, softened
- 50g (¼ cup) light brown sugar
- 2–3 ripe bananas

For the sponge

- 100g (½ cup minus 1 tsp) butter, softened
- 100g (½ cup) light brown sugar
- 2 medium eggs
- 1 tsp vanilla extract
- 1 tbsp maple syrup
- 100g (¾ cup) gluten-free self-raising (self-rising) flour
- 1 tsp gluten-free baking powder
- 50g (1¾oz) chocolate chips (optional)

Now this is a recipe all about how my banana cake got flipped, turned upside down. If you didn't get that reference, just pretend my previous sentence was only a rather strange statement of fact. With sticky, gooey, caramelized bananas on top of an incredibly light and moist sponge cake, packed with chocolate chips, all that's left to do is serve with vanilla ice cream and dig in.

Preheat your oven to 160°C fan / 180°C / 350°F.

For the topping, grab a medium mixing bowl, add the butter and sugar, and cream together until light and fluffy. Spoon into a 20cm (8in) cake tin (pan) and spread the mixture all over the base and up the sides too. Slice your bananas lengthwise and place across the base – as many as will fit!

For the sponge, grab a large mixing bowl and cream together your butter and sugar until light and fluffy. Crack in the eggs, then add the vanilla, maple syrup, flour and baking powder and mix until well combined. Lastly, fold in your chocolate chips, if using.

Pour the mixture over your bananas and spread it out so it's nice and even on top. Bake in the oven for 30–35 minutes until cooked through and golden on top.

Remove from the oven and allow to sit in the tin for around 5 minutes before inverting onto a serving plate – it's ready to serve immediately. Serve warm with vanilla ice cream, or enjoy cold.

TIP:
You can always switch up your toppings from bananas to canned pineapple or sliced pears.

Show-Stopping LATTICE APPLE PIE

SERVES · 12

TAKES · 1 HOUR 10 MINUTES + 30 MINUTES CHILLING

- 1½ quantity of ultimate gluten-free shortcrust pastry (page 206) (if your chilled pastry dough is quite firm, leaving it out at room temperature ahead of time is definitely advised)
- 700g (1lb 9oz) cooking apples, such as Bramley, peeled, cored and thinly sliced
- 1 tbsp lemon juice
- 80g (6 tbsp) light brown sugar
- 30g (2½ tbsp) caster (superfine) sugar
- 20g (2⅔ tbsp) gluten-free plain (all-purpose) flour, plus extra for dusting
- ½ tsp ground ginger
- 1 tsp ground cinnamon
- ¼ tsp ground nutmeg
- 20g (1½ tbsp) butter
- 1 large egg, beaten
- Demerara (turbinado) sugar, for sprinkling

This pie is 'show-stopping' not just because of its golden, buttery lattice, concealing chunks of sweet and sticky caramelized apple, but mainly because it was inspired by my favourite musical: *Waitress.* Of course, I have to change the lyrics to 'sugar, butter, *gluten-free* flour' but that's certainly a change I'm willing to make.

Cut off a generous third of your pastry ball, re-wrap in the cling film (plastic wrap) and return to the fridge – this will be for the lattice top.

Lightly flour your rolling pin and a sheet of non-stick baking parchment, then roll out the larger dough portion on the parchment to a 2mm (1/16in) thickness. Aim for a circular shape but remember not to handle your dough too much as this will make it more fragile.

Grab a 23cm (9in) pie dish and, using the baking parchment to support it, invert your rolled out pastry into the dish, then peel off the parchment. Using your hands, carefully push the pastry in to line the pie dish, leaving overhang around all the edges of around 2cm (¾in). Place in the fridge to keep chilled while you prepare the apple filling.

Place your sliced apple in a large saucepan with the lemon juice and brown sugar. Mix together until well coated. Add the caster sugar, flour, ginger, cinnamon and nutmeg to your pan, stirring it into the apples. Place over a medium heat, add your butter and stir constantly until the apples have softened slightly and the juices have thickened – this should take 5–10 minutes. The apples should still have bite to them and not be mushy. If your apples have softened but the juices haven't thickened to a more syrupy consistency, remove the apples and continue to cook down the juices. Allow the apple filling and syrup to cool.

Spoon the cooled apple filling (including all the syrup) into your pastry case, spread it out evenly, then place back in the fridge to chill.

To make the lattice top, roll out your reserved piece of pastry to a rectangle 4mm (⅙in) thick – slightly thicker than the base and longer than the pie dish diameter. Cut this into long 2cm (¾in) wide strips.

Evenly space half the strips apart on top of the pie, so they overhang on both sides. Pull back every other strip and place down one new strip at right angles to these, then overlap with all the strips you pulled back earlier. Next, pull back all the remaining original strips, then place another new strip at right angles, leaving a gap between this one and the last right angled strip. Once again, overlap with the strips you just pulled back, then continue to do this until you have a complete lattice. Ensure all strips overhang the pastry dish slightly, then trim any excess lattice to be the same length as the overhang from the base. Finally, fold the overhang up and over the edges and crimp with your fingers to seal the pie shut.

Brush the top of your pie with beaten egg, sprinkle on your demerara sugar, then chill in the fridge for 30 minutes. Preheat your oven to 180°C fan / 200°C / 400°F.

Place your pie dish on a baking sheet and bake for 15 minutes, then cover the edges of the pie with foil (these are likely to brown more quickly than the rest of the pie), then reduce the oven temperature to 170°C fan / 190°C / 375°F and bake for a further 25 minutes until golden brown.

Remove from the oven and allow to cool a little before serving warm or cold, with ice cream, cream or custard.

Treacle TART

use dairy-free cream (minimum 30% fat) and a (hard) dairy-free butter alternative

use lactose-free whipping cream (minimum 30% fat)

SERVES · 12

TAKES · 1 HOUR

- 1 quantity of ultimate gluten-free shortcrust pastry (page 206)
- 150g (5oz) gluten-free white bread (ideally stale), roughly torn
- Gluten-free plain (all-purpose) flour, for dusting
- 65g (¼ cup plus 1 tsp) butter
- 415g (1¼ cups) golden syrup
- 15g (¾ tbsp) black treacle (molasses)
- 1 large egg, plus 1 egg yolk
- 2 tbsp double (heavy) cream
- 1 tbsp lemon juice
- 1 tsp ground ginger

This classic tart is something I missed out on for well over a decade, and I can assure you that it was more than worth the wait. After one bite of that flaky pastry, topped with gooey, buttery, almost caramelized sweet filling, you'll never let yourself go without it ever again. Or at least I certainly won't!

If your chilled pastry dough is quite firm, leaving it out at room temperature ahead of time is definitely advised.

Preheat your oven to 180°C fan / 200°C / 400°F and place a baking sheet inside to heat up.

Place the bread in a food processor or blender and pulse until it resembles fine breadcrumbs.

Lightly flour your rolling pin and a large sheet of non-stick baking parchment, then roll out the dough on the parchment to a 2mm (1⁄16in) thickness. Aim to roll out a large circular shape, but remember not to handle your dough excessively as this will make it more fragile.

Transfer the pastry to a 23cm (9in) loose-bottomed fluted tart tin (pan) – I do this by supporting the pastry as I gently invert it into the tin, with equal overhang on all sides. Peel off the baking parchment. Next, use your fingers to carefully ease the pastry into place, so that it neatly lines the tin. Lift the overhanging pastry and, using your thumb, squash 2mm (1⁄16in) of pastry back into the tin. This will result in slightly thicker sides which will prevent your pastry from shrinking when baked. Allow the overhang to do its thing – we'll trim it after chilling. Lightly prick the base of the pastry case several times with a fork then place in the fridge for 15 minutes.

Remove the pastry case from the fridge and use a rolling pin to roll over the top of the tin, removing the overhang and flattening the pastry rim. Loosely line the base with a piece of scrunched up baking parchment and fill with baking beans (or uncooked rice if you don't have any). Place on the hot baking sheet in the oven and bake for 15 minutes, then remove the baking parchment and baking beans and cook for a further 5 minutes. Remove from the oven and reduce the oven temperature to 160°C fan / 180°C / 350°F.

Place your butter, golden syrup and black treacle in a small saucepan and heat so the butter is fully melted and the mixture is warm. Remove from the heat and beat in the egg, egg yolk, cream, lemon juice and ginger, then stir in your breadcrumbs.

Pour the filling mixture into your pastry case and spread it out so it's even. Bake for 25 minutes, then reduce the oven temperature to 140°C fan / 160°C / 325°F and cook for a further 15 minutes until the filling is slightly wobbly but completely set.

Remove from the oven and allow to rest for 15 minutes before serving warm with vanilla ice cream.

Billionaire's NO-BAKE TART

MAKES · 12 SLICES

TAKES · 40 MINUTES + 5 HOURS CHILLING

For the biscuit base

- 350g (12oz) gluten-free digestive biscuits (graham crackers)
- 2 tbsp unsweetened cocoa powder
- 165g (¾ cup minus 1 tsp) butter, melted

For the caramel

- 185g (¾ cup plus 1 tbsp) butter
- 35g (3 tbsp) golden caster (superfine) sugar
- 65g (3 tbsp) golden syrup
- 1 x 397g (14oz) can of condensed milk

For the chocolate ganache top

- 120ml (½ cup) double (heavy) cream
- 50g (1¾oz) dark chocolate, chopped
- 50g (1¾oz) milk chocolate, chopped
- 20g (1½ tbsp) butter, softened

To finish

- 50g (1¾oz) white chocolate, melted, plus extra for grating

Yup, I can assure you that this easy, no-bake tart is a staple part of any billionaire's diet. I mean, with a chocolatey biscuit base, topped with a thick layer of set caramel and a wealth of smooth, rich, chocolatey ganache on top, what else would you rather eat?

Firstly, make your base. In a food processor, blitz your biscuits into a crumb-like texture – not into a fine dust! If you don't have a food processor, pop the biscuits into a zip-lock bag and bash them with a rolling pin. Add the cocoa powder and blitz once more or mix in until your biscuits are a dark brown chocolate colour. Add to a large mixing bowl, pour in your melted butter and mix until well combined.

Spoon the mixture into a 23cm (9in) loose-bottomed fluted tart tin (pan). Compact it into the base and up the sides of the tin using the back of a spoon. Next, press the base of a small jar or cup over the biscuit base and sides to tightly compact, ensuring the sides are a consistent thickness. It should look deceptively similar to a pastry case. Chill in the fridge for at least 30 minutes or up to an hour, while you make your caramel.

For your caramel, place all the ingredients in a small saucepan over a low to medium heat. Allow the butter to melt and sugar to dissolve, then mix well to ensure it doesn't stick to the bottom and is all well combined. Turn the heat up so the mixture starts to bubble a little, then stir continuously for about 5–8 minutes or until it has thickened and turned a dark golden colour.

Pour your caramel on top of your biscuit base, spreading it so that it's level and even. Place in the fridge to set for at least 2 hours. Once chilled, remove from the fridge, ready for the final layer.

To make your ganache, heat your cream in a small saucepan until just before boiling. Add the chopped chocolate and softened butter to a heatproof bowl, then pour in the hot cream. Allow it to sit for about 5 minutes without stirring, then stir together so it's all melted, thoroughly combined and pourable.

Briefly allow to cool, then pour on top of your chilled caramel layer. Return to the fridge for 2–3 hours until the ganache has set. Just before serving, drizzle with melted white chocolate for the final finishing touch, and grate a little extra on if you fancy.

Manchester TART

use dairy-free milk and ensure your custard powder is dairy-free

use lactose-free whole milk and ensure your custard powder is lactose-free

SERVES · 12

TAKES · 1 HOUR + 3 HOURS CHILLING

- 1 quantity of ultimate gluten-free shortcrust pastry (page 206)
- Gluten-free plain (all-purpose) flour, for dusting
- 1 large egg, beaten

For custard filling

- 4 large egg yolks
- 55g (2oz) caster (superfine) sugar
- 60g (2oz) custard powder
- ½ tsp vanilla extract
- 550–750ml (2⅓–3 cups) whole milk (depending on how thick you like your custard)

For the rest of the filling and topping

- 150g (5oz) raspberry or strawberry jam
- 2 large, ripe bananas, peeled and sliced (optional)
- 100g (3½oz) desiccated (dried shredded) coconut
- 1 glacé cherry

Considering I went to University in Manchester to study law (before dropping out because it was too hard) and later lived there, it's a city that will always have a special place in my heart. And a slice of this tart will always have a special place in my belly! Golden pastry filled with jam, fresh banana, custard, topped with coconut and a cherry on top. It's every bit as sweet as the city itself.

If your chilled pastry dough is quite firm, leaving it out at room temperature ahead of time is definitely advised.

Preheat your oven to 180°C fan / 200°C / 400°F.

Lightly flour your rolling pin and a large sheet of non-stick baking parchment, then roll out the dough on the parchment to a 2mm (1⁄16in) thickness. Aim for a large circular shape, but remember not to handle your dough excessively as this will warm it up and make it more fragile.

Transfer the pastry to a 23cm (9in) loose-bottomed fluted tart tin (pan) – I do this by supporting the pastry as I gently invert it into the tin, with equal overhang on all sides. Peel off the baking parchment. Next, use your fingers to carefully ease the pastry into place, so that it neatly lines the tin. Lift the overhanging pastry and, using your thumb, squash 2mm (1⁄16in) of pastry back into the tin. This will result in slightly thicker sides which will prevent your pastry from shrinking when baked. Allow the overhang to do its thing – we'll trim it after chilling. Lightly prick the base of the pastry case several times with a fork then place in the fridge for 15 minutes.

Remove the pastry case from the fridge and use a rolling pin to roll over the top of the tin, removing the overhang and flattening the pastry rim. Loosely line the base with a piece of scrunched up baking parchment and fill with baking beans (or uncooked rice if you don't have any). Place on the hot baking sheet in the oven and bake for 15 minutes, then remove the baking parchment and baking beans and bake for a further 5 minutes.

Remove from the oven, brush the base with beaten egg white and pop back in the oven for a couple of minutes. (The egg wash helps to seal the pastry when filled to prevent it from becoming soggy.) Allow to cool completely.

For the custard filling, grab a large mixing bowl and add the egg yolks, sugar, custard powder and vanilla, then whisk until smooth.

Pour the milk into a medium saucepan and place over a medium heat. Heat until nearly boiling, then reduce to a low heat. Pour a splash of the milk into your mixing bowl and whisk in until well combined, then pour the entire contents of the mixing bowl into the saucepan with the rest of the warm milk. Stir constantly over a low heat until a lovely, thick custard forms.

Spread the base of your pastry case with a layer of jam, then cover the jam with a layer of sliced bananas, if using – I highly recommend doing so! Pour your custard over the top of the bananas, cover with coconut and chill in the fridge for 2–3 hours until the custard is set (bearing in mind that it's quite a soft custard). Finish with a glacé cherry in the middle.

RASPBERRY RIPPLE Arctic Roll

use dairy-free ice cream

ensure your ice cream is both lactose-free and low FODMAP

use lactose-free ice cream

SERVES · 10

TAKES · 35 MINUTES + COOLING AND CHILLING

- 100g (½ cup) caster (superfine) sugar
- 4 large eggs
- 1 tsp vanilla extract
- 100g (¾ cup) gluten-free self-raising (self-rising) flour
- ¼ tsp xanthan gum
- Handful of fresh raspberries, to serve
- A few fresh mint leaves, to serve (optional)

For the filling

- 500g (1lb 2oz) raspberry ripple ice cream (or any flavour you prefer!)
- Icing (confectioners') sugar, sifted, for dusting
- 200g (7oz) raspberry jam

I think I'd sooner move to the Arctic before I found a gluten-free Arctic roll in the supermarket. Fortunately, I can easily make my own at home, so I won't need to feng shui my igloo anytime soon. This is dangerously easy to make and so incredibly satisfying to eat, so I implore you to give it a go ASAP.

Preheat your oven to 180°C fan / 200°C / 400°F. Grease a 35 x 25cm (14 x 10in) Swiss roll tin (pan) and line it with non-stick baking parchment, making sure the parchment fits well as you'll need the full shape of the tin.

Remove your ice cream from the freezer and, on a large sheet of cling film (plastic wrap), larger than your Swiss roll tin (pan), form a long sausage shape that is roughly 3.5cm (just under 1½in) in diameter. Roll it up tightly in the cling film, then place in the freezer to firm up again.

In a large mixing bowl, whisk together your sugar and eggs until light and a little frothy. It should only take a few minutes (I prefer to use an electric hand whisk for this). Add the vanilla extract and briefly whisk in.

Sift in your flour and xanthan gum, then fold this into your mixture carefully using a silicone spatula until fully combined.

Pour the mixture into your tin and spread it right to the edges. Try your best to get it nice and level so it will bake more evenly in the oven. Bake for about 9 minutes; the sponge should have come away a little bit from the sides of the tin and be slightly risen.

Lightly dust another piece of baking parchment with icing sugar. Remove the sponge from the oven and very carefully invert it onto the prepared baking parchment. Carefully peel off the parchment that was lining the tin.

Now, while the sponge is still warm and with a long side closest to you, roll it up with the parchment inside it as you roll. Leave to cool completely while rolled up. (I usually put something heavy against it to ensure it stays fairly tight and doesn't unroll itself.)

Once completely cooled, carefully unroll your sponge and remove the parchment. Spread your jam all over the inside of the unrolled sponge, then remove your ice cream from the freezer. Remove the cling film and place the ice cream along the long side of your sponge, about 2cm (¾in) in, and carefully roll the sponge up around the ice cream. Re-wrap in cling film and place back in the freezer for a couple of hours to firm up.

To serve, remove from the freezer and allow to sit for about 5 minutes, then dust with icing sugar before slicing and serving with fresh raspberries and a few mint leaves, if you like.

MALVA PUDDING

use dairy-free cream (minimum 30% fat) and milk

vegetarian

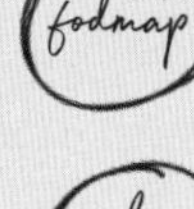

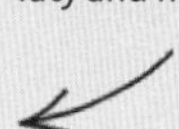

use lactose-free whipping cream (minimum 30% fat) and milk

SERVES · 8

TAKES · 1 HOUR

- 30g (2 tbsp) butter, melted
- 125ml (½ cup plus 1 tsp) milk
- 1 tsp cider vinegar
- 190g (1½ cups minus 1 tbsp) gluten-free plain (all-purpose) flour
- 1 tsp bicarbonate of soda (baking soda)
- 2 large eggs
- 200g (1 cup) caster (superfine) sugar
- 60g (2oz) apricot jam

For the sauce

- 200ml (¾ cup plus 1½ tbsp) double (heavy) cream
- 90g (⅓ cup plus 1 tbsp) butter
- 80g (⅓ cup plus 1 tbsp) caster (superfine) sugar
- 80ml (⅓ cup) water

My dad came to the UK from South Africa when he was 13 and brought his love of Malva pudding with him. Fortunately, it's easy to make gluten-free and you'd never know the difference – so yes, we can still enjoy it together! The pudding is super-light and delicate with a sweet, sticky finish that's perfect with custard. It's basically like the South African equivalent of a sticky toffee pudding, but with cream and custard instead of toffee!

Preheat your oven to 160°C fan / 180°C / 350°F. Lightly grease a 30 x 20cm (12 x 8in) rectangular baking dish or tin (pan).

Put your melted butter, milk and vinegar in a jug (pitcher), mix together and put to one side. Don't allow the butter to resolidify – if it seems like it will, simply heat in the microwave for 5–10 seconds to keep it warm.

Stir the flour and bicarb together in a small bowl.

In a large mixing bowl, add your eggs and sugar and beat together until thick and pale. Add the apricot jam and mix once more. Fold in half your flour, then fold in half your milk mixture. Repeat with the rest of your flour and milk, folding in between each addition until smooth.

Pour the mixture into the prepared baking dish or tin and bake in the oven for 35–40 minutes until dark golden brown and well risen. Check it's done by poking a skewer into the middle – if it comes out clean, then it's done.

While the pudding is baking, prepare the sauce. Add all the ingredients to a small saucepan over a low heat. Allow the butter to melt and the sugar to dissolve, but don't allow it to boil.

When the sponge comes out of the oven, use the skewer to poke lots of holes into the top of it, then pour the hot sauce all over the top and leave it to soak in.

Serve hot or at room temperature with custard or vanilla ice cream.

Banana FRITTERS

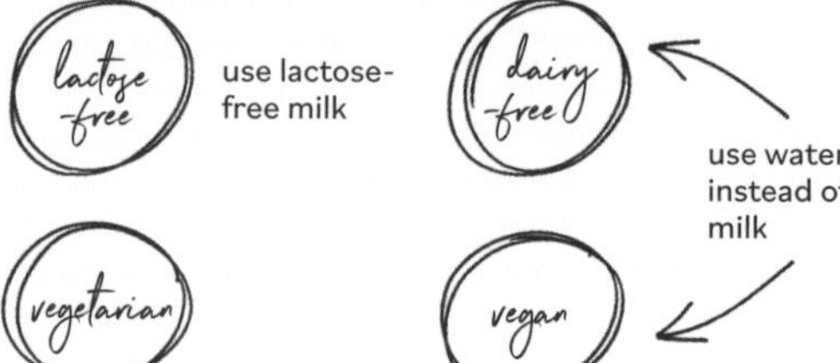

MAKES · 9 (SERVES 3)

TAKES · 30 MINUTES

- Vegetable oil, for deep-frying
- 3 ripe bananas, peeled
- 25g (3 tbsp) gluten-free plain (all-purpose) flour
- 10g (⅓oz) sesame seeds, toasted
- 125g (⅔ cup minus 2 tsp) caster (superfine) sugar

For the batter

- 100g (¾ cup) gluten-free plain (all-purpose) flour
- ½ tsp gluten-free baking powder
- 100ml (½ cup minus 1½ tbsp) milk or water

Here's a classic Chinese takeaway dessert that I missed out on for well over a decade. Think gooey banana in crispy batter, coated in a crunchy caramel, topped with toasted sesame seeds. You can always skip the caramel coating if you prefer, and simply drizzle the battered banana with maple or golden syrup. Serve with vanilla ice cream and enjoy.

Half-fill a large, heavy-based saucepan with vegetable oil and place over a medium heat for 15 minutes or until it reaches 180°C (356°F). If you don't have a digital food thermometer, check the temperature of the oil using the wooden spoon test (page 21).

In a large mixing bowl, whisk the batter ingredients together until smooth and consistent. Allow to rest for 5 minutes until lovely and thick.

Slice each banana into 3 pieces. Spread the flour out on a large dinner plate and roll your banana pieces in it, ensuring coverage on all sides. Transfer half of your banana pieces to the batter and gently toss them around until well coated.

Carefully lower a few of your coated banana pieces into the hot oil – I find that piercing them with a skewer and allowing them to slide off is the easiest way to do this without losing the batter. Cook for 2–3 minutes until golden, using a slotted spoon to move them around and check they're not stuck to the bottom of the pan after 1 minute. Once golden, transfer to a wire rack set over a baking sheet, to drain. Repeat with the rest of your banana slices.

Fill a small mixing bowl with cold water and ideally add a few ice cubes. On a small side plate, spread out your toasted sesame seeds. Add your sugar to a small saucepan and place over a medium heat. As it starts to melt, give it a stir occasionally. Once it starts to crystallize, keep stirring until there are no more lumps and it's completely caramelized. Remove from the heat; if it starts to harden too much in the saucepan as you are coating the bananas, simply heat gently to soften again.

Using a skewer, add your battered banana 3 at a time to the caramel, and turn to coat well. Ensure they don't touch or they'll stick together! One at a time, pierce with a skewer and lightly dab them on the plate of toasted sesame seeds. Then, while still skewered, transfer to the cold water bowl for 5 seconds, to harden the caramel.

Transfer back to the wire rack to drain, ensuring they don't touch any other banana pieces. Repeat with the rest of your battered bananas, then serve up with vanilla ice cream.

TIP:
To clean the saucepan you made your caramel in, simply fill with boiling water. Add in any utensils used too. Bring it to a simmer for 5–10 minutes and all the sugar will magically dissolve into the water. If you use cold water to clean your pan, the caramel will harden and be near impossible to remove!

Making it low FODMAP?
Use lactose-free milk. Ensure that your serving size contains no more than 35g (1¼oz) ripe banana per person.

Triple Chocolate NO-BAKE CHEESECAKE

use lactose-free chocolate, cream cheese, and lactose-free whipping cream (minimum 30% fat)

MAKES · 12 SLICES

TAKES · 30 MINUTES + AT LEAST 5 HOURS CHILLING

For the base

- 320g (11½oz) gluten-free digestive biscuits (graham crackers)
- 2 tbsp unsweetened cocoa powder
- 150g (⅔ cup) butter, melted

For the white chocolate filling

- 125g (4½oz) white chocolate, broken into pieces
- 300g (1⅓ cups) mascarpone
- 50g (5¾ tbsp) icing (confectioners') sugar
- 150ml (⅝ cup) double (heavy) cream

For the dark or milk chocolate filling

- 125g (4½oz) dark or milk chocolate, broken into pieces
- 300g (1⅓ cups) mascarpone
- 50g (5¾ tbsp) icing (confectioners') sugar
- 150ml (⅝ cup) double (heavy) cream

To decorate

- 50g (1¾oz) white chocolate, finely chopped
- 50g (1¾oz) milk chocolate, finely chopped
- 50g (1¾oz) dark chocolate, finely chopped

This no-bake beauty is flavoured with a trilogy of chocolate in a creamy, whipped cheesecake filling, sitting proudly on top of a buttery biscuit base. It's a proper people-pleaser!

Firstly, make your base. In a food processor, add your biscuits and cocoa powder, then blitz into a crumb-like texture – not into a fine dust! If you don't have a food processor, you can always pop the biscuits into a zip-lock bag and bash them with a rolling pin. Place in a large bowl and pour in your melted butter. Mix until well combined.

Spoon your mixture into a 20cm (8in) round, loose-bottomed or springform tin (pan). Compact the mixture into the base to create a nice, even layer. Chill in the fridge for 30 minutes and up to an hour, while you make your filling.

I use a stand mixer for this next part, but you can easily do this using an electric hand whisk too. Doing it by hand is entirely achievable, but in that case it's even more vital that you whisk long enough (as you're far more likely to undermix by hand).

To make your white chocolate filling, melt the white chocolate, either in the microwave (mixing in between short bursts) or in a heatproof bowl set over a saucepan of boiling water, ensuring the bottom of the bowl is not touching the water, and stirring until melted. Allow to cool slightly, but not to solidify.

Place the mascarpone and icing sugar in the bowl of a stand mixer. Mix on a low-medium speed for 10–20 seconds, then add the cream. At a medium speed, mix for 2 more minutes or until the mixture begins to firm up. Pour in the melted white chocolate and briefly mix until combined. Do not overmix as the mixture can split. It should end up as a nice, thick, spoonable consistency, *not* a pourable one. Transfer to a clean bowl and set aside.

Clean the bowl of the stand mixer, and repeat the process for your dark or milk chocolate filling.

To assemble the cheesecake, alternate spooning each filling on top of the chilled biscuit base, 1 heaped tablespoon at a time, occasionally swirling both mixtures to blend them just slightly. Repeat until you've used up both mixtures, then use a palette knife to smooth over the top. Place in the fridge to chill, for at least 5 hours, but ideally overnight. When ready to serve, carefully remove from the tin and transfer to a serving plate. Decorate with finely chopped chocolate in a ring, all around the edge of the cheesecake.

Store in the fridge (ideally covered or in an airtight container) or slice and freeze for up to 3 months.

Making it dairy-free? Or vegan?
Use a (hard) dairy-free butter alternative, dairy-free chocolate, dairy-free cream cheese (minimum 23% fat) and dairy-free cream (minimum 30% fat).

NO-BAKE Strawberry Cheesecake

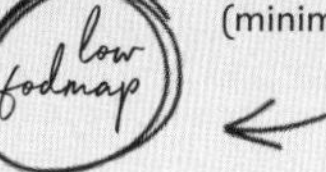

use lactose-free cream cheese and lactose-free whipping cream (minimum 30% fat)

MAKES · 12 SLICES

TAKES · 30 MINUTES + AT LEAST 5 HOURS CHILLING

For the base

- 320g (11½oz) gluten-free digestive biscuits (graham crackers)
- 150g (⅔ cup) butter, melted

For the filling

- 600g (2⅔ cups) mascarpone
- 100g (¾ cup minus ½ tbsp) icing (confectioners') sugar, sifted
- ½ tsp vanilla extract
- 300ml (1¼ cups) double (heavy) cream
- 200g (7oz) strawberries, hulled and chopped

For the sauce

- 150g (5oz) strawberries, hulled and quartered
- 60g (5 tbsp) caster (superfine) sugar
- 2 tbsp water
- 1½ tsp cornflour (cornstarch)

To decorate

- 200g (7oz) strawberries, hulled and halved

I'm not gonna lie, my inspiration for this recipe was a bog-standard, boxed, frozen cheesecake in the supermarket which has screamed 'eat me' at me for the last decade. Sadly, a gluten-free version never came to exist, so I recreated it myself.

Firstly, make your base. In a food processor, blitz the biscuits to a crumb-like texture – not into a fine dust! Alternatively, pop the biscuits into a zip-lock bag and bash them with a rolling pin. Place in a large bowl and pour in your melted butter. Mix well.

Spoon the mixture into a round 20cm (8in) loose-bottomed or springform tin (pan). Compact it into the base in an even layer, then chill in the fridge for 30 minutes and up to an hour, while you make your filling.

I use a stand mixer to make the filling, but you can easily do this using an electric hand whisk. Doing this process by hand is achievable, but in that case it's vital that you whisk long enough (as you're far more likely to undermix by hand).

Place your mascarpone, icing sugar and vanilla extract into the bowl of the stand mixer. Mix on a low to medium speed for 10–20 seconds, then add your cream. At a medium speed, mix for 2 more minutes, or until it begins to firm up. Definitely don't overmix as the mixture can split. It should end up as a nice, thick, spoonable consistency, *not* a pourable one. Gently fold in your chopped strawberries until evenly dispersed.

Spread your filling evenly on top of the chilled biscuit base and place into the fridge to chill for at least 5 hours, but ideally overnight.

For the sauce, place a medium saucepan over a low heat and add the quartered strawberries, sugar and water. Simmer for 10 minutes, or until the sugar has dissolved and the strawberries have softened, then break them down with the back of a wooden spoon. Sieve the mixture into a small bowl and pour the liquid back into the saucepan. Stir in the cornflour and continue to simmer and stir until the mixture thickens, then allow to cool briefly.

Arrange your halved strawberries for decorating on top of the cheesecake, flat-side down. Pour over the strawberry sauce, carefully remove from the tin and serve.

Store in the fridge (ideally covered or in an airtight container) or slice and freeze for up to 3 months.

Making it dairy-free? Or vegan?
Use a (hard) dairy-free butter alternative, dairy-free cream cheese (minimum 23% fat) and dairy-free cream (minimum 30% fat).

Bread

Welcome to the chapter that will remind you of what 'real' bread tastes like. And no, there won't be an enormous hole in the middle when you go to slice it, promise!

This chapter is a continuation of what I started in the bread chapter of my first book *How to Make Anything Gluten Free*. Since then, I've created English muffins, bagels, 'proper' naan bread and tons more that I never thought I'd be sharing here.

But, rather miraculously, I've also had a lot of success in creating yeasted gluten-free dough which is perfect for iced buns, cinnamon rolls and – the holy grail – gluten-free croissants. Yes, I finally did it!

Once you've hopped online and picked up some psyllium husk powder and tapioca starch (page 15), the real fun begins. These two wonder ingredients are the key to that 'real deal' bread texture that's light and tears just how muggle bread should. Trust me, you'll be glad that you ordered them!

Of course, bread isn't just all about fresh loaves, so you'll find pitta breads, proper pizza dough, cornbread and garlic bread baguettes here too.

I hope your reunion with bread is every bit as special as mine was!

Croissants

MAKES · 8 MINI CROISSANTS

TAKES · 1 HOUR + 5 HOURS CHILLING + 3 HOURS PROVING

For the yeast mixture

- 7g (¼oz) dried active yeast (ensure gluten-free)
- 10g (2½ tsp) caster (superfine) sugar
- 130ml (½ cup plus 2 tsp) warm milk

For the dough

- 150g (1 cup plus 2 tbsp) gluten-free plain (all-purpose) flour, plus extra for dusting
- 50g (⅖ cup) cornflour (cornstarch)
- 35g (4½ tbsp) skimmed milk powder
- 10g (⅓oz) psyllium husk powder (ensure gluten-free)
- 1 tsp xanthan gum
- 1 tsp salt
- 40g (3¼ tbsp) caster (superfine) sugar
- 1 large egg, beaten
- 40g (3 tbsp) butter, softened

For the butter sheet

- 210g (¾ cup plus 3 tbsp) butter, softened

To finish

- 1 medium egg, beaten

Making croissants from scratch is already regarded as being rather tricky, but fortunately, gluten-free croissants are no more difficult than making muggle croissants – it's just a little different. But even so, I'd only really recommend this one to more advanced gluten-free bakers – unless you're feeling confident, of course! After one bite of that light, golden, buttery croissant, safe in the knowledge that you can make them again whenever you want… I'm not sure gluten-free baking could possibly get any better.

Put the yeast, sugar and warm milk in a jug (pitcher), then allow to stand for 10 minutes until frothy.

In the bowl of a stand mixer, with the beater attachment in place, add all the dry ingredients for the dough, and briefly mix to combine. With the mixer running, slowly add the egg, softened butter and frothy yeast mixture. Once it forms a smooth, batter-like consistency, continue to mix for 1–2 minutes until completely combined. Remove the bowl from the stand mixer and briefly mix with a silicone spatula to ensure no dry flour is left at the bottom of the bowl. Cover the bowl with cling film (plastic wrap) and chill in the fridge for 4–6 hours.

To create the butter sheet, cut your softened butter into four slices roughly 1cm (½in) thick and arrange in the middle of a sheet of non-stick baking parchment in a square formation. Fold both sides of the baking parchment over the butter, so that the paper is now 15cm (6in) wide. Fold the top and bottom of the baking parchment over to create a perfect 15cm (6in) square parcel of butter.

Flip the parcel over and, using a rolling pin, roll the butter to fill any empty space in the parcel. You should end up with a 15cm (6in) square sheet of butter that's around 4–5mm (⅛–¼in) thick. Place into the fridge to chill for 1 hour, or into the freezer for 10–15 minutes.

When both the dough and butter have chilled, place the dough on a generously floured, large sheet of non-stick baking parchment. Briefly roll the dough in the flour so that it's no longer sticky, then flour the parchment once again. From this point onwards, keep re-dusting the surface/rolling pin as necessary to prevent the dough from sticking. Roll the dough out to a rectangle 15 x 33cm (6 x 13in), 5mm (¼in) thick, then use the baking parchment to lift it onto a large baking sheet. Place in the freezer for 5–10 minutes.

Remove the butter sheet from the fridge or freezer. Ensure that it's cold, but still flexible enough to bend without breaking. If it feels like it might snap instead of bending, allow it to sit out at room temperature until it can flex – remember, it must be cold!

Continued overleaf…

Place the chilled dough on your work surface. With a longer side closest to you, place your butter sheet on the left side of the dough sheet, so that it's perfectly aligned with the left edge of the dough. Fold the right side of the dough over the butter and close it like a book. Trim the edges of the dough if they overhang the butter sheet.

Flip the dough over (re-dusting generously with flour) and press down gently on the folded dough multiple times, from top to bottom, to create several indentations with your rolling pin. This should gradually elongate your dough with each rolling pin press. Now roll out the dough to form a rectangle 5mm (¼in) thick again.

With a longer side of the rectangle closest to you, fold the left and right sides of the dough over so that they both meet in the middle. Then fold in half like you're closing a book. With a shorter side closest to you, repeat the process of using your rolling pin to press down gently on the folded dough multiple times to create several indentations from top to bottom, while gradually elongating the dough. Roll out the dough to a 5mm (¼in) thick rectangle once again, then fold it into thirds like a letter in an envelope.

With a longer side of the dough closest to you, roll the dough out to a rectangle just larger than 23 x 30cm (9 x 12in), then trim the very edges to create neat, straight edges on all sides.

With a longer side of the rectangle closest to you, use a pizza cutter to create 4 strips, each 7.5cm (3in) wide. Then cut them in half diagonally to create eight triangles.

Loosely roll up the triangles, rolling from the wide end of the triangle towards the tip, ensuring you're left with a 1cm (½in) hole in the middle. Repeat with the remaining triangles and transfer to a lined baking sheet, with the tip of the triangle underneath each croissant. Loosely cover with cling film and prove in a warm place for 3–4 hours until noticeably puffy, slightly increased in size and soft to the touch. Ensure your proving place isn't too warm, or the butter can melt and leak out!

Once proved, gently brush with beaten egg and preheat your oven to 200°C fan / 220°C / 425°F.

Remove the cling film and place the croissants in the hot oven. Bake for 10 minutes, or until nicely browned, then cover loosely with foil (shiny-side up) and bake for a further 6–7 minutes until golden brown, crisp and puffy.

Transfer to a wire rack to cool slightly. These are best enjoyed on the day that they're baked, but can be refreshed in the microwave.

TIP:
When making croissants, try to use butter that has a fat content of at least 82% to ensure your croissants come out of the oven looking perfect. This is particularly important for readers in the USA, where the fat content of butter can often be lower than this.

. BAKERY-STYLE .
Iced Buns

use lactose-free milk and coconut milk powder

use dairy-free milk, a (hard) dairy-free alternative to butter and coconut milk powder

MAKES · 8

TAKES · 45 MINUTES
+ 4 HOURS CHILLING
+ 2½ HOURS PROVING

For the dough

- 175ml (¾ cup) warm milk
- 7g (¼oz) dried active yeast (ensure gluten-free)
- 85g (7 tbsp) caster (superfine) sugar, plus 10g (⅓oz)
- 180g (1⅓ cups) gluten-free plain (all-purpose) flour
- 40g (¼ cup) tapioca starch (ensure gluten-free), plus extra for dusting
- 25g (1oz) skimmed milk powder
- 1 tsp xanthan gum
- 1 tsp gluten-free baking powder
- 10g (⅓oz) psyllium husk powder (ensure gluten-free)
- 1 tsp cider vinegar
- 1 large egg, lightly beaten
- 80g (generous ⅓ cup) butter, melted and cooled

For icing and decorating

- 200g (scant 1½ cups) icing (confectioners') sugar, sifted
- 1 tsp vanilla extract
- 2–4 tbsp water
- Pink food colouring paste (optional)
- Gluten-free sprinkles (optional)

I can honestly say that I never valued the humble iced bun until I could no longer eat one. It's such a simple concept – a light, tearable sweet bread topped with a drizzle of icing. But when you're gluten-free, this cheap and cheerful treat suddenly becomes one of the most coveted bakes that we all miss! A little patience is required while you allow the dough to chill and prove, but trust me – good buns come to those who wait!

In a jug (pitcher), stir together your warm milk, yeast and 10g (⅓oz) of sugar. Allow to stand for 10 minutes until frothy.

In a large bowl or the bowl of a stand mixer, mix together your flour, tapioca starch, milk powder, xanthan gum, baking powder, psyllium husk powder and remaining sugar until well combined. Add the vinegar, egg, melted butter and yeast mixture.

Either in a stand mixer fitted with a beater attachment or using an electric hand whisk, mix on a high speed for 3–5 minutes until well combined. It should look thick and sticky. Place in a clean bowl, cover and transfer to the fridge for at least 4 hours (or overnight) to completely chill (or chill in the freezer for 2–3 hours instead). After chilling, I check the dough's internal temperature using a digital food thermometer – it usually gets down to about 8°C–13°C/45°F–55°F. This will ensure the dough is workable and no longer sticky.

Line two 900g (2lb) loaf tins with non-stick baking parchment.

Place your chilled dough on a surface really well dusted with tapioca starch. Gently knead until smooth, then split the dough into 8 even pieces. Roll each piece into a sausage shape and then place them in the two loaf tins. You should have four buns in each tin, placed close together but not quite touching.

Cover loosely with cling film (plastic wrap) and leave to prove in a warm place for 1–2 hours until doubled in size and puffy.

Preheat your oven to 160°C fan / 180°C / 350°F.

Bake in the oven for 25 minutes until golden and cooked through. Halfway through baking, cover with foil (shiny -side up) if they're getting too dark. Remove from the oven and allow to cool completely on a wire rack.

For the icing, grab a mixing bowl and add your icing sugar and vanilla extract. Mix, then add 2–4 tbsp water until it reaches a smooth but thick, spreadable consistency. You can optionally add a small amount of pink food colouring paste until you achieve a pastel pink colour.

Once the buns have fully cooled, drizzle the icing all over the top of them and add some colourful sprinkles, if you fancy.

TIP:
You can also cut these in half and spread a little jam in the middle too for the ultimate finish!

'REAL DEAL' Cinnamon Rolls

use lactose-free milk, lactose-free cream cheese and coconut milk powder

use dairy-free cream cheese (minimum 30% fat), dairy-free milk, a (hard) dairy-free alternative to butter and coconut milk powder

MAKES · 8 LARGE OR 16 SMALL ROLLS

TAKES · 1¼ HOURS + 4 HOURS CHILLING + 2½ HOURS PROVING

For the dough

- 350ml (1½ cups minus 2 tsp) warm milk
- 10g (⅓oz) dried active yeast (ensure gluten-free)
- 170g (¾ cup) caster (superfine) sugar, plus 15g (½oz)
- 360g (2¾ cups) gluten-free plain (all-purpose) flour
- 80g (½ cup) tapioca starch (ensure gluten-free), plus extra for dusting
- 50g (1¾oz) skimmed milk powder
- 2 tsp xanthan gum
- 2 tsp gluten-free baking powder
- 15g (½oz) psyllium husk powder (ensure gluten-free)
- 1 tsp cider vinegar
- 2 large eggs
- 165g (scant ¾ cup) butter, melted and cooled, plus extra for greasing

For the filling

- 70g (⅓ cup) butter, very softened
- 90g (½ cup minus 2 tsp) light brown sugar
- 1 tbsp ground cinnamon

For a cream cheese frosting

- 30g (2 tbsp) butter, softened
- 115g (½ cup) full-fat cream cheese
- 1 tsp vanilla extract
- 200g (1½ cups) icing (confectioners') sugar, sifted
- 1 tbsp milk

For a simple glaze

- 200g (1½ cups) icing (confectioners') sugar, sifted
- 1 tsp vanilla extract
- 2–4 tbsp milk or water

Believe it or not, my cinnamon rolls are soft, oozing with a sticky cinnamon swirl and slathered with frosting (or a simple, quick glaze if you'd prefer). This is definitely not one to be rushed, but after a decade without even being able to eat one of these, a little chilling and proving time is nothing!

In a jug (pitcher), stir together your warm milk, yeast and 15g (½oz) of sugar. Allow to stand for 10 minutes until frothy.

In a large bowl or the bowl of a stand mixer, mix together your flour, tapioca starch, milk powder, xanthan gum, baking powder, psyllium husk powder and remaining sugar until well combined. Add the vinegar, egg, melted butter and yeast mixture.

In a stand mixer fitted with a beater attachment, or using an electric hand whisk, mix on a high speed for 3–5 minutes until well combined. It should look thick and sticky. Place in a clean bowl, cover and place in the fridge for at least 4 hours (or overnight) to completely chill (or chill in the freezer for 2–3 hours). After chilling, I check the dough's internal temperature using a digital food thermometer – it usually gets down to about 8°C–13°C / 45°F–55°F. This will ensure the dough is workable and no longer sticky.

Lightly grease a baking tin (pan), about 28 x 18cm (11 x 7in), or two 20cm (8in) round cake tins.

Place your chilled dough on a surface well dusted with tapioca starch. Knead until smooth then roll out to a rectangle 40 x 25cm (16 x 10in) and 5mm (¼in) thick. Spread the softened butter all over your dough. Mix together the brown sugar and cinnamon, then sprinkle this over the butter. With a long side closest to you, cut the dough into 8 strips (for large rolls), or 16 (for small rolls). Roll each into a tight swirl and place in the tin(s), with a little room between each. If they won't all fit, pop any extra in another tin. Cover and leave to prove in a warm spot (not *too* warm or the butter will melt) for 1–2 hours until doubled in size.

Preheat your oven to 160°C fan / 180°C / 350°F. Bake for 35 minutes until golden. Halfway through baking, cover with foil (shiny-side up) if they're getting too dark. While baking, prepare the frosting or glaze.

For cream cheese frosting, beat together the butter, cream cheese and vanilla extract until smooth. Add the icing sugar and mix well. Add enough milk to achieve a spreadable consistency.

To make a simple glaze, mix the icing sugar and vanilla together, then add enough milk or water so that it is smooth but thick and spreadable.

While the rolls are warm, spoon and spread the frosting on or drizzle over the glaze. Enjoy fresh and warm on the day that they're baked or refresh in the microwave.

Bagels

use a dairy-free butter alternative

use a dairy-free butter alternative, and brush with 2 tbsp dairy-free milk mixed with 1 tsp maple syrup instead of egg white

MAKES · 4–5

TAKES · 1 HOUR + 1½ HOURS PROVING

- 265ml (1 cup plus 2 tbsp) warm water
- 10g (2½ tsp) caster (superfine) sugar
- 7g (¼oz) dried active yeast (ensure gluten-free)
- 250g (2 cups) gluten-free plain (all-purpose) flour, plus extra for dusting
- 35g (4½ tbsp) tapioca starch (ensure gluten-free)
- ½ tsp xanthan gum
- 15g (½oz) psyllium husk powder (ensure gluten-free)
- 1 tsp gluten-free baking powder
- 1 tsp salt
- 55g (4 tbsp) butter, melted and cooled
- 1 tsp apple cider vinegar
- A little oil, for greasing
- 1 tbsp bicarbonate of soda (baking soda)
- 35ml (2 tbsp plus 1 tsp) maple syrup
- 1 medium egg white
- Poppy or sesame seeds, for sprinkling on the tops

You absolutely cannot beat a bagel topped with crunchy seeds, and a soft yet chewy texture that's ready to be crammed full of your favourite fillings. And fortunately, with this recipe, being gluten-free doesn't change that fact!

Put your warm water, sugar and yeast in a jug (pitcher), then stir. Allow to stand for 10 minutes until it becomes nice and frothy.

In a large mixing bowl, mix your flour, tapioca starch, xanthan gum, psyllium husk powder, baking powder and salt until combined. Add the melted butter, vinegar and frothy yeast mixture and mix in until fully combined. It should create a fairly thick, sticky dough.

Transfer your dough to a lightly oiled bowl and cover with cling film (plastic wrap). Leave to prove in a warm place for about 1 hour until noticeably increased in size.

Line a baking sheet with non-stick baking parchment and lightly dust it with flour. Remove your dough from the bowl and place it on the sheet. Split the dough into 4–5 even portions and roll each piece into a ball. Use your thumb to make a 2.5cm (1in) hole in the middle. Space apart evenly, cover with cling film and leave to prove for 30 minutes.

Fill a large saucepan with water and place over a medium heat. Add the bicarb and maple syrup, then bring to the boil. At the same time, preheat your oven to 200°C fan / 220°C / 425°F and line another baking sheet with non-stick baking parchment.

Add one bagel at a time to the boiling water and cook for 30 seconds, then flip and cook for another 30 seconds on the other side. Remove and drain any excess water before transferring to the prepared baking sheet. Repeat with all of your bagels.

Brush egg white over the top of each bagel, then sprinkle with your choice of seeds. Bake in the oven for about 25 minutes until golden and the bottom of each bagel sounds hollow when lightly tapped.

Transfer to a wire rack and allow to cool completely. Enjoy sliced in half and toasted, or simply sliced with all of your favourite fillings.

Once cooled, store in an airtight container, or freeze for 2–3 months. If not eaten on the same day as baking, these can be refreshed in the microwave or oven.

English MUFFINS

use dairy-free milk and a (hard) dairy-free butter alternative

use lactose-free milk

MAKES · 7–8

TAKES · 45 MINUTES + 1 HOUR PROVING

- 300ml (1¼ cups) warm milk
- 10g (⅓oz) dried active yeast (ensure gluten-free)
- 10g (2½ tsp) caster (superfine) sugar
- 300g (2¼ cups) gluten-free plain (all-purpose) flour
- ½ tsp bicarbonate of soda (baking soda)
- 1 tsp xanthan gum
- 1 tsp salt
- 1 large egg
- 25g (scant 2 tbsp) butter, melted
- 2 tbsp lemon juice
- Fine polenta (ensure gluten-free), for sprinkling
- Vegetable oil, ideally in a spray bottle

Is it bad that my most treasured memory of enjoying English muffins is in McDonald's for breakfast? I can almost still taste those soft, fluffy muffins, with crispy bacon, egg, melted cheese and a hash brown on the side. But instead of 'almost tasting' one in my head, these days I much prefer to just create my fave fast-food breakfast at home!

Put your warm milk, sugar and yeast in a jug (pitcher), then stir. Allow to stand for 10 minutes until it becomes nice and frothy.

In a large mixing bowl, mix together your flour, bicarb, xanthan gum and salt until combined. Add the egg, melted butter, lemon juice and frothy yeast mixture, then mix until smooth. Cover the bowl and prove in a warm place for 1 hour until almost doubled in size.

Place a large frying pan over a low heat. Place two 9cm (3½in) crumpet (muffin) rings in the pan and brush or spray oil in the middle and up the sides of each ring. Sprinkle a little polenta to lightly dust the surface inside of each ring, then place 2 tablespoons of the dough mixture in each ring so they are half full. Gently smooth over the tops using the back of a wet spoon to create an even layer, and sprinkle more polenta on top. Cook for 5 minutes, then use a pair of tongs to remove the rings and flip the muffins over. Cook for a further 5 minutes on the other side, then remove from the pan. Repeat until you've used up all of your mixture.

Allow to cool for 15–20 minutes before slicing, toasting and enjoying with your favourite fillings.

TIP:
If your pan is too hot, the outside of each muffin may potentially brown too much before the middle is done. Keeping the heat low is key!

'REAL DEAL'
Garlic & Coriander
NAAN BREAD

use dairy-free milk

use lactose-free milk

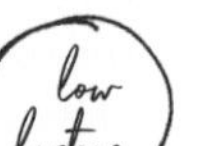

MAKES · 5–6 MINI NAAN BREADS

TAKES · 30 MINUTES + 30 MINUTES RESTING

- 70ml (¼ cup plus 2 tsp) milk
- 60ml (¼ cup) water
- 2 large eggs
- 245g (scant 2 cups) gluten-free self-raising (self-rising) flour, plus extra for dusting
- 50g (⅓ cup) tapioca starch (ensure gluten-free)
- 1 tsp salt

To serve

- Garlic-infused oil
- Handful of fresh coriander (cilantro), chopped

Here's a new and improved version of the gluten-free naan bread recipe you'll find on my blog. These beautiful naans are more 'bready', with lots more bubbles that give it a jaw-droppingly light texture and are utterly indistinguishable from muggle naan breads. Promise!

Put your milk, water and eggs in a jug (pitcher), then beat with a fork until well combined.

Put your flour, tapioca starch and salt in a large mixing bowl. Stir in until evenly dispersed.

Mixing with a silicone spatula, pour in your wet mixture and continue to mix until you have a smooth, wet and sticky mixture. Cover and allow to rest for up to 30 minutes. This gives the mixture much needed time to fully hydrate and thicken.

Place a frying pan over a high heat. The pan may get hotter the more naans you cook, so bear in mind that you may need to reduce the heat slightly for your final few.

Place a large sheet of non-stick baking parchment on a flat surface and generously dust with flour. Take 2 heaped tablespoons of the mixture and dollop into a ball onto the floured baking parchment.

Generously flour your hands and gently move the ball around on the baking parchment until it's lightly covered with flour and no longer sticky. Take the ball in the palm of floured hands and press into a flat, naan bread shape that's around 3mm (1/10in) thick (if they're too thick, they can be a little 'doughy' in texture in the middle, but you can always finish them off in the oven if this is the case). If the dough constantly sticks to your hands, that means you need a little more flour on them.

Lightly dust off any excessively floury parts on your naan and immediately slap the flattened dough straight down into the hot, dry frying pan (do not place it down onto your work surface first, otherwise when you try to pick it up again it'll definitely break!). After around 30 seconds, it should start to bubble up nicely; cook for 30 seconds more. Once the base has browned in places, flip over using a spatula and cook for a further 30 seconds. Repeat until you've used up all of your dough mixture.

Brush all of your naans with garlic-infused oil and sprinkle with chopped coriander.

TIP:
If things get too sticky and messy when flattening your dough into naan shapes, that means you need more flour on your surface and on your hands. But don't overdo it! Excess flour can burn over time in the pan so make sure you dust off the excess before frying.

PITTA Bread

use a dairy-free butter alternative and a thick dairy-free yoghurt

use lactose-free Greek yoghurt

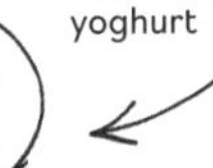

MAKES · 6–8

TAKES · 25 MINUTES + 1½ HOURS PROVING

- 75ml (5 tbsp) warm water
- 10g (2½ tsp) caster (superfine) sugar
- 5g (⅙oz) dried active yeast (ensure gluten-free)
- 225g (1¾ cups) gluten-free plain (all-purpose) flour
- ¼ tsp xanthan gum
- ½ tsp gluten-free baking powder
- ½ tsp salt
- 150g (⅔ cup) Greek yoghurt
- 20g (1½ tbsp) butter, melted
- A little oil, for greasing

With a pocket ready for filling with whatever your heart desires, these pittas are flexible, soft and surprisingly easy to make. Gluten-free lunch options can be hard to come by when you're out and about, so save yourself the hunting and enjoy a proper pitta instead.

Put your warm water, sugar and yeast in a jug (pitcher), then stir. Allow to stand for 10 minutes until it becomes nice and frothy. Line two large baking sheets with non-stick baking parchment.

In a large mixing bowl, put your flour, xanthan gum, baking powder, salt, yoghurt, melted butter and frothy yeast mixture. Mix to combine fully until a sticky mixture forms, then transfer to a lightly oiled bowl and cover with cling film (plastic wrap). Allow to prove in a warm place for 1 hour, until slightly bigger and a little spongy.

Lightly flour your hands, rolling pin and a large sheet of non-stick baking parchment, then take a portion of the dough (roughly one-sixth to one-eighth). Use the rolling pin to push the dough out to an oval pitta shape around 15cm (6in) long, 10cm (4in) wide, and 5mm (¼in) thick. Place on a baking sheet and repeat with the rest of the dough.

Cover the pittas loosely with cling film and allow to prove in a warm place for around 30 minutes; you might start to see some bubbles on the surface.

Preheat your oven to 220°C fan / 240°C / 465°F. Line another large baking sheet with non-stick baking parchment and carefully transfer two of your pittas onto it. Bake in the oven for 4–5 minutes until completely puffed up.

Remove from the oven and transfer to a wire rack, then cover with a tea (dish) towel while you repeat with the rest of the pittas.

Cheese & Jalapeño

CORNBREAD

use dairy-free milk and cheese, and a (hard) dairy-free alternative to butter

use lactose-free milk

vegetarian

MAKES · 9 SLICES

TAKES · 35 MINUTES + 30 MINUTES RESTING

- 170ml (¾ cup minus 2 tsp) milk
- 1 tbsp lemon juice
- 150g (1 cup plus 2 tbsp) gluten-free plain (all-purpose) flour
- 150g (1 cup) fine polenta (ensure gluten-free)
- 50g (¼ cup) light brown sugar
- 1 tsp bicarbonate of soda (baking soda)
- ½ tsp xanthan gum
- 1 tsp salt
- 100g (½ cup minus 1 tbsp) butter, melted
- 2 large eggs
- 25g (1oz) jalapeños, chopped
- 125g (4½oz) extra-mature Cheddar cheese, grated

Cornbread wasn't something I grew up with, yet now I can't live without it. It only requires 15 minutes of effort, plus resting and cooking time, but best of all, it's utterly indistinguishable from its gluten-containing counterpart. With a fluffy texture, and a subtle sweet and spicy, cheesy flavour, I now enjoy this regularly with soup or just for a light lunch with butter.

Grease a 23cm (9in) square baking tin (pan) with butter or oil.

In a jug (pitcher), combine the milk and lemon juice and allow to rest for 10 minutes. It should become a little lumpy – that's when you know it's ready to use!

Put the flour, polenta, sugar, bicarb, xanthan gum and salt in a large mixing bowl. Stir together until well combined.

In a separate mixing bowl, put the melted and slightly cooled butter, then crack in the eggs and pour in your milk mixture. Beat together until well combined.

Add your wet ingredients to your dry mixture and mix until it reaches a smooth, thick consistency. Once it reaches this point – stop! Make sure you don't overmix this one.

Add your chopped jalapeños and two-thirds of your grated cheese, then fold in using a silicone spatula until evenly dispersed. Transfer the batter into the baking tin and use your spatula to ensure it's nice and level. Sprinkle over the remaining grated cheese, cover loosely with a tea (dish) towel and allow to rest for 30 minutes. Preheat your oven to 200°C fan / 220°C / 425°F.

Bake the cornbread in the hot oven for 20 minutes until lovely and golden on top. Remove from the tin and transfer to a wire rack to cool for 10–20 minutes.

Once slightly cooled, simply slice and enjoy warm with butter or alongside your favourite soup. Once fully cooled, store in an airtight container and microwave to refresh.

· MINI ·
SUN-DRIED TOMATO & ROSEMARY
Focaccias

use 20g (¾oz) sun-dried tomatoes and ensure they don't contain garlic – 1 mini focaccia is a safe low FODMAP serving size

use 4 tbsp aquafaba (whisked until frothy) in place of the egg

lactose free

MAKES · 4 MINI FOCACCIAS

TAKES · 1 HOUR + 1 HOUR PROVING

- Garlic-infused oil, for greasing and topping
- 280ml (1 cup plus 2½ tbsp) warm water
- 7g (¼oz) dried active yeast (ensure gluten-free)
- 15g (4 tsp) caster (superfine) sugar
- 260g (2 cups) gluten-free plain (all-purpose) flour, plus extra for dusting
- 2 tsp xanthan gum
- 15g (½oz) psyllium husk powder (ensure gluten-free)
- 6g (¼oz) salt
- 1 large egg
- 1 tsp cider vinegar
- 50ml (3½ tbsp) olive oil
- 70g (2½oz) sun-dried tomatoes, roughly chopped

For the top

- Fresh rosemary sprigs
- Flaky sea salt

In supermarkets, gluten-free bread only seems to come in white, brown or a variation of the two, but that only makes something like this ten times more enjoyable. With sun-dried tomatoes, garlic-infused oil and fresh rosemary infusing this light and fluffy focaccia, one is never enough.

Grease a baking sheet with garlic-infused oil, then drizzle more over the base and set aside.

Put your warm water, yeast and sugar in a jug (pitcher), then stir. Allow to stand for 10 minutes until it becomes nice and frothy.

In a large bowl, or the bowl of a stand mixer, mix together your flour, xanthan gum, psyllium husk powder and salt until well combined. Add your egg, vinegar, olive oil, sun-dried tomatoes and frothy yeast mixture.

Either in a stand mixer with a beater attachment or with an electric hand whisk, mix on a high speed for 2–3 minutes until well combined. It should look like a very thick, sticky batter. Leave to rest for 10 minutes.

Weigh out 170g (6oz) of your rested mixture per focaccia. (I place cling film/plastic wrap on the scales so they don't get sticky while I'm weighing the mixture out.)

Flour your hands and a large sheet of non-stick baking parchment. Transfer your sticky dough portion to the floured parchment and roll it lightly in the flour so that it's no longer sticky. Mould it with your hands into a flat, oval shape then place on the prepared baking sheet. Repeat with the rest of your dough.

Cover loosely with cling film and allow to prove in a warm place for 1 hour until noticeably risen and puffy.

Preheat your oven to 210°C fan / 230°C / 450°F.

Make several deep dimples in each risen dough portion, using oiled fingers, then generously drizzle garlic-infused oil all over the top and fill the dimples. Push sprigs of rosemary into the dimples and sprinkle with flaky salt before baking in the oven for 15 minutes until golden.

Remove from the oven and lightly tap the base of each focaccia to check that it feels and sounds hollow – if so, then they're done. Drizzle some extra oil on top and transfer to a wire rack to cool completely.

Once cooled, store in an airtight container, or freeze for 2–3 months. If not eaten on the same day as baking, these can be refreshed in the microwave or oven.

Super Seeded SANDWICH LOAF

MAKES · 15 SLICES

TAKES · 1½ HOURS + 1 HOUR PROVING

- 445ml (2 cups minus 2½ tbsp) warm water
- 10g (⅓oz) dried active yeast (ensure gluten-free)
- 25g (2 tbsp) caster (superfine) sugar
- 150g (1¼ cups) buckwheat flour (ensure gluten-free)
- 150g (1 cup plus 2 tbsp) gluten-free plain (all-purpose) flour
- 70g (½ cup minus 1½ tbsp) tapioca starch (ensure gluten-free)
- 2 tsp xanthan gum
- 25g (1oz) psyllium husk powder (ensure gluten-free)
- 6g (1 tsp) salt
- 80g (3oz) egg white (about 2 large eggs)
- 2 tsp cider vinegar
- 1 medium egg, beaten (optional; or use water)
- 160g (6oz) seeds (mixture of sesame, pumpkin, poppy)

I'm probably the proudest of this loaf, purely because of how close it comes to the real deal. The buckwheat flour and mixed seeds add an instant injection of flavour and the tapioca starch helps it to tear like real bread as you rip and pull it apart – something that's hard to find in gluten-free bread. It's super crusty too and would most definitely be on sale in my imaginary gluten-free bakery, every day!

In a jug (pitcher), stir together your warm water, yeast and sugar. Allow to stand for 10 minutes until frothy. Grease and line a Pullman loaf tin (pan) – mine is 21.5 x 12.3 x 11.4cm (8½ x 5 x 4½in). Or grease and line a large loaf tin – mine is 26 x 12 x 8cm (10 x 5 x 3in). If you've greased your tin thoroughly, lining it with non-stick baking parchment isn't necessary.

In a large bowl or the bowl of a stand mixer, add both flours, the tapioca starch, xanthan gum, psyllium husk powder and salt. Mix together until well combined, then add the egg whites, vinegar and yeast mixture.

Either in a stand mixer fitted with a beater attachment or using an electric hand whisk, mix on a high speed for 3–5 minutes until well combined. It should look like a very thick, sticky batter. Mix in 125g (4½oz) of your seeds so they're well incorporated. Allow to rest for about 10 minutes – this bread batter is very wet, and resting it is important.

Transfer your rested mixture into the lined tin, ensuring that it's nicely smoothed out and level. Cover loosely with cling film (plastic wrap) and leave to prove in a warm place for 1 hour, until noticeably risen.

Preheat your oven to 230°C fan / 250°C / 480°F. Place a large roasting dish at the bottom of the oven, and boil a kettle. Brush the top of the loaf with the beaten egg or a little water and sprinkle the rest of your seeds on top. Place in the hot oven and immediately add a mug of boiling water to the roasting dish. Bake for 20 minutes, then reduce the oven temperature to 200°C fan / 220°C / 425°F and bake for a further 45 minutes. If the seeds are getting too brown, cover the bread loosely with foil (shiny-side up).

Remove from the oven. Carefully remove from the tin and tap the base to check that it feels and sounds hollow – if so, then it's done (see the tip on page 155 for more advice on how to check if your loaf is done). Place onto a wire rack and allow to cool completely before slicing.

This loaf is best enjoyed fresh, on the day it was baked, but it will last 2–3 days stored in an airtight container. It's also perfect for slicing and freezing.

TIPS:
If you want an even crustier crust, once the loaf is cooked, remove it from the tin and allow it to cool in the warm oven with the door open.

Pictured on page 157.

TIGER *Bread*

MAKES · 12 SLICES

TAKES · 1 HOUR 10 MINUTES + 30 MINUTES PROVING

- 425ml (1¾ cups) warm water
- 9g (⅓oz) dried active yeast (ensure gluten-free)
- 25g (2 tbsp) caster (superfine) sugar
- 180g (1½ cups) gluten-free white rice flour
- 190g (1½ cups minus 1 tbsp) gluten-free plain (all-purpose) flour, plus extra for dusting
- 2 tsp xanthan gum
- 25g (1oz) psyllium husk powder (ensure gluten-free)
- 6g (¼oz) salt
- 2 tsp cider vinegar
- 80g (3oz) egg white (about 2 large eggs)

For the topping

- ½ tsp easy bake yeast (ensure gluten-free)
- 1 tsp golden caster (superfine) sugar
- 1½ tsp sesame oil
- ¼ tsp salt
- 75g (⅔ cup) gluten-free white rice flour
- 90ml (6 tbsp) warm water

Nothing is more satisfying than the smell or taste of freshly baked tiger bread, especially when it's gluten-free. This loaf has that distinctive crusty, cracked top, with a light and airy crumb.

In a jug (pitcher), stir together your warm water, yeast and sugar. Allow to stand for 10 minutes until frothy.

In a large bowl or the bowl of a stand mixer, add both flours, the xanthan gum, psyllium husk powder and salt. Mix together until well combined, then add your vinegar, egg white and frothy yeast mixture.

Either in a stand mixer fitted with a beater attachment or using an electric hand whisk, mix on a high speed for 3–5 minutes until well combined. It should look like a very thick, sticky batter. Allow to rest for 10 minutes – this bread batter is very wet, and resting it is important.

Grab a proving basket and add 1 tablespoon of flour to it. Rotate the basket so that the flour lightly coats all of the base and sides. (If you don't have a proving basket, grease the insides of a 20cm (8in) mixing bowl with oil and proceed with the steps outlined for a proving basket.)

Transfer the mixture into the prepared basket, ensuring that it's smoothed out and level. Loosely cover with cling film (plastic wrap) and allow to prove in a warm place for 30–45 minutes until noticeably risen. Proving can take longer on a cold day, so keep an eye on it!

While your dough is proving, prepare your topping. Place all ingredients in a small bowl and mix together until well combined. Put to one side for later, ensuring it's prepared at least 10 minutes ahead of baking time.

Preheat your oven to 240°C fan / 260°C / 500°F, or as hot as it will go. Place a roasting dish in the bottom of the oven, and boil the kettle.

Once your dough has risen, carefully invert the basket onto a sheet of non-stick baking parchment in one quick motion. Use the parchment to gently transfer the dough into a 28cm (11in) skillet or ovenproof frying pan.

Carefully spread the tiger paste all over the top of your dough, then smooth over with the back of a spoon – ensure you go down the sides too.

Transfer to the hot oven and immediately add a mug of boiling water to the roasting dish. Bake for 15 minutes, then cover with foil (shiny-side up) and bake for a further 15 minutes. Reduce the oven temperature to 200°C fan / 220°C / 425°F and bake for another 20 minutes, until golden.

Remove from the oven. Carefully remove from the skillet and tap the base to check that it feels and sounds hollow (see tip) – if so, then it's done. Place on a wire rack and allow to cool completely before slicing.

TIP:
Apart from tapping the base of the loaf to check if it's done, you can also check the internal temperature of the loaf with a digital food thermometer – it should be around 95–100°C/205–210°F. Also, if you weigh your bread mixture in the tin before baking, the weight should decrease by around 15% once baked.

Pictured on page 156.

STAINLESS STEEL
Prestige
MADE IN ENGLAND

HOT DOG Rolls

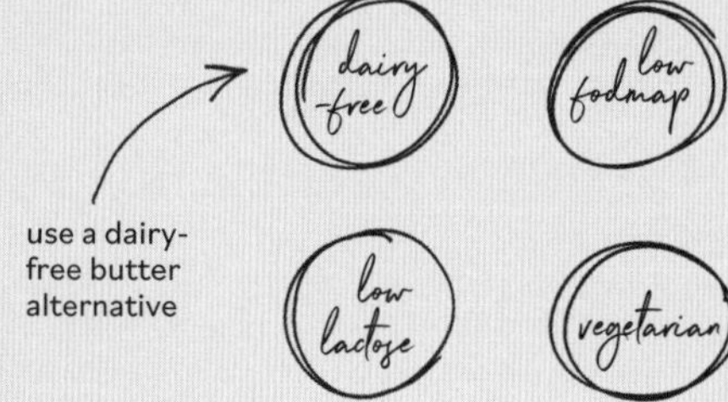

MAKES · 10–11

TAKES · 50 MINUTES + 1¾ HOURS PROVING

- 360ml (1½ cups) warm water
- 10g (⅓oz) dried active yeast (ensure gluten-free)
- 25g (2 tbsp) caster (superfine) sugar
- 335g (2½ cups) gluten-free plain (all-purpose) flour or gluten-free bread flour
- 80g (½ cup) tapioca starch (ensure gluten-free), plus extra for dusting
- 2 tsp xanthan gum
- 15g (½oz) psyllium husk powder (ensure gluten-free)
- 6g (¼oz) salt
- 1 tsp cider vinegar
- 3 large egg whites
- 30g (2 tbsp) butter, melted, plus an extra 2 tbsp, for brushing the tops
- A little oil, for greasing

Q: Is a hot dog really a hot dog without the bun? A: No, it's just a sausage. Yet so often, at BBQs, or when eating out, I crave a hot dog and end up with just a sausage. Well, that all ends now.

Check out the variation at the end of the method if you fancy using this recipe to make crusty sub rolls too – you'll just need a little polenta in addition.

Line a large baking sheet with non-stick baking parchment.

In a jug (pitcher), stir together your warm water, yeast and sugar. Allow to stand for 10 minutes until frothy.

In a large bowl or the bowl of a stand mixer, put the flour, tapioca starch, xanthan gum, psyllium husk powder and salt. Mix until well combined, then add the vinegar, egg whites, melted butter and yeast mixture.

In a stand mixer fitted with a beater attachment or using an electric hand whisk, mix on a high speed for 3–5 minutes. It should look like a very thick, sticky batter. Transfer the batter to a lightly oiled bowl, cover with a damp tea (dish) towel or cling film (plastic wrap) and leave to prove in a warm place for 1 hour, until noticeably increased in size.

Dust the work surface and your hands lightly with tapioca starch, then divide the proved dough into 10 or 11 portions, 75–80g (2½–3oz) each – I pull off portions straight from the bowl one at a time and place cling film on the scales to avoid them sticking.

Transfer one portion to the floured surface and roll it lightly in the starch so that it's no longer sticky. Mould it with your hands into a sausage shape around 10–12.5cm (4–5in) long, then place on the lined baking sheet. Repeat with the rest of the dough portions, spacing them 1.5cm (⅔in) apart. Loosely cover with cling film and prove in a warm place for 45–60 minutes until increased in size.

Preheat your oven to 190°C fan / 210°C / 410°F.

Remove the cling film and brush the rolls with a little melted butter. Bake for 20–22 minutes until golden brown, then remove from the oven and allow to cool briefly on the sheet before transferring to a wire rack to cool completely.

If not eaten on the same day as baking, these can be refreshed in the microwave or oven. Once cooled, store in an airtight container or freeze for 2–3 months.

VARIATION:
CRUSTY SUB ROLLS
MAKES · 8

Grease a 4-wave baguette tray with a little butter. If you don't have one, you can bake these on a baking sheet lined with baking parchment.

Follow the recipe as directed, but divide the proved dough into 8 portions, each 105g (3¾oz), and roll each in a little polenta to coat the outside and prevent it from sticking. Roll into sausage shapes about 15cm (6in) long and 6cm (2.5in) wide and place in the baguette trays. Prove as directed above, then preheat your oven with a large roasting dish at the bottom, and boil a kettle. Place the baguette trays in the oven then immediately add a mug of boiling water to the roasting dish. Bake for 20 minutes, then reduce the oven temperature to 170°C fan / 190°C / 375°F and bake for another 15 minutes. Proceed as above.

Pictured on page 157.

ITALIAN HERBS & CHEESE

No-Yeast Loaf

MAKES · 12 SLICES

TAKES · 50 MINUTES + 30 MINUTES RESTING

- 345ml (1½ cups minus 1 tbsp) milk
- 5 tbsp lemon juice
- 300g (2¼ cups) gluten-free plain (all-purpose) flour
- 1 tsp xanthan gum
- 1 tsp bicarbonate of soda (baking soda)
- 2 tbsp dried oregano
- ½ tsp salt
- 30g (1oz) extra-mature Cheddar, finely grated

For the topping

- 2 tbsp dried oregano
- 1 tbsp gluten-free plain (all-purpose) flour
- 25g (1oz) extra-mature Cheddar, finely grated

Meet my SUPER-easy-to-bake gluten-free loaf that only needs seven simple ingredients and a little salt – no yeast required. This was not surprisingly inspired by my favourite bread at Subway which I unfortunately haven't eaten in well over a decade (cue sad music). This one is incredibly beginner-friendly, and having a proving basket makes the job even simpler!

In a jug (pitcher), stir together your milk and lemon juice and allow to stand for 10–15 minutes until it becomes thicker and a little lumpy.

In a large mixing bowl, put your flour, xanthan gum, bicarb, dried oregano and salt, and mix until well combined. Mix in your grated cheese until well coated in the flour mixture.

Pour in the milk mixture and stir well with a wooden spoon, mixing until thick and slightly lumpy, ensuring there are no clumps of flour left. This is a very wet mixture, so don't expect it to form a dough.

If using a proving basket, add the dried oregano and flour for the topping to it. Briefly mix it all up and spread it around so that it coats the base and sides. This will not only top your bread, but also prevent it from sticking to the proving basket. If you don't have a proving basket, grease the insides of a 20cm (8in) mixing bowl with oil and proceed with the steps outlined for a proving basket.

Transfer your dough mixture into the prepared proving basket or bowl and smooth over the top. Cover loosely with a tea (dish) towel and allow to rest for at least 30 minutes.

Preheat your oven to 240°C fan / 260°C / 500°F (or as hot as your oven will go) and place a 20cm (8in) skillet or ovenproof frying pan in the oven to heat up. Place a roasting dish at the bottom of the oven.

Once the oven has fully preheated, cut a 30cm (12in) square sheet of non-stick baking parchment and scrunch it up, then open it back up and flatten it back out on your work surface. This will help the paper to line your skillet without creating creases! Boil a kettle.

Carefully invert the dough out onto the baking parchment in one quick motion. Do your best not to disturb the mixture – you'll lose all the lovely bubbles hiding inside! Top with the grated cheese. Remove the skillet or frying pan from the oven. Use the baking parchment to lift the dough into the hot skillet or pan. Score three slashes on the top of your dough using a sharp, wet knife. Place in the oven, add two mugs of boiling water to the roasting dish at the bottom of your oven and bake for 10 minutes, then reduce the oven temperature to 200°C fan / 220°C / 425°F and bake for a further 18–20 minutes.

Remove from the oven. Carefully remove from the skillet or pan, and the baking parchment, then tap the base to check that it feels and sounds hollow – if so, then it's done (see the tip on page 155 for more advice on how to check if your loaf is done). Place on a wire rack and allow to cool completely before slicing. Store in an airtight container or slice and freeze.

Pictured on page 156.

Garlic BREAD

use a (hard) dairy-free butter alternative

use garlic-infused oil instead of garlic

MAKES · 2 LONG BAGUETTES

TAKES · 1 HOUR + 45 MINUTES PROVING

- 330ml (1 cup plus 6 tbsp) warm water
- 10g (⅓oz) dried active yeast (ensure gluten-free)
- 25g (2 tbsp) caster (superfine) sugar
- 410g (3 cups plus 1 tbsp) gluten-free plain (all-purpose) flour
- 2 tsp xanthan gum
- 15g (½oz) psyllium husk powder (ensure gluten-free)
- 6g (¼oz) salt
- 3 large egg whites
- 1 tsp cider vinegar
- 30g (2 tbsp) butter, melted, plus extra for greasing

For the garlic filling

- 250g (1 cup plus 2 tbsp) butter, softened
- 4 tsp chopped parsley
- 1 tsp salt
- 4 tbsp garlic-infused oil or 2 tsp minced garlic

Garlic bread used to be a side that I never thought twice about. But after embarking on a gluten-free diet, it suddenly became something I could only dream about. With a crisp crust and a light crumb that's slathered in garlic butter, I guess my dreams finally came true! Awkwardly enough, I'm actually intolerant to garlic, so I use garlic-infused oil instead, but you can also use minced garlic (from a jar) for a stronger flavour, if you can tolerate it.

Put your warm water, yeast and sugar in a jug (pitcher), then stir. Allow to stand for 10 minutes until it becomes nice and frothy.

In a large bowl or the bowl of a stand mixer, mix together your flour, xanthan gum, psyllium husk powder and salt until well combined. Add your egg whites, vinegar, melted butter and frothy yeast mixture.

Either in a stand mixer with a beater attachment or with an electric hand whisk, mix together on a high speed for 3–5 minutes until well combined. It should look like a very thick, sticky batter. Leave to rest for about 10 minutes.

Grease your baguette tray with a little butter.

Divide your mixture evenly between the two recesses of the baguette tray. As the mixture is fairly sticky, I'd recommend first wetting your fingers and a palette knife, then using them to smooth and shape the batter until you achieve two long baguette shapes. Loosely cover with cling film (plastic wrap) and leave to prove in a warm place for 45 minutes until noticeably risen.

Preheat your oven to 200°C fan / 220°C / 425°F. Place a large roasting dish at the bottom of the oven. Boil the kettle.

Once your baguettes are risen, remove the cling film and slash each baguette 3–4 times diagonally, using a sharp knife. Place in the hot oven and immediately add a mug of boiling water to the roasting dish. Bake for 40 minutes until golden brown, reducing the oven temperature after 20 minutes to 160°C fan / 180°C / 350°F. If your baguettes are browning a little too much, cover loosely with foil (shiny-side up) for the last 10 minutes.

Remove from the oven and allow to cool briefly in the baguette tray before transferring to a wire rack to cool completely.

Preheat your oven to 200°C fan / 220°C / 425°F. In a small bowl, mix all the ingredients for the garlic butter. If using garlic oil, ensure it's all well incorporated and smooth.

Cut each baguette into two equal lengths. Without cutting all the way through, slice as many 2cm (¾in) slices as you can in each. Smear the cut slices and tops with garlic butter and wrap each portion separately in foil. Transfer to a baking sheet and bake for 15 minutes, or until lovely and golden.

'REAL DEAL' Pizza Dough

MAKES · 2 PIZZA BASES

TAKES · 45 MINUTES + 1 HOUR PROVING

- 185ml (¾ cup plus 1 tsp) warm water
- 12g (1 tbsp) caster (superfine) sugar
- 10g (⅓oz) dried active yeast (ensure gluten-free)
- 200g (1½ cups) gluten-free plain (all-purpose) flour
- 50g (⅓ cup) tapioca starch (ensure gluten-free)
- 1 tsp xanthan gum
- ½ tsp gluten-free baking powder
- 1 tsp salt
- 1 tbsp olive oil
- 1 tsp apple cider vinegar
- Fine polenta (ensure gluten-free), for dusting

Meet my best-ever gluten-free pizza base! This yeasted dough results in a lighter base and a more bread-like flavour, while the tapioca starch gives it a lovely texture that tears just like the real deal, alongside a super-crisp finish. So, get your favourite toppings at the ready! If you've got my first book, *How to Make Anything Gluten Free*, there's a simple pizza sauce recipe in there you can happily use here too.

Put your warm water, sugar and yeast in a jug (pitcher), then stir. Allow to stand for 10 minutes until it becomes nice and frothy.

In a large mixing bowl, mix your flour, tapioca starch, xanthan gum, baking powder and salt until combined. Add the olive oil, vinegar and frothy yeast mixture and mix until fully combined. It should create a fairly thick, sticky dough.

Transfer your dough to a lightly oiled bowl and cover with cling film (plastic wrap). Leave to prove in a warm place for about 1 hour until noticeably increased in size.

Preheat your oven to 220°C fan / 240°C / 465°F and place two round, non-stick pizza baking sheets in the oven to heat up.

Lightly dust a sheet of non-stick baking parchment with fine polenta and turn your dough out onto it. Cut your dough in half, return one portion to the bowl and cover with the cling film.

Keep your hands lightly oiled or floured and carefully push the dough on the parchment outwards to form a circular shape, using your fingertips and the palms of your hands. You can make your pizza as thin or as thick as you like, and don't forget to make the edges a little thicker if you want more of a crust. Lightly dust another sheet of non-stick baking parchment with fine polenta and repeat with the other portion of your dough.

Allow both bases to rest for about 10 minutes while you sort out your toppings. After 10 minutes, spread your pizza sauce on the base, add your toppings, then brush the crust lightly with oil and sprinkle with a little more fine polenta.

Remove your hot pizza sheets from the oven and use the baking parchment to lift your pizzas onto them. Bake for 15-18 minutes until golden.

SAVOURY

So often, us gluten-free folks are always drawn in first by bread and sweet treats, but when you think about it... deep down, we love savoury bakes as much as anyone else! That's why this chapter aims to reunite you with all your favourite savoury pies, pasties and tarts.

I've spent a ton of time perfecting my ultimate gluten-free shortcrust pastry (page 206) and rough puff pastry (page 207), which you'll find used a lot in this section, so head over to the essentials section to familiarize yourself with those first.

CREAMY CHICKEN

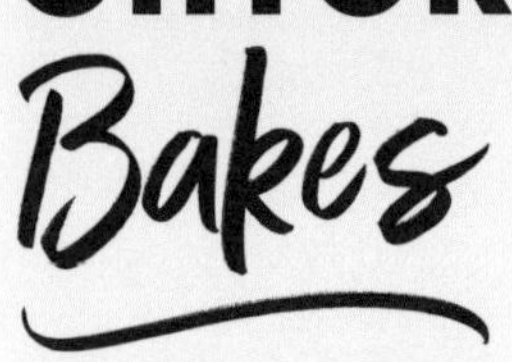

use dairy-free cream and cream cheese, stirring in both after the filling has slightly cooled

use lactose-free whipping cream (minimum 30% fat) and cream cheese

use lactose-free whipping cream (minimum 30% fat) and cream cheese, and a low FODMAP stock cube

MAKES · 4–5

TAKES · 40 MINUTES

- 1 quantity of gluten-free rough puff pastry (page 207)
- 1 medium egg, beaten

For the filling

- 200g (7oz) chicken breast fillet
- 1 tbsp vegetable oil
- 1½ tbsp gluten-free plain (all-purpose) flour
- 200ml (generous ¾ cup) gluten-free chicken stock
- 50g (3½ tbsp) full-fat cream cheese
- ½ tsp salt
- ½ tsp ground black pepper
- 3 tbsp double (heavy) cream

Not surprisingly, this savoury hand pie was inspired by a certain chain of bakeries that still somehow manages to serve almost zero gluten-free options. Fortunately, when you can make your own golden, flaky, puffy pastry and creamy chicken filling at home, there's no need to complain to said bakery on social media about it. But I still do anyway.

Firstly make your filling. Chop your chicken into small chunks, around 1 x 2cm (¾ x 1¼in).

In a large pan, heat the oil over a medium heat, add your chicken and fry until sealed. Add your flour and stir until all the chicken is evenly coated. Pour in your stock, cream cheese, and salt and pepper. Bring to the boil and simmer until it reduces to form a nice, thick sauce. Turn off the heat, stir in the cream and allow to briefly cool.

Preheat your oven to 200°C fan / 220°C / 425°F. Line a large baking sheet with non-stick baking parchment.

Place the pastry dough on a large sheet of non-stick baking parchment and cut the dough in half widthways. Re-wrap one portion in cling film (plastic wrap) and place back into the fridge for later. Roll out the other portion into a large rectangle, around 20 x 30cm (8 x 12in) and 2mm (1⁄16in) thick.

Keep flouring the surface if it gets sticky – this often happens on warmer days or if you have warm hands! Cut your pastry into rectangles of about 10.5 x 9cm (4 x 3½in) – you'll need two rectangles per bake. Brush the edges of one of the rectangles with beaten egg.

Spoon a good tablespoon of filling into the middle of your rectangle, then place your second rectangle of pastry on top, pressing it down around all the edges. Use a fork to seal the edges of each bake. Score 6 wavy lines across the top of each bake with a sharp knife (make sure you don't cut right through the pastry) and then brush the top with a little more beaten egg. Transfer to the lined baking sheet.

Bake in the oven for 20 minutes until golden. Repeat using the rest of your pastry and filling. Enjoy served warm.

TIPS:

Freeze these for up to 3 months, then defrost before reheating in a moderate oven.

Remember that when using rough puff pastry, you cannot simply just re-roll it (or any off-cuts) into a ball. You'll destroy the layers you've spent time creating! If you do have any off cuts, you can always top them with cheese and bake until golden for an easy snack.

Making it veggie?

Simply use the filling from my curry puffs recipe over on page 167 to make a veggie curry bake.

Ham & Cheese PASTRIES

use dairy-free cheese

use dollops of pesto instead of ham

MAKES · 12

TAKES · 35 MINUTES

- 1 quantity of gluten-free rough puff pastry (page 207)
- Gluten-free plain (all-purpose) flour, for dusting
- 250g (9oz) extra-mature Cheddar
- 125g (4½oz) thick ham, diced
- 1 medium egg, beaten
- Handful of fresh parsley, chopped

All you need to make these wonderfully, crisp, flaky and buttery ham and cheese pastries are... ham, cheese and pastry! This is a really easy one to whip up and you can easily make them out of scraps of rough puff pastry too – no need to fold them over in that case.

Preheat your oven to 200°C fan / 220°C / 425°F. Line a baking sheet with non-stick baking parchment.

Cut the pastry in half widthways, re-wrap one half in cling film (plastic wrap) and keep in the fridge for later.

On a well-floured surface, roll the pastry out to a rectangle about 20 x 30cm (8 x 12in) and 2mm (1⁄16in) thick. Keep flouring the surface if it gets sticky – this often happens on warmer days or if you have warm hands! Cut your pastry into six 10cm (4in) squares.

Generously sprinkle each square with some grated cheese, then top with some diced ham. Fold in two corners so that they meet in the middle, and gently press them together to seal the ends.

Place on the lined baking sheet and brush any exposed pastry with beaten egg. Bake in the oven for 20 minutes until golden. Repeat with the other half of your pastry and filling.

Sprinkle with chopped parsley and serve warm.

Store in an airtight container in the fridge, or freeze for up to 3 months. Once defrosted, bake in the oven to refresh.

TIP:
Remember that when using rough puff pastry, you cannot simply just re-roll it (or any off-cuts) into a ball. You'll destroy the layers you've spent time creating! If you do have any off cuts, you can always top them with chopped ham and cheese and bake until golden for an easy snack.

Pictured on page 165.

· MARK'S ·

Curry Puffs

use a low FODMAP curry powder and the green parts of the spring onion (scallion) only

MAKES · 14

TAKES · 50 MINUTES

- 1 quantity of ultimate gluten-free shortcrust pastry (page 207)
- 2 tbsp garlic-infused oil
- 350g (12oz) potato, peeled and finely cubed
- 1 tbsp mild curry powder
- 500ml (2 cups plus 1½ tbsp) boiling water
- 1 tsp gluten-free soy sauce
- 1 tsp sugar
- ½ tsp salt
- ¼ tsp ground black pepper
- 4 tbsp frozen peas
- Handful of spring onion (scallion) greens, thinly sliced
- Gluten-free plain (all-purpose) flour, for dusting
- 1 medium egg, beaten
- Vegetable oil for deep-frying (if frying rather than baking)

I asked Mark to describe his curry puffs and all he said was 'my childhood on a plate'. So I thought I'd elaborate on his behalf! Curry puffs are a popular Malaysian snack, somewhere between a pasty and a samosa, which not surprisingly Mark enjoyed (a lot) whenever he visited his family as a kid. For an authentic finish, Mark recommends deep-frying them for crisper, flakier pastry, but he also insists on showing you how to bake them in the oven for ease too. The choice is yours.

If your chilled pastry dough is quite firm, remove from the fridge and allow to rest at room temperature whilst you prepare the filling.

For the filling, place a large pan over a medium heat and add the garlic-infused oil. Add your potato and fry for 4–5 minutes until softened, then add the curry powder and continue to fry for 2 minutes.

Add the boiling water, soy sauce, sugar, salt and pepper, bring to the boil and simmer until the potato is cooked and the water has reduced to a thickened sauce – this should take 15–20 minutes. Stir in the peas and spring onion greens and cook for 2–3 minutes until all the sauce has evaporated. Set aside to cool.

Divide your pastry evenly into 14 small, golf ball-sized pieces, each weighing 40g (1½oz). Remember not to handle your dough excessively as this will warm it up and make it more fragile. Place in a small bowl, cover with cling film (plastic wrap) and return to the fridge.

Flour a large sheet of non-stick baking parchment and a small rolling pin. (Rolling out a small portion of dough is trickier with a large rolling pin, so use a small one if you have one!)

Roll one ball of pastry out to a small circle, 2mm (1⁄16in) thick. Spoon a modest tablespoon of filling on one side of the pastry, ensuring it's at least 1cm (½in) in from the edge. Flatten the filling a little as this will make it easier to seal.

Brush a little beaten egg around the filling, then fold over the pastry and lightly press together. Crimp the edge by folding over a small section at a time, then pinching to seal, repeating all along the edge. Repeat with the remaining pastry and filling.

If baking your curry puffs, preheat your oven to 180°C fan / 200°C / 400°F. Transfer all of your curry puffs to a baking sheet lined with non-stick baking parchment, and generously brush with beaten egg. Bake for 18 minutes until golden.

Alternatively, if deep-frying them, half-fill a large, deep, heavy-based saucepan with vegetable oil and place over a medium heat for 15 minutes or until it reaches 170°C (340°F). If you don't have a digital food thermometer, check the temperature of the oil using the wooden spoon handle test (page 21). While waiting for the oil to heat, generously brush all of your curry puffs with beaten egg. Carefully lower each curry puff into the hot oil, in batches of 4, placing them slightly apart – they should gently sizzle. Fry for 5–6 minutes or until lovely and golden brown. Remove them to a wire rack suspended over a baking sheet, to drain.

Enjoy warm as a snack. Store in an airtight container in the fridge, or freeze for up to 3 months. Once defrosted, bake in the oven to refresh.

Cornish Pasties

use carrot instead of onion

omit the beef and replace with 175g (6oz) extra-mature Cheddar, grated

MAKES · 2 LARGE PASTIES

TAKES · 45 MINUTES

- 1 quantity of ultimate gluten-free shortcrust pastry (page 206)
- 1 tbsp vegetable oil
- 1 small potato, peeled and finely cubed
- 50g (1¾oz) swede (rutabaga), peeled and finely cubed
- 1 small carrot, peeled and finely cubed (or 60g/2oz diced onion, if you can tolerate it)
- 200g (7oz) beef skirt (flank), cubed (or 220g/7¾oz rib-eye steak, cubed, any tough parts removed)
- 1 tsp salt
- Pinch of ground black pepper
- Gluten-free plain (all-purpose) flour, for dusting
- 1 medium egg, beaten

Here's my gluten-free version of a British classic that's packed full of tender beef and chunky veg, encased in golden, buttery pastry. Beef skirt (flank) is the traditional cut of choice, but it can be hard to source in supermarkets; a rib-eye steak makes for a great substitute. Opt for onion for a more traditional filling, but since I can't tolerate it, it's carrot instead for me!

Preheat your oven to 180°C fan / 200°C / 400°F. Line a large baking sheet with non-stick baking parchment.

If your chilled pastry dough is quite firm, remove from the fridge and allow to rest at room temperature whilst you prepare the filling.

Heat the oil in a large frying pan over a medium heat. Add all the diced vegetables to the pan and fry for 4–5 minutes until slightly softened. Add to a mixing bowl, along with the beef, season with the salt and pepper, then set aside.

Cut your pastry ball in half, take one portion and cover the other in cling film (plastic wrap), then lightly flour your rolling pin. Remember not to handle your dough excessively as this will warm it up and make it more fragile.

On a sheet of non-stick baking parchment, roll out the dough portion to a large, round circle, around 3mm (⅛in) thick. Cut out a circle that's 20cm (8in) in diameter – I find that cutting around a baking tin (pan) or a side plate to be the easiest way to do this.

Spoon half of the filling onto one side of the pastry circle, leaving a 1cm (½in) gap between the filling and the edge. Brush all around the edge of the pastry circle with beaten egg, then fold the pastry over the filling so that it meets the edge on the other side. Seal the pasty shut by pinching the pastry together, then crimping all along the edge with your fingers. Repeat with the other half of your pastry and remaining filling to create two pasties. Transfer both pasties to the lined sheet and generously brush with beaten egg.

Bake in the oven for 25–30 minutes until the pastry is light and golden. Remove from the oven and allow to rest for 10 minutes before enjoying warm.

Once cooled, store in an airtight container in the fridge, or freeze for up to 3 months. Once defrosted, bake in the oven to refresh.

TRIPLE CHEESE & ONION *Quiche*

use dairy-free cheese and a thick dairy-free yoghurt instead of cream

use the green parts of spring onion (scallion) only and lactose-free Greek yoghurt instead of cream

low lactose

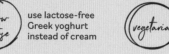

use lactose-free Greek yoghurt instead of cream

use extra Cheddar instead of Parmesan and Comté

SERVES · 8

TAKES · 1 HOUR

- 1 quantity of ultimate gluten-free shortcrust pastry (page 206)
- Gluten-free plain (all-purpose) flour, for dusting
- 240ml (1 cup) double (heavy) cream
- 3 large eggs
- 1 tsp salt
- Pinch of ground black pepper
- 1 bunch (about 130g/4½oz) spring onions (scallions), thinly sliced
- 50g (1¾oz) extra-mature Cheddar, grated
- 50g (1¾oz) Parmesan, grated
- 50g (1¾oz) Comté, grated

Once you've made your pastry, you actually only need 6 simple ingredients to mix together the filling... and three of those are just different types of cheese! The pastry is light and golden (no soggy bottoms in sight) and the classic combo of cheese and onion won't fail to put a smile on your face.

Preheat your oven to 180°C fan / 200°C / 400°F. Place a large baking sheet in the oven to heat up. Remove your chilled pastry dough from the fridge. If it feels really firm, leave it out at room temperature briefly before rolling it.

Lightly flour your rolling pin.
On a sheet of non-stick baking parchment, roll out the dough into a large circle, 2mm (1/16in) thick.

Transfer the pastry to a 23cm (9in) loose-bottomed fluted tart tin (pan) – I do this by supporting the pastry as I gently invert it into the tin, with equal overhang on all sides. Peel off the baking parchment. Next, use your fingers to carefully ease the pastry into place, so that it neatly lines the tin. Lift the overhanging pastry and, using your thumb, squash 2mm (1/16in) of pastry back into the tin. This will result in slightly thicker sides which will prevent your pastry from shrinking when baked. Allow the overhang to do its thing – we'll trim it after chilling. Lightly prick the base of the pastry case several times with a fork, then place in the fridge for 15 minutes.

After chilling, use a rolling pin to roll over the top of the tin, instantly removing the overhang and flattening down the pastry.

Loosely line the base with a piece of scrunched up baking parchment and fill with baking beans (or uncooked rice if you don't have any). Place on the hot baking sheet in the oven, bake for 15 minutes, then remove the baking parchment and baking beans and bake for a further 5 minutes.

Meanwhile, in a large jug (pitcher), beat together the cream and eggs, then season with the salt and pepper. Stir in the spring onions and grated cheeses, reserving a little cheese for the top.

Remove the pastry case and the baking sheet from the oven. Work quickly from this point so the baking sheet doesn't lose its heat! Pour the egg mixture into the pastry case, then top with your reserved cheese. Carefully place back into the preheated oven (ensuring you don't spill any!), still on the hot baking sheet, and bake for 25–30 minutes, until lovely and golden brown on top, a little risen and not 'jiggly'.

Allow to cool for 5 minutes before removing from the tin and serving warm. Alternatively, allow to cool completely and enjoy at room temperature, or straight from the fridge. Once cooled, store in an airtight container in the fridge, or slice and freeze for up to 3 months (in which case, always reheat from frozen in a moderate oven for 20–30 minutes).

TIPS:
Feel free to use all extra-mature Cheddar instead of the mixture of cheeses. Also, if you can tolerate onion, you can also replace the spring onion with a whole regular onion, sliced and lightly fried.

'Proper' Salmon EN CROÛTE

use lactose-free cream cheese

SERVES · 4

TAKES · 1 HOUR

- 1 quantity of ultimate gluten-free shortcrust pastry (page 206)
- Gluten-free plain (all-purpose) flour, for dusting
- 1 tbsp Dijon mustard
- 1 medium egg, beaten

For the filling

- 2 tbsp garlic-infused oil
- 100g (3½oz) baby leaf spinach
- 200g (1 cup minus 1½ tbsp) full-fat cream cheese
- 2 tbsp chopped fresh dill
- Grated zest of 1 lemon
- ½ tsp salt
- ½ tsp ground black pepper
- 500g (1lb 2oz) side of salmon

The day that I'm able to order this in a restaurant is probably also the same day that I pass out in disbelief multiple times before I even place my order. Until that day comes, I can fortunately just make it at home in no time instead. Think golden, light pastry concealing tender, chunky salmon with a creamy, lemon and spinach topping – no passing out required.

If your chilled pastry dough is quite firm, remove from the fridge and allow to rest at room temperature whilst you prepare the filling.

Heat the garlic-infused oil in a large frying pan over a low heat. Add the spinach and stir until completely wilted. Remove from the pan, roughly chop, then transfer to a mixing bowl and allow to cool. Once cooled, add the cream cheese, dill and lemon zest, season with the salt and pepper and mix until well combined.

Preheat your oven to 200°C fan / 220°C / 425°F.

Lightly flour your rolling pin, and remember not to handle your dough excessively as this will warm it up and make it more fragile. On a sheet of non-stick baking parchment, roll out your dough into a long rectangle that's around 2mm (1/16in) thick. Ensure that the shorter sides of the rectangle are roughly the diameter of your salmon side, plus 5cm (2in). Using a sharp knife, cut the pastry rectangle in half crosswise, to create two shorter rectangles of pastry.

Spoon your mustard into the middle of one of the pastry sheets and spread it out, leaving a 2.5cm (1in) clear border. Place your salmon on top, then top with the spinach mixture. Brush beaten egg around the edge of the salmon and place the other pastry sheet on top, then gently but tightly seal all around the salmon. Trim off any excess pastry so that you're left with a 1cm (½in) border of pastry, and crimp the edges shut with a fork.

Lastly, brush with beaten egg and, if you fancy, use a metal spoon to gently create a lovely fish-scale effect, starting at the edge closest to you and working your way up towards the opposite side. You don't need to press too hard as the pastry can tear, so just aim to create subtle lines of scalloped indentations.

Lift the salmon parcel onto a baking sheet, using the baking parchment to lift it (transfer to a fresh sheet of baking parchment if there's lots of flour left from rolling). Trim off any excess parchment that may flap about in the oven, then bake for 30–35 minutes until the pastry is golden.

Serve with mashed potatoes and tartar sauce.

Making it dairy-free?
Omit the cream cheese and proceed with the recipe as directed. I'm yet to find a dairy-free cream cheese that doesn't completely liquify when baked, so it's best to omit it entirely.

Roasted Veggie & Feta TARTS

use dairy-free cheese and pesto

ensure pesto is low FODMAP

ensure pesto is vegetarian

MAKES · 12

TAKES · 35 MINUTES

- 1 quantity of gluten-free rough puff pastry (page 207)
- Gluten-free plain (all-purpose) flour, for dusting

For the topping

- 1 courgette (zucchini), thinly sliced into rounds
- 1 yellow (bell) pepper, sliced into thin strips
- Handful of cherry tomatoes, sliced in half
- 40ml (2½ tbsp) garlic-infused oil
- 50g (1¾ oz) pesto
- 200g (7oz) feta, crumbled
- Fresh basil leaves
- Salt and ground black pepper

For me, the savory tarts in bakeries are often just as tempting as all of the wonderful sweet treats available. After one bite of buttery, golden, rough puff pastry, topped with colourful veg, bookended with pesto and creamy feta, it's hopefully not hard to see why.

Preheat your oven to 200°C fan / 220°C / 425°F. Line a baking sheet with non-stick baking parchment.

Place the sliced veg in a large mixing bowl. Add the garlic-infused oil with salt and pepper to taste, and mix until everything is well coated.

Cut the pastry in half widthways, rewrap in cling film (plastic wrap) and keep one portion in the fridge for later.

On a well-floured surface, roll the pastry out into a rectangle 2mm (1/16in) thick. Keep flouring the surface if it gets sticky – this often happens on warmer days or if you have warm hands!

Cut your pastry into six 10cm (4in) squares. Spread pesto in the middle of each square, leaving a 1cm (⅓in) pastry border. Top with some of your veg mixture, then a few pieces of crumbled feta.

Place each pastry square on the lined baking sheet and brush the edges of each pastry with beaten egg. Bake in the oven for 20 minutes until golden. Repeat with the remaining pastry and toppings.

Top with fresh basil leaves and serve immediately.

Store any leftover tarts in an airtight container in the fridge, or freeze for up to 3 months. Once defrosted, bake in a moderate oven for a few minutes to refresh.

TIP:
Remember that when using rough puff pastry, you cannot simply just re-roll it (or any off-cuts) into a ball. You'll destroy the layers you've spent time creating! If you do have any off cuts, you can always top them with crumbled feta and bake until golden for an easy snack.

MINI BEEF

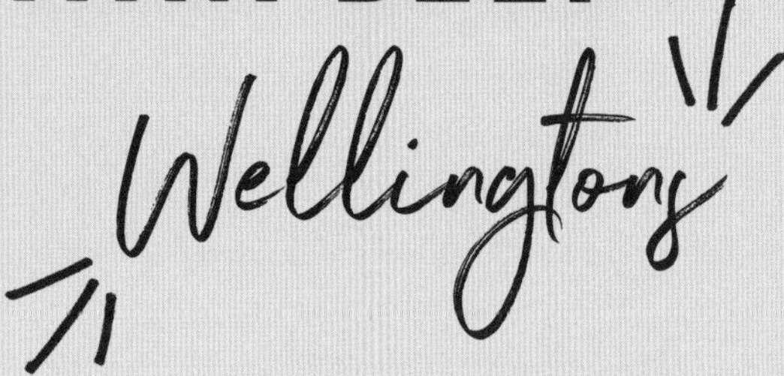

use oyster mushrooms

SERVES · 4

TAKES · 1 HOUR

- 1 quantity of ultimate gluten-free shortcrust pastry (page 206)
- Gluten-free plain (all-purpose) flour, for dusting
- 1 medium egg, beaten

For the beef and filling

- 2 x 200g (7oz) beef fillet (tenderloin) steaks (about 3cm/1¼in thick)
- Vegetable oil, to coat the steaks
- 200g (7oz) chestnut mushrooms
- 3 tbsp garlic-infused oil
- 1 tbsp fresh thyme leaves
- 50ml (3 tbsp plus 1 tsp) dry white wine
- 6–8 slices of prosciutto
- Salt and ground black pepper

My golden, buttery pastry conceals incredibly tender, infinitely flavoursome beef fillet, coated in prosciutto that's flanked with a garlic and herb mushroom duxelle. Making mini beef Wellingtons means you don't need to hunt (or shell out) for a big hunk of beef fillet (tenderloin) – you can easily find beef fillet steaks in the supermarket.

If your chilled pastry dough is quite firm, remove from the fridge and allow to rest at room temperature whilst you prepare the filling.

Drizzle your steaks with a little vegetable oil, massage until covered, then season on both sides with salt and pepper. Place a large frying pan over a medium heat. Once the pan is hot, add both steaks and cook for 4 minutes, then flip and cook for another 3 minutes or until both sides have a dark golden crust. Remove from the pan and allow to cool.

Chop your chestnut mushrooms as finely as possible, aiming for a breadcrumb-like consistency – I prefer to pulse in a food processor; definitely don't overmix and purée them though!

Heat your garlic-infused oil in a large frying pan over a medium heat, add the mushrooms and fry for 5 minutes until softened. Add the thyme, ½ teaspoon of salt and a pinch of pepper, then add the wine and simmer for another 10 minutes, until thick and paste-like.

Preheat your oven to 180°C fan / 200°C / 400°F and line a baking sheet with non-stick baking parchment.

Place another piece of parchment on your work surface and lay 3–4 slices of prosciutto on top, overlapping slightly. Spoon a quarter of the mushroom mixture on the ham and flatten a little, then pop one of your steaks on top. Spread another quarter of the mushroom mixture on top of the steak, then use the baking parchment to carefully wrap the steak in the prosciutto. Repeat with the remaining prosciutto, mushroom mixture and steak, then set aside.

Lightly flour your rolling pin. Cut your dough in half and return one portion to the cling film (plastic wrap). Remember not to handle your dough excessively as this will warm it up and make it more fragile.

On a sheet of non-stick baking parchment, roll out your dough into a long rectangle about 3mm (⅛in) thick. Ensure that the shorter sides are comfortably longer than your wrapped steaks, and the longer sides are at least three times wider.

Place a wrapped steak on top, then brush beaten egg over the pastry around the steak and fold the pastry over the steak as though you were closing a book. Gently press around the steak to seal it, trim off any excess pastry so that you're left with a 1cm (½in) rim, then crimp the edges shut with a fork. Lastly, brush with beaten egg and use a sharp knife to lightly score three diagonal lines in the top of the pastry. Repeat with the remaining pastry and steak.

Carefully transfer both Wellingtons to the prepared baking sheet and bake for 30 minutes until the pastry is golden. Allow to rest for 15–20 minutes before cutting in half and serving with mashed potato and gluten-free gravy.

Steak & SPUD PIE

use low FODMAP stock cube and carrot instead of onion

SERVES · 4–6

TAKES · 3 HOURS

- 1½ quantity of ultimate gluten-free shortcrust pastry (page 206)
- Gluten-free plain (all-purpose) flour, for dusting
- 1 medium egg, beaten

For the filling

- 3 tbsp garlic-infused oil
- 1kg (2lb 3oz) beef braising (chuck) steak, cubed
- 2 medium carrots, peeled and chopped (or 1 onion, chopped, if you can tolerate it)
- 4 tbsp gluten-free plain (all-purpose) flour
- 1½ tsp salt
- 1 tsp ground black pepper
- 250ml (generous 1 cup) gluten-free beef stock
- 250ml (generous 1 cup) red wine (or more beef stock)
- ¼ tsp gravy browning (ensure gluten-free)
- 2 tsp dried rosemary
- 2 medium potatoes, peeled and cubed

This crowd-pleaser is full to the brim with incredibly tender, chunky beef and veggies that soak up all that lovely, thick gravy. It's encased in a golden pastry that no human could detect as gluten-free – feel free to test that part for yourself. You'll need to make an extra half quantity of my pastry for this one, so bear that in mind before you start.

If your chilled pastry dough is quite firm, remove from the fridge and allow to rest at room temperature whilst you prepare the filling.

Preheat your oven to 200°C fan / 220°C / 425°F.

For the filling, add the garlic-infused oil to a large, flameproof casserole dish that has a lid. Place over a medium heat and, once hot, add the beef. Fry until browned on all sides, then add the carrots (if using rather than onion) and continue to fry for 1–2 minutes. If using onion instead of carrots, remove the beef from the pan, add a little more oil, chuck in the chopped onion and fry until slightly browned, then add the beef back in and continue.

Add the flour, salt and pepper and stir in until everything is well coated. Add the stock, wine (if using), gravy browning and dried rosemary. Bring to the boil, pop the lid on and place in the oven for 1 hour. Remove from the oven, take off the lid and add your cubed potatoes. Replace the lid and return it to the oven for a further 1 hour, then open the lid and check to ensure the gravy is lovely and thick. If it's not quite there, give it a quick blast on the stove over a medium heat until it thickens up. Set aside to cool slightly.

Cut off a generous third of your pastry and cover it in cling film (plastic wrap), then lightly flour your rolling pin. Remember not to handle your dough excessively as this will warm it up and make it more fragile.

On a sheet of non-stick baking parchment, roll out the larger portion of your dough to a large circle, around 3mm (⅛in) thick.

Grab a 23cm (9in) pie dish and, using the baking parchment to support it, invert your rolled out pastry into the dish, then peel off the parchment. Using your hands, carefully push the pastry in and line the pie dish, leaving overhang around all the edges. Brush the overhang with beaten egg and fill with your slightly cooled pie filling, right to the top.

Grab the piece of non-stick baking parchment you used earlier and roll out your reserved dough to a large circle, again around 3mm (⅛in) thick. Lightly flour your rolling pin again, if needed. Invert on top of your pie dish and peel off the parchment once again to create a lid.

Using a sharp knife, trim all of the overhang off and crimp the edges of your pie shut using a fork. Generously brush the top of the pie with egg and cut a couple of slits in the middle of the lid. Use any offcuts to fashion together some decoration for the top if you fancy. Just ensure you remember to egg wash these too.

Transfer the pie dish to a baking sheet and bake in the oven for 35 minutes until the pastry is lovely and golden.

Serve up with gluten-free gravy and Yorkshire puddings, with veggies on the side.

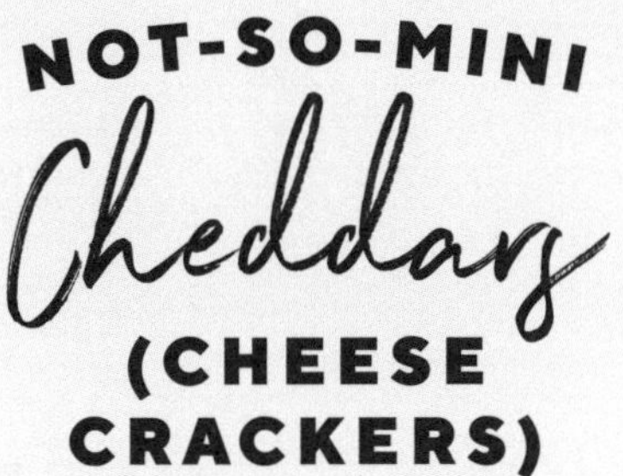

NOT-SO-MINI Cheddars (CHEESE CRACKERS)

use a (hard) dairy-free butter alternative, and dairy-free cheese

vegan

SERVES · 6–8

TAKES · 30 MINUTES + 45 MINUTES CHILLING

- 225g (1¾ cups) gluten-free plain (all-purpose) flour, plus extra for dusting
- ½ tsp xanthan gum
- 1½ tsp gluten-free baking powder
- 90g cold butter (⅓ cup plus 1 tbsp) cubed
- 65g (2¼oz) extra-mature Cheddar, grated
- ½ tsp salt
- ½ tsp sugar
- 30ml (2 tbsp) vegetable oil, or olive oil
- 40ml (2 tbsp plus 2 tsp) cold water

To finish

- 25g (1¾ tbsp) butter, melted
- Flaky salt, for sprinkling

Crackers aren't often something I ever even contemplated baking as, fortunately, there's always a healthy supply of gluten-free crackers in supermarkets (though in my experience, some often tend to crumble into dust, which isn't ideal). But after one bite of these light, flaky and undeniably cheesy crackers, I now bake them myself as often as I can. They just cannot be beat!

Mix together the flour, xanthan gum and baking powder in a large mixing bowl, then add your cold, cubed butter and rub it in with your fingertips until you achieve a breadcrumb-like consistency (you could also use a food processor to speed things up a bit).

Stir in your grated cheese, salt and sugar until evenly distributed. Add your oil, followed by your water, cutting them in with a knife so it gradually starts to come together. Use your hands to bring the mixture together into a ball, wrap in cling film (plastic wrap) and chill in the fridge for 45 minutes.

Preheat your oven to 160°C fan / 180°C / 350°F. Line a baking sheet with non-stick baking parchment.

On a lightly floured piece of non-stick baking parchment, roll out your dough to a 4mm (⅙in) thickness and use a 5cm (2in) round or fluted cutter to cut shapes out of your dough. Reroll the dough as necessary to cut out as many shapes as possible.

Transfer the shapes to your prepared baking sheet, ideally using a small palette knife, then prick a few holes in each of them using a fork. Bake in the oven for about 12 minutes until golden.

Remove from the oven, brush with melted butter and sprinkle with some flakes of salt. Allow to cool completely on the baking sheet.

TIP:
This is an incredibly versatile savoury cracker dough. If you prefer a different flavouring, feel free to leave out the cheese and add dried herbs of your choice.

Christmas

I'll never forget my first gluten-free Christmas... mainly because I felt miserable and I missed out on eating almost everything worth eating!

Leaving the dramatics aside, back then, I was just happy to survive the day without gluten gatecrashing the party. But now, I've realized that Christmas doesn't have to mean missing out on a single thing, and the same applies to you – especially as this chapter aims to make sure of it!

So here's a collection of festive favourites from the blog, as well as a few new surprises you won't find anywhere else.

Have a Merry (gluten-free) Christmas!

PIGS IN BLANKETS

Sausage Rolls

omit cranberry sauce

use vegetarian cocktail sausages

MAKES · 18

TAKES · 35 MINUTES

- 1 quantity of gluten-free rough puff pastry (page 207) or ultimate gluten-free shortcrust pastry (page 206)
- 1 medium egg, beaten
- 18 gluten-free pigs in blankets
- Handful of poppy seeds
- Cranberry sauce, to serve

These are perfect for party canapés, or just epic gluten-free snacks on Christmas day. The combo of crisp, flaky pastry wrapped around pigs in blankets never fails to be a proper people-pleaser. You can always make your own pigs in blankets by wrapping (raw) gluten-free cocktail sausages in rashers of streaky bacon, if you can't find any. Or just use gluten-free cocktail sausages and enjoy these all year round.

Preheat your oven to 200°C fan / 220°C / 425°F. Line two large baking sheets with non-stick baking parchment.

Place the pastry dough on a large sheet of non-stick baking parchment. Cut the dough in half widthways, re-wrap one portion in cling film (plastic wrap) and place back in the fridge. Roll out the second dough portion into a large rectangle, about 15 x 35cm (6 x 14in) and 2mm (1/16in) thick. Use a pizza cutter to cut it into 9 rectangles, each 5 x 11.5cm (2 x 4½in), then brush both of the shorter edges of each with beaten egg.

Place a pig in blanket in the middle of each rectangle. Fold over both sides, ensuring that they overlap slightly to form a seam, and gently press all along the seam to seal it completely. Transfer to a lined baking sheet, seam-side down. Brush each sausage roll with beaten egg and top with poppy seeds. Repeat with the other portion of your pastry and pigs in blankets.

Bake in the oven for 25 minutes until golden brown, then transfer to a wire rack to cool for 15–20 minutes.

Serve with cranberry sauce for dipping.

TIPS:

These will puff in the oven, so ensure you create a nice, secure seam or they'll open up as they bake!

Remember that when using rough puff pastry, you cannot simply just re-roll it (or any off-cuts) into a ball. You'll destroy the layers you've spent time creating! If you do have any off cuts, you can always top them with cheese and bake until golden for an easy snack.

CHRISTMAS LEFTOVERS

use dairy-free cream

use lactose-free cream and a low FODMAP stock cube

use lactose-free cream

SERVES · 4–6

TAKES · 1 HOUR

- 1½ quantity of ultimate gluten-free shortcrust pastry (page 206)
- 2 tbsp garlic-infused oil
- 1 medium carrot, diced
- 350g (12oz) cooked turkey meat, diced
- 200g (7oz) cooked ham, diced
- 4 tbsp gluten-free plain (all-purpose) flour, plus extra for dusting
- 400ml (1⅔ cups) gluten-free chicken stock
- 1 tbsp dried sage
- ½ tsp black pepper
- 50g (1¾oz) frozen peas
- 3 tbsp double (heavy) cream
- 1 medium egg, beaten

Meet the pie that'll instantly transform Christmas day leftovers into a Boxing day dinner to remember. It's creamy, packed with flavour and you wouldn't believe how mind-blowingly tender leftover turkey could taste. Encased in my super buttery shortcrust pastry, even Santa wouldn't know (or care) that it's gluten-free.

If your chilled pastry dough is quite firm, remove from the fridge and allow to rest at room temperature whilst you prepare the filling.

Place a large pan over a medium heat and heat your garlic-infused oil. Add the carrot and fry for 2–3 minutes until softened, then throw in the cooked turkey and ham. Add the flour and mix until everything is nicely coated, then add the stock, dried sage and pepper. Bring to the boil and simmer for 5 minutes, then add the frozen peas. Simmer for 2–3 more minutes until the gravy has nicely thickened. Remove from the heat and allow to cool for 5 minutes, then stir in the cream and leave to cool further.

Preheat your oven to 200°C fan / 220°C / 425°F.

Cut off a generous third of your pastry and cover in the cling film (plastic wrap) and set aside. Lightly flour your rolling pin. Remember not to handle your dough excessively as this will warm it up and make it more fragile.

On a sheet of non-stick baking parchment, roll out the larger portion of your dough to a large, round circle, around 2mm (1/16in) thick.

Grab a 23cm (9in) pie dish and, using the baking parchment to support it, invert your rolled out pastry into the dish. Using your hands, carefully push the pastry in to line the pie dish, leaving overhang around all the edges. Brush the overhang with beaten egg and fill with your slightly cooled pie filling, right to the top.

Grab the piece of non-stick baking parchment you used earlier and roll out your reserved portion of dough to a large, round circle, again around 2mm (1/16in) thick. Use this as a lid and invert on top of your pie dish. Using a sharp knife, trim all of the overhang off, then crimp the edges of your pie shut using a fork. Generously brush the top of the pie with egg and cut a couple of slits in the middle of the lid.

Use any off-cuts to fashion together some decoration for the top, if you fancy. Just ensure you remember to egg wash these too.

Transfer the pie dish to a baking sheet and bake in the oven for 35 minutes until the pastry is lovely and golden.

Serve up with leftover roast potatoes, veggies, cranberry sauce and gluten-free gravy.

TIP:
You can actually make this all year round! Just use cooked, chopped boneless chicken thighs instead of turkey.

(GERMAN CHRISTMAS COOKIES)

use a (hard) dairy-free butter alternative

one cookie is a safe serving size

MAKES · 12

TAKES · 40 MINUTES + 30 MINUTES CHILLING

- 90g (3oz) blanched hazelnuts
- 65g (½ cup plus 2 tbsp) ground almonds (almond flour)
- 300g (2¼ cups) gluten-free plain (all-purpose) flour
- ¼ tsp xanthan gum
- ½ tsp gluten-free baking powder
- ¼ tsp bicarbonate of soda (baking soda)
- 2 tsp ground cinnamon
- 1 tsp ground ginger
- ½ tsp ground cloves
- 3 tbsp unsweetened cocoa powder
- 50g (3½ tbsp) butter, softened
- 175g (¾ cup plus 2 tbsp) dark brown sugar
- 170g (6oz) maple syrup
- Grated zest of 1 orange or lemon
- 2 large eggs

For the icing

- 400g (2 cups) icing (confectioners') sugar, sifted
- 50ml (3 tbsp plus 1 tsp) lemon juice

For me, I never truly feel like I've 'stepped into Christmas' until I've taken a bite of one of these, while watching *Elf*. The icing is packed with an intense, sweet, lemony kick and the cookies are delightfully soft, crammed with tons of warming, festive spice.

Place your hazelnuts, ground almonds and half your flour in a food processor. Pulse until the hazelnuts have broken down. Add the rest of your flour, the xanthan gum, baking powder, bicarb, cinnamon, ginger, cloves and cocoa powder to the processor. Pulse once more so everything is mixed together. (Alternatively, you can do all this by hand, bashing the hazelnuts on their own in a zip-lock bag, using a rolling pin, until a fine, consistent dust. Then add to a bowl and stir in the remaining dry ingredients.)

In a large mixing bowl, cream together your butter, sugar, maple syrup and orange or lemon zest until completely smooth (I prefer to use an electric hand whisk for this). Beat your eggs in one at a time, then gradually add your dry mixture to the bowl, mixing in between each addition.

Place your mixture in the fridge to chill for 30 minutes. Preheat your oven to 160°C fan / 180°C / 350°F. Line two baking sheets with non-stick baking parchment.

As the dough is fairly sticky, I use an ice-cream scoop to transfer the mixture to the baking sheets – one large scoop per cookie. Make sure you leave space between each dollop, as they will spread a bit.

Bake in the oven for about 12 minutes until a dark golden colour. Briefly allow to cool on the baking sheet before transferring to a wire rack to cool completely.

To make your icing, sift your icing sugar into a large mixing bowl and gradually stir in lemon juice until a thick, spreadable icing is formed. If it becomes too runny, just sift in more icing sugar and mix in.

Once your cookies have cooled, spoon icing on top of them, right in the middle. It should run very slowly towards the edges and spread all over the cookies. Leave the icing to set for a few hours.

Store in an airtight container for up to 5 days, or freeze for up to 3 months.

DEEP-FILLED Mince Pies

use oil for greasing

MAKES · 12

TAKES · 40 MINUTES (+ 12 HOURS SOAKING AND 2 HOURS COOKING IF MAKING THE MINCEMEAT)

- 1 quantity of ultimate gluten-free shortcrust pastry (page 206)
- Butter or oil, for greasing
- 1 medium egg, beaten
- Caster (superfine) sugar, for sprinkling

For the mincemeat filling (or use store-bought)

- 200g (7oz) raisins
- 150g (5oz) currants
- 150g (5oz) candied mixed peel
- 150g (5oz) gluten-free vegetable suet
- 200g (1 cup) dark brown sugar
- 2 tsp ground mixed spice
- 1 tsp ground cinnamon
- ½ tsp ground nutmeg
- Grated zest and juice of 1 lemon
- Grated zest and juice of 1 orange
- 1 cooking apple, such as Bramley, cored, peeled and finely chopped
- 50ml (generous 3 tbsp) brandy (optional)

What would Christmas be without mince pies? Fortunately, I never struggle to find gluten-free mince pies in the supermarket, but trust me - you absolutely can't beat making your own, especially when it comes to pastry. Feel free to use store-bought mincemeat from the supermarket , which speeds up the process massively - just ensure it's gluten-free.

For the mincemeat, combine all the ingredients except the brandy in a large, lidded ovenproof dish. Cover and leave to soak for at least 12 hours.

Preheat your oven to 100°C fan / 120°C / 250°F. Transfer the mincemeat dish to the oven and cook for 2–3 hours, then give it a good stir and leave to cool. Once completely cooled, give it another good stir, then stir in the brandy, if using.

Preheat your oven to 180°C fan / 200°C / 400°F and lightly grease a 12-hole muffin or cupcake tin (pan).

If your chilled pastry dough is quite firm, leaving it out at room temperature ahead of time is definitely advised. Remember not to excessively handle your dough as this will warm it up and make it more fragile.

Place the pastry dough on a large sheet of non-stick baking parchment and roll out to a large rectangle, around 3mm (⅛in) thick. Use a 9cm (3½in) round cookie cutter to cut out 12 circles for the bases of your mince pies. Carefully ease them into the holes of the muffin tin, pressing them in gently.

Spoon around 2 teaspoons of your mincemeat filling into each pastry case, level with the top of the case. Brush the edges of each pastry case with beaten egg.

Re-roll the remaining pastry to a similar thickness as before. Use a 7.5cm (3in) round cookie cutter to cut out 12 lids. Carefully press the lids on top of the filled pastry cases to seal them, then brush the tops of each pie with a little more beaten egg. Generously sprinkle sugar on top of each mince pie, then, using a sharp knife, cut two small slits in the lid of each.

Bake in the oven for about 20 minutes until the pastry is lovely and golden. Allow to cool before removing from the tin.

Best Ever CHRISTMAS PUDDING

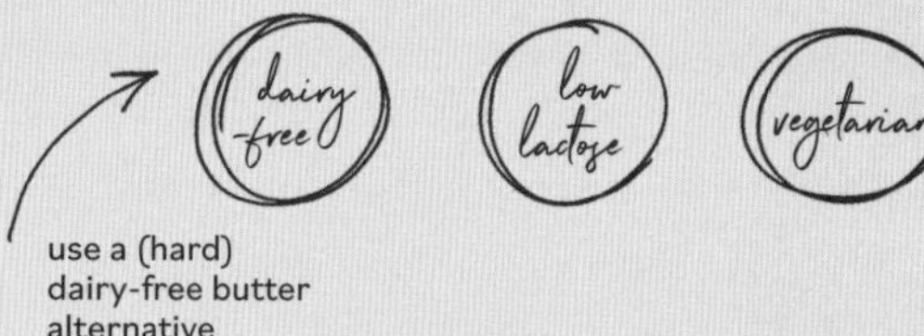

use a (hard) dairy-free butter alternative

SERVES · 6–7

TAKES · 45 MINUTES + 2 HOURS SOAKING + 8 HOURS STEAMING

For the soaked fruit

- 150g (5oz) raisins
- 150g (5oz) currants
- 150g (5oz) candied mixed peel
- 1 small cooking apple, such as Bramley, peeled, cored and roughly chopped
- Grated zest and juice of 1 lemon
- 4 tbsp brandy or sherry

For the pudding batter

- 75g (⅓ cup) butter, softened, plus extra for greasing
- 150g (¾ cup) light muscovado sugar
- 2 large eggs
- 90g (⅔ cup) gluten-free plain (all-purpose) flour
- 1 tsp gluten-free baking powder
- ½ tsp xanthan gum
- 1 tsp ground nutmeg
- 2 slices of gluten-free bread, blitzed into breadcrumbs

For the brandy butter

- 125g (generous ½ cup) butter, softened
- 200g (scant 1½ cups) icing (confectioners') sugar, sifted
- Grated zest of ½ orange
- 4 tbsp brandy, plus an extra 4 tbsp to serve

My gluten-free Christmas pud is proof that everything tastes better when you make it yourself... because this is the only Christmas pudding I will actually eat! It's like taking one big bite out of Christmas. This couldn't be easier to make, and while the pudding is enjoying a luxurious steam, you can get back to wrapping pressies.

Place the raisins, currants, mixed peel and apple in a large bowl. Add the lemon zest and juice, the brandy or sherry and leave to soak for at least 2 hours, or ideally overnight.

Grease a 1.4l (3 pint) pudding basin and line the base with non-stick baking parchment. If your pudding basin doesn't have a lid, create one by cutting a circle of foil and baking parchment that's roughly 4cm (1½in) larger than the basin's diameter. Place both circles on top of one another (foil on top) and fold a pleat down the middle. Set aside.

In a large mixing bowl, cream the butter and sugar, then add the eggs, one by one, mixing in between each addition. Add the flour, baking powder, xanthan gum, nutmeg and breadcrumbs, and mix until well combined. Lastly, mix in all the soaked fruit, plus any soaking liquid.

Spoon the mixture into the pudding basin. Compact it down and ensure it is flat on top. Secure the lid, or use string to secure your parchment and foil in place. If your pudding basin has a lid, I'd suggest wrapping the whole thing in foil after popping it on, just to be safe. Place in a large saucepan and add boiling water to come halfway up the basin. Place the lid on the pan, bring to the boil then reduce the heat and simmer for 5 hours, keeping an eye on it and topping up the water when needed.

Remove the pudding basin from the water, take off the lid and allow to cool completely in the basin. Cover and store in a cool, dry place until Christmas day.

On Christmas day, put the lid back on your pudding basin; if you made your own, you'll need to create a new one. Place in the large saucepan again and add boiling water to come halfway up the pudding basin. Pop the lid on, bring to the boil, reduce the heat and simmer for 2 hours.

Meanwhile, whip up your brandy butter. Place the butter in the bowl of a stand mixer (or use an electric hand whisk) and mix on a medium speed for 5 minutes until pale. Add the icing sugar and mix until incorporated, then add your orange zest and brandy and mix once more. Transfer to a serving dish and keep refrigerated until needed.

To serve, turn out your Christmas pud onto a lipped serving dish. Warm up the extra brandy in a small saucepan (don't let it boil) and then pour it over the hot Christmas pudding. Carefully set light to it and serve as soon as the flames have died down, with brandy butter.

Pictured on pages 186–7.

CLASSIC CHRISTMAS
· Cake ·

use a dairy-free butter alternative

MAKES · 20 SLICES

TAKES · 4¾ HOURS + 12 HOURS SOAKING

For the soaked fruit
(The total weight of your mixed dried fruit should be 850g/1lb 14oz. I use the following, but use what you have to hand/is available.)

- 350g (12oz) currants
- 150g (5oz) sultanas (golden raisins)
- 125g (4½oz) raisins
- 125g (4½oz) glacé cherries
- 50g (2oz) candied mixed peel
- 50g (2oz) dried cranberries
- 120ml (½ cup) Amaretto or brandy, plus extra for 'feeding'
- Grated zest of 2 lemons, and the juice of 1

For the cake

- 225g (1 cups plus 2 tbsp) dark brown sugar
- 225g (1 cup) butter, softened, plus extra for greasing
- 4 large eggs
- 1 tbsp black treacle (molasses)
- 1½ tsp ground mixed spice
- 225g (1¾ cups) gluten-free plain (all-purpose) flour
- ½ tsp xanthan gum
- 25g (¼ cup) ground almonds (almond flour)
- 50g (1¾oz) blanched almonds, chopped

To finish

- 5 tbsp apricot jam
- 400g (14oz) marzipan
- 700g (1lb 9 oz) white fondant icing
- Icing (confectioners') sugar, for dusting
- Red and green fondant icing, for a holly decoration

My classic gluten-free Christmas cake proved to be a huge hit during the festive season, so here it is in all its glory. For me (as a professional procrastinator) the only hard part is ensuring you make this as early as possible. That'll give this beauty ample time to mature and develop, guaranteeing an intense flavour that only comes from feeding across weeks and months. I promise it's worth the wait!

Place your dried fruit in a large bowl and ensure that any larger chunks of dried fruit are finely chopped – dried cherries especially, if using. Pour over your Amaretto or brandy and the lemon juice, then stir in your lemon zest. Cover and allow to soak for at least 12 hours.

Preheat your oven to 120°C fan / 140°C / 285°F. Grease a 20cm (8in) loose-bottomed, deep, round cake tin (pan) and line the base with non-stick baking parchment. Then line the sides, ensuring the parchment is slightly taller than the tin itself. Finally, wrap a double layer of baking parchment around the outside of the tin and secure round the middle with string, with the parchment about 5cm (2in) taller than the top of the tin. (This prevents the sides of the cake from burning during the long bake.)

Add all the cake ingredients to a large mixing bowl. Mix until fully combined, ideally with an electric hand whisk. Gradually stir in all your soaked, dried fruit thoroughly, using a spatula or wooden spoon. Spoon into your prepared tin, making sure it's all nice and level.

Cover the top of your cake with a square of baking parchment with a hole in the middle of it – the hole helps with steam and the covering helps prevent the cake from burning. Bake in the oven for around 4 hours – it will be a dark golden colour and fairly firm. Allow the cake to fully cool in the tin.

Continued overleaf...

Once cooled, poke all over with a skewer (until about halfway down) and spoon over a little extra Amaretto or brandy. Remove the cake from the tin and wrap in two layers of baking parchment followed by two layers of kitchen foil. Store in an airtight container for up to 3 months, feeding the cake every few weeks by pouring over a tablespoon of Amaretto or brandy.

A week before serving, remove the cake from its baking parchment/foil wrapping and turn it upside down so that its flat end is facing upwards. Spread all over with a thin layer of slightly warmed apricot jam.

Generously dust your work surface with icing sugar and briefly knead your marzipan until softer and more workable. Dust your surface once again and your rolling pin too. Roll out your marzipan to a large circle, around 4mm (⅙in) thick, ensuring it's big enough to cover the entire cake. Use your rolling pin to lift up the marzipan and cover your cake with it. Carefully press it onto the top and down the sides so that it's lovely and smooth. Trim any excess marzipan around the base, using a sharp knife.

Dust your surface once more with icing sugar, then roll out your white fondant icing to a large circle, around 4mm (⅙in) thick. Again, use your rolling pin to the lift up the icing and cover the cake with it. Trim off any excess.

Decorate the cake however you wish with edible or non-edible decorations, such as ribbons or festive figures. I used a little red and green fondant to make holly leaves and berries, using a little water to stick them in place.

Yule LOG

use dairy-free milk and a (hard) dairy-free butter alternative

use lactose-free milk

SERVES · 10

TAKES · 40 MINUTES

- 100g (½ cup) caster (superfine) sugar
- 4 large eggs
- 65g (½ cup) gluten-free self-raising (self-rising) flour
- ¼ tsp xanthan gum
- 40g (½ cup minus 1 tbsp) unsweetened cocoa powder
- Icing (confectioners') sugar, for dusting
- Red and green fondant icing, for the holly decoration

For the chocolate buttercream

- 675g (4¾ cups) icing (confectioners') sugar
- 45g (½ cup minus 2 tsp) unsweetened cocoa powder
- 65g (¼ cup plus 1 tsp) butter, softened, plus extra for greasing
- 2 tsp vanilla extract
- 125ml (½ cup plus 1 tsp) milk

You wouldn't believe just how incredibly flexible and strong a gluten-free sponge could be until you've made this. The sponge is super-soft and light, yet strong enough to roll and hold all that lovely, chocolatey buttercream. I loved seeing all your photos of your yule logs last year, so keep tagging me in them on Instagram (@beckyexcell) if you make this!

Preheat your oven to 180°C fan / 200°C / 400°F. Grease a 35 x 25cm (14 x 10in) Swiss roll tin (pan), and line it with non-stick baking parchment.

In a large mixing bowl, whisk together your caster sugar and eggs until light and a little frothy – I use an electric hand whisk for this. Sift in your flour, xanthan gum and cocoa powder. Fold this into your mixture carefully until fully combined. Pour the mixture into your prepared Swiss roll tin, ensuring it spreads right to the edges. Try your best to get it as even as possible.

Bake for about 9 minutes; the sponge should have come away a little from the sides of the tin and be slightly risen.

Remove from the oven and very carefully invert the sponge onto another piece of baking parchment that's lightly dusted with icing sugar. Carefully peel off the parchment that was lining the tin.

Now, while the sponge is still warm, roll it up from a longer side, with the parchment inside it as you roll. Place to one side and leave it to cool completely, while rolled up. I usually put something heavy against it to ensure it stays fairly tight and doesn't unroll itself.

While your sponge is cooling, make your buttercream. Add all the ingredients to the bowl of a stand mixer (an electric hand whisk will do the job just fine too, but if making by hand, ensure you mix for longer), sifting in the icing sugar and cocoa powder. Start the mixer on low and then increase to a higher speed as it all begins to come together into a lovely, smooth, spreadable consistency. If it's not coming together, add a little extra milk very slowly, while mixing.

To assemble, carefully unroll the sponge and remove the baking parchment.

Spread a layer of buttercream about 1cm (½in) thick over the sponge, leaving a 5mm (¼in) clear border. Carefully roll the sponge back up and transfer to a serving plate.

Your rolled-up sponge will probably now look a little long. To create a 'branch', cut a quarter off at a 45-degree angle, then simply place it against the main cake. Trim the angled end off the main log so both ends are straight once again.

Cover the sponge with the remaining buttercream and use a fork or sharp knife to create a wood-like pattern. Dust with icing sugar and, to finish, use a tiny amount of red and green fondant to create a holly leaf decoration or two. Cut the ends off to reveal your swirl, and enjoy.

CHRISTMAS Meringue Wreath

use dairy-free cream (minimum 30% fat)

use lactose-free whipping cream (minimum 30% fat)

SERVES · 8

TAKES · 1½ HOURS + COOLING

For the meringue and filling

- 6 large egg whites
- 350g (1¾ cups) caster (superfine) sugar
- 2 tsp cornflour (cornstarch)
- 2 tsp white wine vinegar
- 600ml (2½ cups) double (heavy) cream
- 3 tbsp icing (confectioners') sugar
- 1 tsp vanilla extract

For the raspberry coulis

- 120g (½ cup plus 3 tbsp) caster (superfine) sugar
- 3 tbsp orange juice or water
- 200g (7oz) raspberries
- 1 tsp cornflour (cornstarch)

To serve

- Fresh raspberries, strawberries, blueberries, blackberries
- Gold leaf (optional)

At Christmas, I often find myself needing an easy peasy crowd pleaser and this festive wreath is exactly that. Each bite is packed with crunchy meringue, fluffy whipped cream, fresh berries and a drizzling of sweet, sharp raspberry coulis, all of which comes as Santa-approved – yes, I know him.

Preheat your oven to 140°C fan / 160°C / 325°F. Line a large baking sheet with non-stick baking parchment and use a large dinner plate to draw a 30cm (12in) circle in the middle of the paper. Place a 15cm (6in) small bowl upside down in the middle of the drawn circle.

Add the egg whites to the bowl of a stand mixer (an electric hand whisk will do the job just fine too, and if making by hand, ensure you mix for longer) and whisk at a medium speed until it reaches soft peaks. Add your caster sugar in three stages, whisking at a higher speed until it reaches stiff peaks. Lastly, mix the cornflour with the vinegar and add to the egg whites, mixing in until combined.

Spoon your meringue mixture all around the small bowl on the baking parchment, right up to the edges of the larger circle. Use a spoon to create a shallow trench where the filling will sit. Remove the bowl.

Place in the oven and reduce the oven temperature to 120°C fan / 140°C / 285°F. Bake for 1 hour, until the meringue is lovely and crisp on the outside. Turn the oven off and leave the wreath in the oven with the door shut to cool completely, ideally overnight.

Place all the ingredients for the coulis in a small saucepan, mix thoroughly and place over a medium heat. Bring to the boil, then simmer for 10 minutes until everything is broken down. Pour the mixture through a sieve, using a silicone spatula to push any chunkier bits through.

When ready to serve, whip the cream, icing sugar and vanilla extract together in a large mixing bowl until stiff peaks form. Spoon the cream on top of the meringue, then top with the fruit and drizzle over the coulis. Apply gold leaf for the ultimate finishing touch, if using.

TIP:
If using lactose-free or dairy-free cream, it must be 30% fat or higher or it will never whip. You learn something new every day!

You can also use store-bought raspberry coulis if you feel like you've done enough hard work already.

Gingerbread PEOPLE

use a (hard) dairy-free butter alternative

one gingerbread person is a safe serving size

MAKES · 15

TAKES · 40 MINUTES + AT LEAST 30 MINUTES CHILLING

- 350g (2⅔ cups) gluten-free plain (all-purpose) flour, plus extra for dusting
- ¼ tsp xanthan gum
- 3 tsp ground ginger
- 1 tsp ground cinnamon
- ¾ tsp bicarbonate of soda (baking soda)
- 125g (½ cup plus 1 tbsp) cold butter, cubed
- 175g (¾ cup plus 2 tbsp) light brown sugar
- 1 large egg
- 4 tbsp golden syrup
- 1 quantity of royal icing (page 214)
- Sprinkles (ensure gluten-free)

Nothing says Christmas like a fun, festive baking project! The gingerbread is lovely and crisp on the outside, but soft in the middle with lots of festive fiery flavour. It's perfect if you have little helpers, and feel free to unleash your creative side when it comes to decorating! This type of gingerbread isn't suitable for making a gingerbread house, so if that's what you're looking for check out my blog for the perfect mini gingerbread house recipe.

Mix your flour, xanthan gum, ginger, cinnamon and bicarb in a large mixing bowl. Rub in your cold, cubed butter until you achieve a breadcrumb-like consistency. (You can speed up this process by using a food processor.) Stir in your sugar.

Crack the egg into a small bowl, add your syrup and beat together. Gradually add this to your dry ingredients, mixing between each addition.

Transfer your mixture to a lightly floured surface, then briefly knead it together into a ball. Split your dough into two, then cover both dough portions with cling film (plastic wrap) and chill in the fridge for 30 minutes, and up to 2 hours. The longer you chill the dough the better, as chilling helps to prevent your gingerbread from spreading in the oven.

Preheat your oven to 160°C fan / 180°C / 350°F. Line two baking sheets with non-stick baking parchment. Prepare 2 large sheets of baking parchment, dusting a little flour onto one of them.

Place one of your dough portions on the flour-dusted baking parchment and place your other sheet of parchment on top. Roll the dough out to 5mm (¼in) thickness, then use gingerbread-people cutters to cut out your shapes. Reroll the dough scraps until you've cut out as many shapes as possible.

Place the gingerbread shapes onto your prepared baking sheets, leaving space between each to allow for any minor spread, and bake in the oven for 12 minutes, or until golden. (Smaller ones may need less time than this; check after 8 minutes.)

Leave to cool for 10 minutes on the baking sheet before transferring to a wire rack to cool completely. Repeat with the other portion of the dough, or keep it stored in the fridge for 2–3 days.

Use your royal icing (page 214) to create simple line decorations. You can also use line and flood icing to create more intricate designs of your choice, for example by adding festive jumpers to your gingerbread people. Stick on sprinkles while the icing is still wet, to give them an added flourish. The sky's the limit!

Baked and iced biscuits pictured on pages 194–195.

STOLLEN

use dairy-free milk and a (hard) dairy-free butter alternative

use lactose-free milk

MAKES · 15–20

TAKES · 30 MINUTES

- 340g (2⅔ cups) gluten-free self-raising (self-rising) flour, plus extra for dusting
- 1 tsp gluten-free baking powder
- ¼ tsp xanthan gum
- 85g (⅓ cup plus 2 tbsp) very cold butter, cubed
- 60g (5 tbsp) caster (superfine) sugar
- 50g (½ cup) ground almonds (almond flour)
- 150g (5oz) marzipan, grated
- 100g (3½oz) sultanas (golden raisins), finely chopped
- Grated zest of 1 lemon or orange
- 150ml (⅝ cup) milk
- 3 tsp lemon juice
- 1 large egg
- 2 tsp almond extract
- Icing (confectioners') sugar, sifted, for dusting

I've given up waiting for Santa to bring me a gluten-free stollen, so I've made my own bite-sized version instead. They're incredibly quick and easy to make, packed with tons of festive flavour with a 'snowy' dusting of icing (confectioners') sugar on top, just like the ones I always see in supermarkets that we can never eat!

Preheat your oven to 200°C fan / 220°C / 425°F. Line a baking sheet with non-stick baking parchment.

Mix your flour, baking powder and xanthan gum in a large mixing bowl. Add your cold, cubed butter and rub it into the flour with your fingertips until it forms a breadcrumb-like consistency. Stir in your caster sugar, ground almonds, grated marzipan and sultanas. Stir in the lemon or orange zest.

Gently warm your milk in a jug (pitcher) – I do this in the microwave at full power for about 35 seconds, but ensure that it remains warm and doesn't get hot. Add your lemon juice to the milk and allow to stand for 1–2 minutes – it should turn slightly curdled and lumpy. Add the egg and almond extract to the milk mixture and beat together until well combined.

Make a well in the middle of your dry mixture. Pour in the wet mixture and work it in using a metal fork or knife. Keep working it till it forms a slightly sticky dough.

Lightly dust your work surface and hands with a little flour. Take dough ball-sized amounts of your mixture and roll into slightly flattened balls (not *too* flattened as they spread a little in the oven). Place on your lined baking sheet, allowing a 2.5cm (1in) gap between each.

Bake in the oven for 12–15 minutes until golden. Allow to cool briefly on the sheet before transferring to a wire rack to cool completely. Dust well with icing sugar and enjoy cold, or slightly warm if you can't wait!

ESSENTIALS

This chapter doesn't just contain the recipes that any aspiring gluten-free baker needs in their back pocket, but also all the recipes that are essential for baking, full-stop. After all, if you want to create bakes that nobody would ever know were gluten-free, you'll need all the proper finishing touches to get the job done, right?

So dive right into all my best pastry recipes, as well as all the buttercream, frosting, fillings and icing you'll need throughout your gluten-free baking journey. You'll find that I refer back to the recipes in this chapter a lot, so you definitely won't be short of ideas on how to use them.

GLUTEN-FREE Plain (All-Purpose) FLOUR

MAKES · 1KG (6½ CUPS)

TAKES · 2 MINUTES

- 500g (3 cups) white rice flour
- 150g (1 cup) tapioca starch (ensure gluten-free)
- 150g (¾ cup) potato starch
- 150g (1¼ cups) cornflour (cornstarch)
- 50g (scant ½ cup) buckwheat flour

If you live in the UK, you can easily find gluten-free plain (all-purpose) flour in supermarkets; in which case, you don't need this recipe! This recipe is for anyone who can't easily source gluten-free plain flour where they live or for anyone who has had mixed results using their country's equivalent. As commercial blends contain flours/starches in specific quantities, they can vary wildly depending on where you live in the world – and so can your baking results. So here's a blend you can rely on for using in this book – you can easily purchase these starches and flours online.

Simply combine all the ingredients in a large mixing bowl and mix thoroughly. Store in an airtight container. Consider labelling it so you can tell it apart from other flour.

Use whenever a recipe calls for gluten-free plain flour.

GLUTEN-FREE Self-Raising (Self-Rising) FLOUR

MAKES · 450G (3¼ CUPS)

TAKES · 2 MINUTES

- 450g (3¼ cups) gluten-free plain (all-purpose) flour (opposite)
- 6 tsp gluten-free baking powder
- 1 tsp xanthan gum

Gluten-free self-raising flour is readily available across all supermarkets in the UK. But if you can't find it where you live, you can easily make your own using this simple recipe. Can't find gluten-free plain (all-purpose) flour? You can easily make your own using the recipe opposite. It might be wise to double the quantities of this to ensure you don't have to make it too often.

Simply combine the ingredients in a large mixing bowl and mix thoroughly, then store in an airtight container. Consider labelling it so you can tell it apart from other flour.

Use whenever a recipe calls for gluten-free self-raising (self-rising) flour.

ULTIMATE GLUTEN-FREE Shortcrust Pastry

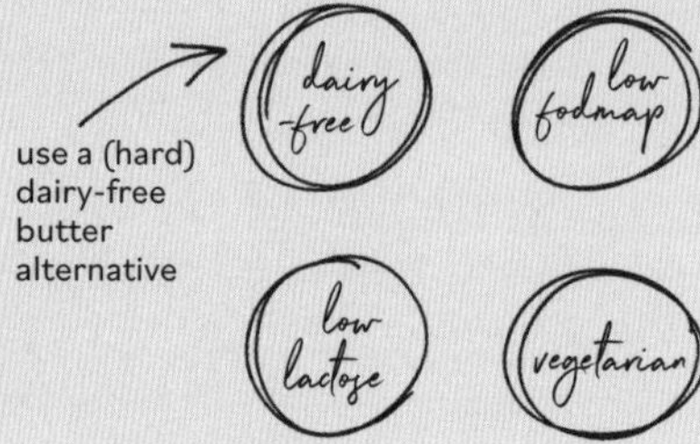

MAKES · 560G (1LB 4OZ)

TAKES · 15 MINUTES + 30 MINUTES CHILLING

- 300g (2¼ cups) gluten-free plain (all-purpose) flour
- 1½ tsp xanthan gum
- 145g (⅔ cup) very cold butter, cut into 1cm (½in) cubes
- 3 tbsp caster (superfine) sugar (for sweet pastry only)
- 1 tsp salt (for savoury pastry only)
- 2 large eggs, beaten

This incredibly versatile pastry is halfway between shortcrust (pie crust) and rough puff pastry and absolutely perfect for sweet or savoury baking. Not only is it incredibly easy to work with, but it also has a taste and texture that I never thought possible in gluten-free pastry. It has a flaky quality that instantly livens up any pie, quiche or tart. Best of all, it's tried and tested by hundreds of you lovely gluten-free folks!

In a large mixing bowl, mix together your flour and xanthan gum.

Make sure your butter is really cold; if not, put it in the fridge or freezer until nicely chilled. Add the cubes to the bowl and mix it into the flour. Using your fingertips, rub the butter into the flour to form a breadcrumb-like consistency. Make sure your hands are cool, as we want to avoid the butter getting warm! (You can also achieve the same result by using a food processor to blitz the ingredients together.)

If making sweet pastry, stir in the sugar, or if making savoury pastry, stir in the salt.

Add your beaten egg and, using a knife, carefully cut it into the mixture until it comes together. It should form a ball and not be crumbly – it will be a little sticky to touch but not unmanageable.

Wrap the dough in cling film (plastic wrap) and leave to chill in the fridge for around 30 minutes before using. You can freeze this pastry for up to 2 months; defrost fully before using.

TIP:
Chill! Using cold butter and chilling the dough makes your gluten-free pastry stronger and more workable. Making any type of pastry on an incredibly hot day isn't advisable as the warmer your dough is, the more fragile it will become. However, make sure that, once chilled, you allow your pastry to warm up a bit before rolling, otherwise it can be very hard to work with.

Use for recipes like my lemon meringue pie (page 106), Cornish pasties (page 169) and triple cheese & onion quiche (page 170), plus loads more!

ROUGH PUFF *Pastry*

MAKES · 650G (1LB 7OZ)

TAKES · 30 MINUTES + 1¼ HOURS CHILLING

- 295g (scant 2¼ cups) gluten-free plain (all-purpose) flour, plus extra for dusting
- 1 tsp xanthan gum
- Pinch of salt
- 225g (1 cup) very cold butter, cut into 1cm (½in) cubes
- 1 medium egg white
- Ice-cold water

My gluten-free rough puff pastry is back with lots of golden, buttery flaky layers that magically puff up in the oven. Once you've nailed the folding method, you'll be surprised how quickly you can make this. And while it chills... so can you!

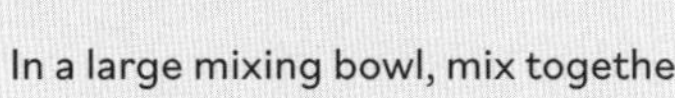

In a large mixing bowl, mix together your flour, xanthan gum and salt.

Make sure your butter is really cold; if not, put it in the fridge or freezer until chilled. Add the cubes to the bowl and stir it into the flour. With cool hands, gently squeeze the butter with your fingertips to break the cubes down a little. Definitely don't try and rub them into the flour as we want to see chunks of butter in the mix at all times.

Add your egg white to a jug (pitcher) and add ice-cold water to the jug until the mixture reaches 130ml (4½fl oz) in total. Give it a mix. Gradually add three-quarters of the wet mixture to your mixing bowl, tossing the mixture with your hands, or using a knife to cut it in, between pouring. This will allow the mix to hydrate, but don't try to form a dough at this point.

Once you've added three-quarters of the wet mixture, start to add it in even smaller quantities, still tossing in between. If your dough doesn't come together after adding all of it, you might need to add up to an extra tablespoon of water. Bear in mind that you may need to add more or less water – this just serves as a rough guide. Once a dough starts to form, only then begin bringing it together with your hands – you don't want it to be too dry or sticky, just somewhere in between.

Using your hands, form a rectangle with the dough and wrap in cling film (plastic wrap). It should have visible streaks of butter in it. Place in the fridge for about 15 minutes.

Lightly flour a large sheet of non-stick baking parchment. Remove your dough from the fridge and remove the cling film. Roll it out on the parchment until just over 1cm (½in) thick. Fold over the bottom of the dough so it meets the middle, then fold the top of the rolled out dough over that, like a letter in an envelope. Try to get the layers fairly evenly folded, but at this stage, it doesn't matter if it looks messy.

Return the dough to the fridge for about 15 minutes, to chill. Repeat the rolling, folding and chilling 3 more times, turning the pastry 90 degrees each time you roll. On its last trip to the fridge, chill it for no less than 30 minutes before using.

You can freeze this pastry for up to 2 months; defrost fully before using.

TIPS:

Chill! Using cold water, cold butter and chilling the dough makes your gluten-free pastry stronger and more workable. Making any type of pastry on an incredibly hot day isn't advisable as the warmer your dough is, the more fragile it will become.

Remember that when using rough puff pastry, you cannot simply just reroll it (or any off-cuts) into a ball. You'll destroy the layers you've spent time creating! If you do have any off-cuts, you can always bake them and roll them in cinnamon sugar for a sweet, buttery treat.

Use for my creamy chicken bakes (page 164), ham & cheese pastries (page 166), roasted veggie & feta tarts (page 173) and pigs in blankets sausage rolls (page 180).

Making it dairy-free?
Use a (hard) dairy-free butter alternative. I find that hard margarine is a little too soft for rough puff, so use a block that feels very firm when chilled.

Choux PASTRY

use dairy-free milk and a (hard) dairy-free butter alternative

vegetarian

low fodmap

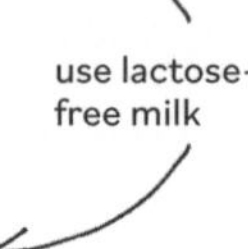

use lactose-free milk

MAKES · 14 ÉCLAIRS OR 8–10 CHOUX BUNS

TAKES · 30 MINUTES

- 150g (1 cup plus 2 tbsp) gluten-free plain (all-purpose) flour
- ½ tsp xanthan gum
- 2 tsp caster (superfine) sugar
- ¼ tsp salt
- 150ml (⅝ cup) milk
- 150ml (⅝ cup) water
- 100g (½ cup minus 1 tbsp) butter, cubed
- 4 large eggs, beaten

Every gluten-free baker needs to learn to embrace choux pastry for two very valid reasons: 1) it's identical to muggle choux pastry in terms of method, and 2) in terms of taste and texture it's identical to gluten-containing choux. And there's not many things I can say that for, so absolutely make sure you get to grips with this one – it's easy!

Sift your flour, xanthan gum, sugar and salt into a mixing bowl. Place to one side.

Add your milk, water and cubed butter to a small to medium saucepan and place over a low to medium heat. Gently heat until the butter has melted, then bring to a gentle simmer and, as soon as it is simmering, take off the heat and immediately add your dry mixture to the pan. Mix immediately and vigorously until everything comes together into a dough that almost resembles mashed potato. Place your pan back onto a medium heat for 2 minutes, stirring until it forms more of a ball and releases more moisture. We don't want the mixture to be wet, but of course, don't let it stick to the bottom of the pan!

Place the dough in a large mixing bowl and allow to cool for 10–15 minutes. Once cooled, add your beaten eggs a little at a time to the dough, mixing thoroughly between each addition until smooth. Watch the consistency of the dough as you add the egg, as you don't want it to go too runny – it needs to be thick enough to be a pipeable consistency that can hold its shape, and you might not need all of the egg. You can add the egg by hand using a wooden spoon quite easily but it's a proper workout! I use an electric hand whisk on a low speed.

Transfer your dough to a piping bag – refer to your recipe of choice as to which type of nozzle you'll need attached.

Use for my no-yeast banoffee beignets (page 91), ring doughnut éclairs (page 99), maple pecan cruller doughnuts (page 103), coffee & cream éclairs (page 119) and XL profiterole buns (page 120).

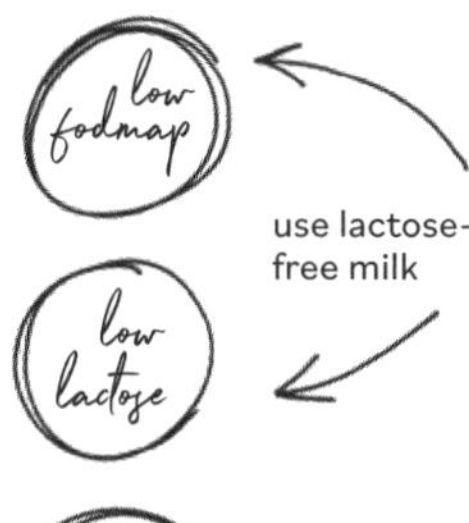

MAKES · ENOUGH TO ICE 16 CUPCAKES OR TO FILL AND TOP A TWO-TIERED SPONGE CAKE

TAKES · 10 MINUTES

- 200g (¾ cup plus 2 tbsp) butter, softened
- 400g (3 cups) icing (confectioners') sugar, sifted
- 1 tsp vanilla extract
- 1–3 tsp milk, if needed

This is the base whenever I use buttercream throughout this book. I often mix it up by changing the extract to suit whatever it is that I'm baking, plus I sometimes add food colouring paste to give it a vibrant colour. It's creamy and buttery, delightfully sweet and is seriously stable - use for sandwich cakes or on cupcakes, whenever you need sweet, fluffy buttercream.

I use a stand mixer whenever I make icing, but an electric hand whisk will do the job just fine too. If making by hand, ensure you mix for longer, until everything is well combined and consistent.

Place your butter in the bowl of a stand mixer and mix on a medium speed for about 5 minutes until it has turned a lot paler in colour.

Add your icing sugar in two or three stages, beating for about 3 minutes between each addition. Start your mixer slowly (to avoid creating a mini icing sugar explosion) then increase the speed to medium-high for each of your 3-minute mixing intervals. Add in your vanilla extract and mix until fully combined.

If your buttercream feels a little stiff, just mix in a teaspoon of milk (dairy-free or lactose-free if necessary) at a time until you achieve a smooth, pipeable consistency.

TIP:
Feel free to switch up the extracts and add additional flavourings as you please. You can easily add citrus zest and juice for a lemon or lime twist, ground cinnamon for a warming flavour, a generous drizzling of caramel sauce or even melted chocolate or cocoa powder for a chocolatey finish. This recipe is incredibly versatile, so make it your own!

Use for my Viennese fingers and whirls on page 74.

SWISS MERINGUE
Buttercream

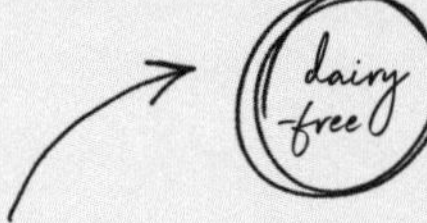

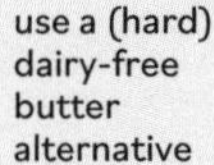

MAKES · ENOUGH TO TOP 16 CUPCAKES OR TO FILL AND TOP A TWO-TIERED SPONGE CAKE

TAKES · 20 MINUTES + COOLING

- 4 large egg whites (about 150ml/⅝ cup)
- 300g (1½ cups) caster (superfine) sugar
- 300g (1⅓ cups) butter, softened
- 2 tsp vanilla extract

This white buttercream is a delightfully buttery version of Swiss meringue, which unlike traditional buttercream won't form a thin crust when exposed to air. Like meringue, it's incredibly light and whippy, yet it's surprisingly stable, meaning it can be used however you like. I use it as a filling in my whoopie pies (page 28), but it's also perfect for icing cakes or cupcakes too.

In a large heatproof bowl, add your egg whites and sugar, then mix until well combined. Place over a saucepan of gently boiling water, making sure the base of the bowl is not touching the water. Keep stirring until the sugar has fully dissolved. You can test it's ready by rubbing a little of the mixture between your fingers – if you don't feel any sugar granules, then it's done. If you have a digital cooking thermometer, you can be certain the sugar has dissolved once the temperature reaches around 70°C (158°F).

Once the egg white mixture is ready, remove from the heat and pour it into the bowl of a stand mixer (an electric hand whisk will do the job just fine too). Using the whisk attachment at a medium-high speed, whisk to stiff peaks and wait until the mixture is completely cooled. You must not add the butter until it's cold, so be patient!

Once cooled, set your mixer to a medium speed and add your (very) softened butter, a chunk at a time, allowing the butter to mix in a little before adding the next piece. The mixture might start to look like it's going to curdle but don't worry, keep the mixer going at the same speed and it will come back around. Once it does, briefly increase the speed to high, until smooth and thick.

Finally, mix in your vanilla extract until well combined. Use straight away, or store in the fridge until needed, bringing it back to room temperature before using.

TIP:
Feel free to flavour and colour this buttercream however you like, using different flavour extracts and food colouring pastes of your choice.

Use for my whoopie pies on page 28.

Chocolate FROSTING

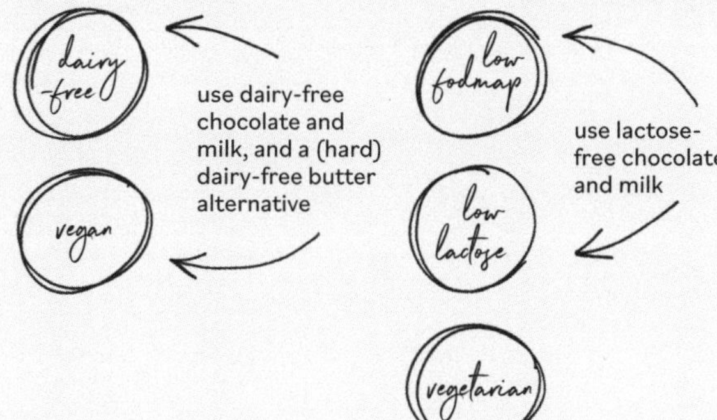

MAKES · ENOUGH TO TOP 16 CUPCAKES OR TO FILL AND TOP A TWO-TIERED SPONGE CAKE

TAKES · 10 MINUTES

- 110g (3½oz) dark chocolate
- 250g (1 cup plus 2 tbsp) butter, softened
- 185g (1¼ cups) icing (confectioners') sugar
- 55g (½ cup) unsweetened cocoa powder
- 1–3 tsp milk, if needed

Over the years, I've iced my chocolate cakes with what feels like every variation of chocolate frosting in existence. And out of all of them, this is my favourite. It's creamy, sweet and the combo of cocoa powder and dark chocolate adds an intense, rich chocolatey finish. It doesn't taste like dark chocolate, so don't worry if you're not a fan! Use for sandwich cakes or cupcakes that need a wonderful, chocolatey finish, or use it in my chocolate courgette (zucchini) cake on page 53.

I use a stand mixer whenever I make icing, but an electric hand whisk will do the job just fine too. If making by hand, ensure you mix for longer, until everything is well-combined and consistent.

Firstly, melt your dark chocolate (I do this in the microwave, mixing in between short bursts until melted), then put to one side and allow to cool slightly while you make the rest of the buttercream.

Place your butter in the bowl of a stand mixer and mix on a medium speed for about 5 minutes until fluffy and paler in colour. Add your icing sugar in three stages, beating for about 3 minutes between each addition. Start your mixer slowly (to avoid creating a mini icing sugar explosion) but then increase the speed to medium-high for each of your 3-minute mixing intervals. Sift in your cocoa powder and then mix again until fully combined.

Add in your slightly cooled, melted chocolate and mix until fully incorporated. If your chocolate frosting feels a little stiff, just mix in a teaspoon of milk (dairy-free if necessary) at a time until you achieve a smooth, pipeable consistency.

Use for my chocolate courgette cake (page 53) and my zebra cake (page 47).

CREAM CHEESE

use lactose-free cream cheese

MAKES · ENOUGH TO ICE 16 CUPCAKES OR TO FILL AND TOP A TWO-TIERED SPONGE CAKE

TAKES · 10 MINUTES

- 150g (⅔ cup) butter, softened
- 150g (1 cup) icing (confectioners') sugar, sifted
- 300g (1⅓ cups) full-fat cream cheese
- 1 tsp vanilla extract

When it comes to icing a carrot cake or red velvet cake, only a thick and fluffy cream cheese frosting will do. Fortunately, it's no harder to make than buttercream and adds a more indulgent, creamier finish to any of your bakes lucky enough to be paired with it.

I use a stand mixer whenever I make icing, but an electric hand whisk will do the job just fine too. If making by hand, ensure you mix for longer, until everything is well-combined and consistent.

Place your butter into the bowl of a stand mixer and mix on a medium speed for about 5 minutes until it has turned a lot paler in colour. Add your icing sugar and mix for a further 5 minutes. If you're scaling up the quantities to make more, I'd recommend adding the icing sugar in two or three separate stages to avoid creating an icing sugar explosion!

Before you add the cream cheese, ensure that there is no excess liquid in the tub (if buying in a tub) – simply drain it off, if needed. Add the cream cheese to the bowl with the vanilla extract and mix for 2-3 more minutes until well combined, and the icing is light and fluffy, without lumps.

If not using at once, keep covered and chilled in the fridge until you need it. Bear in mind that cakes with cream cheese frosting need to be stored in the fridge. Cream cheese frosting can be frozen and then defrosted in the fridge overnight before use.

Use for my carrot cake cupcakes (page 65) and red velvet cupcakes (page 68).

Crème Pâtissière (PASTRY CREAM)

use dairy-free milk

use lactose-free milk

MAKES · ENOUGH TO FILL 14 ÉCLAIRS

TAKES · 20 MINUTES + 2–3 HOURS CHILLING

- 20g (3 tbsp) cornflour (cornstarch)
- 50g (¼ cup) caster (superfine) sugar
- 60g (2oz) egg yolks (3–4 yolks)
- 250ml (1 cup) whole milk
- 1 tsp vanilla extract

Don't let the fancy name put you off – this is basically the lovely, thick, vanilla custard you'll find in filled doughnuts and proper éclairs. Unlike regular custard, it's richer in flavour and, crucially, thicker, which allows it to hold its shape better when used as a filling. After one taste, you'll want to use it in everything! See the variations on how to transform your custard into crème diplomate (perfect for piping or spreading onto cakes and cupcakes) or crème mousseline (a more buttery, luxurious and stable version of creme pat, also used for filling profiteroles and doughnuts).

Put your cornflour and half your sugar in a small bowl, then mix together to combine. In a large mixing bowl, beat your egg yolks to break them all up, then add your flour/sugar mixture in two stages, mixing in between each addition (I prefer to use an electric hand whisk for this). Set aside.

In a small saucepan, add your milk, vanilla extract and the remaining sugar, and whisk until well combined. Place over a low heat until it just starts to boil, then immediately pour a third of the milk mixture into your mixing bowl and whisk constantly to combine. Follow this with another third of your milk mixture, whisking once more until well incorporated.

Pour the contents of your mixing bowl back into your saucepan with the remaining third of the milk and whisk constantly over a medium heat until it thickens. It will be frothy on top to start with but as it starts to thicken, this will disappear and a lovely thick custard will develop – turn the heat to low at this point. Keep whisking constantly until you see large bubbles form on top of the custard. This lets you know that the cornflour is cooked.

Remove from the heat and transfer the custard to a bowl to cool. Cover with cling film (plastic wrap) so that it is touching the surface of the custard; this will prevent a skin from forming as it cools. Place in the fridge for 2–3 hours to completely cool and further thicken.

When you want to use your crème pâtissière, remove from the fridge and mix thoroughly to return it to a smooth consistency, as when it cools it becomes more jelly-like (I prefer to use an electric hand whisk to do this).

Use for my 'real deal' doughnuts (page 94), duffins (page 95), finger doughnuts (page 98), ring doughnut éclairs (page 99), coffee & cream éclairs (page 119) and XL profiterole buns (page 120).

VARIATIONS:

For crème diplomate, whip 150ml (⅝ cup) double (heavy) cream to very soft peaks, then stir into your cooled crème pâtissière. Use lactose-free or dairy-free cream (minimum 30% fat) if necessary.

For crème mousseline, gradually whisk in 125g (generous ½ cup) very soft butter to the cooled crème pâtissière – be careful not to split the mixture.

·ROYAL· Icing

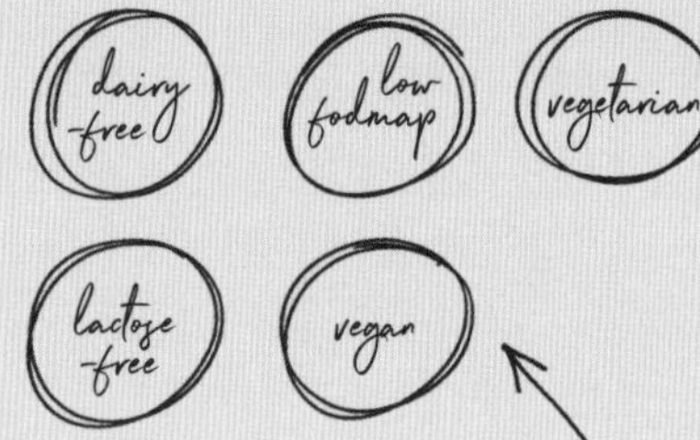

use 150ml (⅝ cup) aquafaba instead of the eggs (whisked until frothy)

MAKES · ENOUGH TO ICE 20 SMALL BISCUITS/ COOKIES

TAKES · 5 MINUTES

- 3 medium egg whites
- 675g (5 cups) icing (confectioners') sugar, sifted
- Food colouring paste, in colours of your choice

Meet the ultimate icing when it comes to icing gingerbread (page 199) or my vanilla biscuits (78). It takes minutes to whip up and the sky's the limit when it comes to using it to create beautiful, edible designs. Follow the instructions below on how to use it for line and flood icing, as well as how to colour it. Using food colouring paste (not liquid food colouring) is important when making coloured icing as it doesn't dilute your mixture.

I use a stand mixer whenever I make icing, but an electric hand whisk will do the job just fine too. If making by hand, ensure you mix for longer, until everything is well-combined and consistent.

Add your egg whites and icing sugar to the bowl of a stand mixer. Starting on a low speed, mix for 5 minutes until you have a thick, smooth paste with a toothpaste-like consistency.

Keep covered in the fridge if you don't intend to use it immediately.

If you intend to pipe white line icing, transfer to a piping bag with a small, round nozzle (around a 2mm/¹⁄₁₆in opening) and pipe away. Allow line icing to set for 5 minutes.

HOW TO FLOOD YOUR BISCUITS/COOKIES WITH WHITE ICING

Split the icing into two bowls and add 1–3 teaspoons of cold water to one of them until you achieve a *slightly* runnier consistency – this is your flood icing. The other bowl is your line icing. Transfer to two piping bags each with a small, round nozzle (around a 2mm/¹⁄₁₆in), ensuring you know which is which.

Use your line icing to pipe a line all around the edge of your biscuit and allow it to set for 5 minutes. Then pipe a generous amount of flood icing in the middle of the biscuit, leaving a 5mm (¼in) gap from the line you piped earlier. Use a cocktail stick to 'drag' the flood icing to meet all of the edges of the line icing. At this point, you can spice up the design a little by adding gluten-free sprinkles of your choice.

You can either allow the flood icing to air-dry for an hour in a warm place, or place them on a baking sheet and pop them in the oven at 55°C fan / 75°C / 170°F for 20 minutes.

HOW TO PIPE LINE ICING IN MULTIPLE COLOURS

Grab as many bowls for as many colours that you intend to use. Split the white icing evenly between the bowls, then mix enough food colouring paste into each to achieve your desired colours. Transfer the icing into separate piping bags with small, round nozzles (around a 2mm/1⁄16in opening) and you're good to go. Allow line icing to set for 5 minutes.

HOW TO FLOOD YOUR BISCUITS/COOKIES WITH MULTIPLE COLOURS

Grab as many bowls for as many colours that you intend to use. Split the white icing evenly between the bowls, then mix enough food colouring paste into each to achieve your desired colours.

To create flood icing, split your coloured icing once again so you now have two bowls of each colour. Add 1–2 teaspoons of cold water to each of your newly split bowls to create a *slightly* runnier mixture – these bowls now contain your flood icing. The original bowls contain your line icing.

Transfer your line icing into separate piping bags with small, round nozzles (around a 2mm/1⁄16in opening) and your flood icing into separate piping bags also with small, round nozzles, making sure you keep track of which is which.

Use one colour of line icing to pipe a shape onto your biscuit and allow to set for 5 minutes. Then pipe a generous amount of the same coloured flood icing in the middle of your shape, leaving a 5mm (1⁄4in) gap from the line you piped earlier. Use a cocktail stick to 'drag' the flood icing to meet all of the edges of the line icing. You can either allow the flood icing to air-dry for an hour in a warm place or place them onto a baking sheet and pop them in the oven at 55°C fan / 75°C / 170°F for 20 minutes.

You can use this method, for example, to pipe the outline of a jumper on a gingerbread person, then use the same colour flood icing to fill it. Then you could use a different coloured line icing to pipe the outline of a hat, then use the same colour flood icing to fill it, etc. Or, you could also line and flood the entire biscuit, allow it to set, then pipe further designs on top of it using line icing.

The sky's the limit, or rather, the number of bowls you have at your disposal is the limit!

TIPS:

Don't pipe line icing like you're drawing with a pen! Start with the piping bag touching the cookie, and as soon as the first little blob of icing makes contact and sticks, raise your piping bag slightly above the cookie for the rest of the outline. Continue that line, allowing it to constantly fall into place as you move the piping bag around the edge of the cookie. Practice makes perfect!

If you don't have enough small, round nozzles, simply snip a 2mm (1⁄16in) opening off the end of your piping bag.

Use for my vanilla biscuits (page 78) and gingerbread people (page 199).

EGG CONVERSION GUIDE

Did you know that a large egg in the UK is actually bigger than in the USA, Canada and Australia? Me neither! That's why I thought I'd pop in a handy egg conversion guide in the back of this book to help make things simple.

That way, when a recipe calls for a small, medium or large egg, you can use the table below to work out exactly what that means for you. I've used UK egg sizes in all my recipes, so just convert from there.

	UK	USA	Canada	Australia
Small	53g and under	42.5g / 1½oz	42g / 1½oz	N/A
Medium	53-63g	49.6g / 1¾oz	49g / 1¾oz	43g
Large	63-73g	56.7g / 2oz	56g / 2oz	52g
Extra large	73g and over	63.8g / 2¼oz	63g / 2¼oz	60g
Jumbo	N/A	70.9g / 2½oz	70g / 2½oz	68g

And just in case you're too lazy to look at anything presented in a table (like I am), here's your cheat sheet! Maybe we can call a meeting of all our world leaders and agree on a uniform egg size in future?

So when a recipe in this book calls for a **small egg**, you should use a:

USA: medium egg
Canada: medium egg
Australia: large egg

When a recipe in this book calls for a **medium egg**, you should use a:

USA: large egg
Canada: large egg
Australia: extra-large egg

When a recipe in this book calls for a **large egg**, you should use a:

USA: extra-large egg
Canada: extra-large egg.
Australia: jumbo egg

OVEN CONVERSION GUIDE

Here's a helpful table for oven temperature conversions depending on the kind of oven you use.

Celsius (fan)	Celsius	Fahrenheit	Gas mark
100	120	250	½
120	140	285	1
130	150	300	2
140	160	325	3
160	180	350	4
170	190	375	5
180	200	400	6
200	220	425	7
210	230	450	8
230	250	480	9
240	260	500	10

INDEX

Thank you

I find it almost impossible to express just how grateful I am for all the support, love and positivity on the publication of my first and now second book. For some reason, everytime I try to, my brain has a mini gratitude meltdown and can only default to the same two words over and over again – 'thank you'! So, at risk of saying it more often than your average cash machine, I thought I'd try and say thank you in as many different languages as possible instead.

Merci to all the team at Quadrille Publishing for all their painstaking hard work, endless expertise and constant support throughout my first and now second book. I want to give you all a great big hug, but that's hard over a video call or from a 2-metre distance! This book is now my second that was written, designed and shot across multiple lockdowns but once again, nobody would be any the wiser... and that's utterly mesmerising to me. Hopefully we'll be able to have a proper book launch celebration in the future and of course, you're all invited!

Danke schön to publishing director Sarah Lavelle for trusting in me to commission not just one, but now two books. That's two whole books more than I could have ever dreamed of, by the way. I greatly look forward to seeing what our working future entails and thank you for always believing in me.

Bedankt to Harriet Webster for being my superstar editor and for so, so much more than you get credit for. For example, if it wasn't for you, I'm 99.9% sure that I would have turned up for the photoshoot in a hoodie and joggers for a lack of a better fashion sense. Of course, my wardrobe now thanks you too.

Dzięki to copy editor Sally Somers for your sage wisdom and for the insurmountable bravery it must take to be one of the first people to proofread my writing.

Tusen takk to Emily Lapworth for working your design magic once again and for always taking time out to sit in on the photoshoots; something which I'm sure explains why everything visually ties together so seamlessly throughout this book. Hopefully I'll finally get to meet you in person one day and not just across a video call!

A big *arigato* to photographer, Hannah Hughes, who not only captured vital evidence that gluten-free food can look like 'regular' food, but who also takes photos of me which make me look like a 'regular' human. That's not an easy task, trust me.

Grazie to Emily Kydd, Susanna Unsworth and Alice Ostan (who I recently discovered does an amazing impression of the creepy old man on *Family Guy*) for their jaw-dropping food-styling prowess.

Grazie mille to Rebecca Newport for the stunning prop styling – I was so pleased to hear you could work on my second book again. And many congratulations in advance on the new addition to the Newport family.

Obrigada to Cat Parnell and Dani Hooker for your wonderful hair and make-up artistry. The juxtaposition of how I look in this book versus how I looked on a daily basis throughout lockdown is testament to how good you are as make-up artists!

Diolch to 'Team Laura' (Laura Willis and Laura Eldridge) and Ruth Tewkesbury for magically making my book pop up in more places than I can count. Both my mum and Mark's mum now have an ever-growing pile of newspapers and magazines that feature my recipes, so I'm sure they'd like to join me in thanking you too.

As a massive fan girl, I can't believe I'm about to write this next bit: *muchas gracias* to Nigella Lawson. It meant the world to me that you were such a huge supporter of my first book and even went on to induct it into the coveted 'Cookbook Corner' on nigella.com. And as if that wasn't outrageously kind enough already, she even gave me her own personal endorsement on the front of this book to boot... I still have to pinch myself every 10 seconds just to make sure this isn't all a dream. I hope that when the world returns to normality, our paths will cross so I can thank you in person myself.

Xièxiè to my boyfriend Mark, also known as my chief 'muggle' taste-tester, the reluctant hero of recipe testing, voluntary pot washer, impromptu proofreader, plus many more titles that I can't remember right now. Once again, he contributed so much more to this book than he wishes to take credit for. He even learned to bake just so he could help me test the recipes! He'd only ever baked scones in food tech lessons at school before I wrote this book, but he now seems to be able to bake anything. So hopefully that's good news for any beginners who own this book!

Woof woof ('thanks' in dog-speak) to Peggy who sat and kept me company through many hours of recipe testing and proofreading, even though you were asleep for most of it.

Dankie to my mum and dad – firstly for looking after Peggy whilst Mark and I were in London attending the photoshoot for this book! But most of all, it means so much to me to know that I've (hopefully) done you proud. Please pass my sincere apologies along to all of your immediate friends who probably had a copy of my first book thrust upon them without much choice.

Terima kasih to my brother Charlie and his girlfriend Gemma (and her mum, dad and brother, Matthew too) for all being my most dedicated recipe testers. This service does come for free, right?!

Gum xia to Mark's mum, dad and sister, Lisa, for always cheering me on and having to constantly listen to me talking about cake! If you do ever fancy a slice of cake, you know where I am, though I'm sure Mark smuggles you too much already.

Mahalo to my hairdresser Nicky (hey look - I spelled your name correctly this time) for sorting my hair ready for the photoshoot, something which I'm sure was a real mission after several months of lockdown. I really appreciate all your advice and positivity on the scary new road I find myself on and it has been so nice just to chat to you about it.

But most of all, a great, big *mulțumesc* to everyone who has a copy of my first (and hopefully now second!) book sitting on your shelves at home. I have to say, seeing all the photos of your books arriving, as well as all the wonderful things you've made from it, has been my favourite part of becoming an author. So please, please keep sharing them and tagging me in them! I hope this book brings back a little joy to being gluten-free and once again reunites you with the foods you really miss.

Becky x

Publishing Director
Sarah Lavelle

Junior Commissioning Editor
Harriet Webster

Copy Editor
Sally Somers

Art Direction and Design
Emily Lapworth

Photographer
Hannah Hughes

Food Stylist
Emily Kydd

Prop Stylist
Rebecca Newport

Make-up Artists
Cat Parnell and Danielle Hooker

Head of Production
Stephen Lang

Senior Production Controller
Katie Jarvis

First published in 2021 by Quadrille Publishing Limited

Quadrille
52–54 Southwark Street
London SE1 1UN
quadrille.com

Cataloguing in Publication Data: a catalogue record for this book is available from the British Library.

Reprinted in 2024 (twice)
10 9 8 7 6 5 4 3

ISBN: 978 1 78713 663 2

Printed in China using vegetable-based inks

This book is not intended as a substitute for genuine medical advice. The reader should consult a medical professional in matters relating to their health, particularly with regard to symptoms of IBS and coeliac disease.

BECKY EXCELL is a full-time gluten-free food writer with a following of over 350,000 on her social media channels and 1 million monthly views on her award-winning blog. She's been eating gluten-free for over 10 years and has written recipes for numerous online publications, as well as doing cooking demos at events including the Cake and Bake Show. She gave up a career working in PR and marketing to focus on food full-time, with an aim to develop recipes which reunite her and her followers with the foods they can no longer eat. She lives in Essex, UK.

Becky's recipes tried and tested,
And all are gluten-free,
Easy to follow, nice to taste,
You've bought this book? You'll see.

Paul

Becky's recipes literally save the day. I wanted a gluten-free afternoon tea with my family in the garden for my birthday. My mum baked me scones and cakes from Becky's book, without loads of experience baking gluten-free. They were amazing – **HER RECIPES JUST NEVER FAIL**. She is the Queen of Gluten-Free!

Rachael

I'm so happy we accidentally found Becky. My mum's life turned upside down nearly two years ago and she thought she would never eat 'normal' food again. **YOU HAVE GIVEN MY MUM A LOVE FOR FOOD AGAIN** just like before she was coeliac. It's even better that I can bake for her, as the recipes are so easy and delicious, and work every time. You can't even tell that they're gluten-free!

Sarina

I was lost on my gluten-free journey until I came across Becky's AMAZING recipes! Now when someone says 'you can't have that' I simply reply... **'YES I CAN, AND 100 TIMES BETTER!'**

Louise

Becky's recipes have **NEVER FAILED ME**. She is the angel of gluten-free baking! Amazing recipes from an equally amazing woman.

Hannah

Easy-to-follow recipes with everyday ingredients that have literally changed my life. **WHAT'S NOT TO LOVE?!**

Sandra

Becky has been a revelation. Delicious food that tastes divine! My family don't even know that what I've baked is gluten-free. **THIS LADY IS MAGIC**. Thank you so much.

Nina

The most frequent question in our house when I serve food is **'IS THIS A BECKY?'** We all love the recipes!

Ruth

With Becky's help my daughter has found **A NEW LOVE FOR BAKING** and cooking, which has helped her pass her GCSE cooking classes with flying colours.

Rachel